Poor Women, Powerful Men

About the Book and Author

Poor Women, Powerful Men chronicles the achievements and subsequent failure of the Louisiana Family Health Foundation, the most extensive family planning program ever to operate in the United States. Martha C. Ward's even-handed account reveals the mechanisms—of politics, poverty, and public health policies—at work in the perpetual controversies surrounding reproductive rights and the delivery of health care services to the poor.

Ward's book begins in the early 1960s when Louisiana was among the most underdeveloped states and ranked at the bottom of all scales measuring illiteracy, illegitimacy, and infant mortality. Despite the free statewide Charity Hospital system, many routine preventive medical and public health services were not available to poor women and their children, particularly if they were black. But in the mid-1960s, a visionary group of doctors and health care practitioners began to clear the hurdles erected by law, church, and the medical-political establishment. By 1970 they had set up the first statewide family planning program for poor people in the United States.

The Louisiana experiment was a spectacular success. The Ford, Rockefeller, and Kellogg Foundations poured millions of dollars into the program. The Great Society and War on Poverty programs placed a high priority on the health of poor mothers and infants. With the help of the population lobby—including Planned Parenthood and the Agency for International Development—the Family Health Foundation moved into Latin America and other developing areas.

But in 1974, the bubble burst. Accusations of fiscal mismanagement, fraudulent statistics, patronage, and political payoffs led to federal indictments and jail sentences for top officials. Poor women and powerful men, the black and white communities, and the liberal and conservative medical factions were pitted against each other. With the collapse of the program, methods for handling the epidemic of adolescent pregnancies and the high infant mortality rate reverted to the state bureaucracies.

Poor Women, Powerful Men is the first book-length account of the Louisiana experiment. In a clear and dispassionate voice, Ward demonstrates that many of the questions raised by the experiment persist. Is family planning an answer to the cycle of poverty, teenage pregnancies, and infant mortality? How can the conflict between private and public delivery of medical care be resolved? Where do the reproductive rights of women fit into governmentally supported birth control programs? We seem no closer today to answering these questions than the Louisiana Family Health Foundation was more than a decade ago.

Martha C. Ward is professor of anthropology at the University of New Orleans. She has done extensive fieldwork in the U.S. Trust Territory of Micronesia on the relationship of social change and stress diseases and has published *Them Children: A Study in Language Learning* (1971), a book about black family structure and language in Louisiana.

Poor Women, Powerful Men

America's Great Experiment in Family Planning

MARTHA C. WARD

Westview Press / Boulder and London

Copyright © 1986 by Westview Press, Inc.

Published in 1986 in the United States of America by Westview Press, Inc.; Frederick A. Praeger, Publisher; 5500 Central Avenue, Boulder, Colorado 80301

Library of Congress Cataloging-in-Publication Data
Ward, Martha Coonfield.
  Poor women, powerful men.
  Bibliography: p.
  Includes index.
  1. Family Health Foundation (La.) 2. Birth control—
Louisiana. 3. Birth control—Government policy—
Louisiana. I. Title.
HQ766.5.U5W32 1986   363.9′6′09763   86-5557
ISBN 0-8133-0366-4 (alk. paper)
ISBN 0-8133-0367-2 (pbk.: alk. paper)

Printed and bound in the United States of America

The paper used in this publication meets the requirements of the American National Standard for Permanence of Paper for Printed Library Materials Z39.48-1984.

10   9   8   7   6   5   4   3   2   1

*This book is dedicated to
my mother, Moselle;
my grandmother, Tommie Louise;
my daughter, Marlowe Amanda;
and to the continuity of generations*

Contents

Illustrations

Preface

This is a true story about poor women and dead babies, about visions realized and visions failed, about money, about science in action, about politics, population, poverty, and public health policy. In the mid-1960s, the federal government made a commitment to provide specialized health services to indigent women, but no one knew exactly how to fulfill the ideals of these health services. In Louisiana, an experiment of extraordinary proportions centered around family planning, then a new concept that went far beyond the ordinary conventions of birth control. For many women the program offered the first exposure to public health services and preventive medicine and to a type of control over their lives. Family planning became synonymous with the civil rights of poor women to medical care. Family planning was a new form of medicine.

Some regard the Louisiana family planning program as the number one health service success story in the United States. It challenged the assumptions of how health care to the poor should be organized. It brought in millions of dollars. Eventually called the Family Health Foundation, it was one of the most lavishly funded programs under federal antipoverty legislation. Today when family planners gather, they model their philosophies and techniques after the Louisiana program and ask themselves why it succeeded and what really happened to it. They wonder why and how it could have ended in scandals that rocked the community and reflected on the national family planning movement.

Many of the questions raised by this experiment are at the heart of major social issues. Is family planning an answer to the cycle of poverty, teenage pregnancies, and infant mortality? Can birth control, as Margaret Sanger claimed, improve "the quality of life itself"? How can the conflict between private and public delivery of medical care be resolved? Where do the reproductive rights of women fit into governmentally supported birth control? Do poor or minority women really want birth control? Discussions on questions like who shall pay for health care for the poor are as explosive as debates over overpopulation, abortion, involuntary sterilizations, genocide, and sex education. Sometimes people ask why nothing can be done about major social problems such as mothers on welfare or the feminization of poverty. Here is a story of a vision made practical, of a program that tried to answer these questions.

Part of this story focuses on a life and death issue with a dull name—health care delivery systems. Medical care in the United States is not distributed evenly; access depends on class, race, sex, and ability to pay or manipulate the system. If expectant mothers increase the incidence of infant mortality, prematurity, and mental retardation by avoiding good prenatal care, is it because they are ignorant or willful? Is it because they are denied access to that care in ways that are not immediately apparent? Would education along with systemic reforms of health care solve this dilemma? Conflicting views on how health care should be organized and what factors really cause disease or death are at the root of the controversies in this book.

Sometimes the diseases that afflict a society are not caused by germs or cured by pills. How people define disease, determine its symptoms, and organize the treatment are matters of custom, history, economics, vested powers, and above all the cultural values surrounding human life. For example, premature babies are defined as sick because they are underweight and vulnerable to infections and often have underdeveloped lungs or metabolic problems. Hospitals provide intensive care, advanced technology, and trained specialists for newborns. That is one answer to the "illness" of being premature. Another very different approach is to examine the fact that prematurity occurs far more often in poor families, in which adequate diet or prenatal care is lacking, or to unwed teenage mothers. Since this illness largely follows the lines of economic status, it has been suggested that the "cure" will not be found in improved brands of technology but in preventing prematurity at a societal level. In this view, the fragmentation and specialization within health care systems, as well as a limited comprehension of social reality within the medical community, contribute to the rates of a serious disease in infants.

The scope of health care has been enlarged by such groups as medical anthropologists and sociologists to include indigenous health beliefs and behavior, nutritional patterns, reproductive beliefs and behavior, and the social organization of medicine, particularly as applied to public health and clinical care delivery systems. The experiences of cultural anthropologists in implementing health delivery systems for non-Western peoples are being increasingly applied to modern, heterogenous societies. For example, research has been extended from the challenge of persuading a group of people to adopt a particular birth control technique to the development of cultural specifications for whole new systems of delivering family planning. The current study of health care also encompasses both basic and applied research in such areas as using professionals or nonprofessionals, recruiting patients, evaluating results, financing health care, and tackling the problems of racial, sexual, or class biases. A further topic being analyzed is the interaction among patients and professionals from diverse cultures.

With a background in cultural anthropology, I have approached the history of the Louisiana Family Planning, Inc., as an impartial observer, describer, and explainer, not as an apologist or biased actor. Although I have lived in New Orleans for twenty years and witnessed some of the events described in the book, I played no official role in any of them. But living in the community under study has enabled me to interview and check sources with ease. I first did fieldwork in a black village in St. James Parish, near New Orleans, in 1968. Although the aim of this project was to analyze language socialization and family structure, I collected other data as well, some of which are reflected in the material on the folklore of the Charity hospitals, birth control, and abortion. Later research in the U.S. Territory of Micronesia taught me to look at the comparative organization of health systems, their real impact on the lives of ordinary people, and the role of traditional or alternative medical systems. I had long been interested in the question of how women find medical services, especially ones as important as fertility management, which is both controversial and confidential. When I talked to friends in Louisiana about these questions, the focus of the discussions quickly turned to the nature of medical care available to poor women within the state-supported system and the opportunities for middle- and upper-class women within the private system. Then, inevitably, the discussions turned to the now defunct Louisiana Family Planning, Inc., and the Family Health Foundation and their impact on the state.

I have interviewed many people—the patients, doctors, nurses, and administrators who were involved in these events—to learn what they knew, thought, or experienced during those dramatic times. In addition to these human resources, I have had access to rich but scattered documentation, much loaned from private holdings: unpublished materials, films, newspapers, grant applications, government documents, and files of correspondence, minutes, and memoranda. Although enormous amounts of research and program justification, including abundant statistics, have been published, no archive or repository for this material exists. Most of the program and patient data were lost during the collapse of the foundation in 1974; the rest were dispersed randomly. Some papers are in garages or the dusty filing cabinets of obscure bureaucracies. Because of the initial immediacy of the family planning program and later the speed with which the scandals unraveled, no one followed the historian's approach of saving materials about an important set of events.

Telling this story is like drawing an elephant from the proverbial blind men's descriptions. Each source has a true perspective—but from only one angle. I have tried to portray the entire elephant while doing justice to the insights and experiences of each person who actually touched it. I have not identified all the speakers: Because portions of this material are extremely sensitive, some people interviewed requested that their names not be mentioned. Because they confirmed important elements in the story off the record, I wish to protect their confidentiality. Sometimes I have used verbatim quotes for the sheer delight of the language or to show the strength of feelings.

Because this story is about ordinary people and not about a mystery, I have made no effort to dig up the civic skeletons that some people are convinced lie buried in Louisiana or to pass judgment on the public uproar (some of which is covered in Chapters 5 and 6). I find more drama in the story about poor women and the politics of birth control than in revelations of peccadilloes in high places. It is certainly part of the story that people believe in these skeletons or focus principally on the lurid issues. To the anthropologist, such folklore, values, belief systems, and the anecdotes that illustrate them are an important source of data.

During the course of this research, I have interviewed or requested the assistance of many people. I would like to acknowledge my debt to the following who shared their knowledge and insights so graciously:

Dr. Joseph D. Beasley, Brunswick Medical Center and Bard College, New York; Dr. Bruce Everist, Green Clinic, Lincoln Parish, Louisiana; Dr. Arthur T. Fort, Louisiana State Medical Center, Shreveport; Dr. Richard P. Dickey; Dr. Andrew B. Dott; Dr. Gerald Weiner; Dr. Ben Freedman; Dr. Cesar Corzantes, New Orleans.

Jacqueline Harvey and Joan Smith of Louisiana Family Planning, Department of Health and Human Resources; Annie Joseph, Roxy Wright, and Nell Lipscomb, formerly of the Family Health Foundation.

Audrey Collins, Roland Baptiste, and Joan Hertzberg of the Louisiana Department of Health and Human Resources.

Corinne Barnwell, Mayor's Office of Human Rights (New Orleans); Terri Bartlett, Planned Parenthood of Louisiana; Peggy Cottel, Delta Women's Clinic (New Orleans); Susan Andrews, Banks College, New York.

Virginia Ktsanes, Dr. William Bertrand, and Dr. Elizabeth Bennett of the School of Public Health and Tropical Medicine, Tulane University.

Dr. May Wells Jones, Dr. Hugh Floyd, and Warren Gravois of the University of New Orleans.

Jesse Smallwood, Dorothy Bolding, and Missy Rowley.

Doris Antin and Wilber E. Meneray of the Howard-Tilton Library, Tulane University.

My appreciation is extended to all these people as well as to others who made significant contributions but asked to remain unnamed. I would like to thank all the women who shared their stories about birth control, abortions, doctors, Charity Hospital, and trips to a family planning program that treated them with dignity. I have tried to represent fairly all the insights and different opinions that emerged from this research. However, the responsibility for the analysis and the interpretations in this book is exclusively mine.

I would like to pay special tribute to the late Dr. Ann Fischer, a mentor and colleague who planted seeds of interest she never saw harvested. My late friend and neighbor, Jane Lindsey, offered me a sunny office, many cups of coffee, unstinting good humor, and stern criticism. Patty Andrews edited the manuscript and saved me from the worst excesses of rhetoric. Other friends, too numerous to mention, have supported me in many ways.

My thanks to the staff of the Howard-Tilton Library of Tulane University, the Katherine Dexter McCormick Library in New York City, the Tulane University Medical School Library, and the Louisiana State University Medical Center Library. I owe a special debt of gratitude to the faculty and staff of the University of New Orleans Earl K. Long Library who have been wonderful, above and beyond the call of scholarly duty. They found obscure materials and gave unfailingly professional advice.

It has been a delight to work with the staff at Westview Press. The technical aspects of publication would have been tedious without the encouragement and support of Miriam Gilbert, Dean Birkenkamp, and Lynn Malkinson and the editorial assistance of Kathy Streckfus and Pat Peterson.

I would also like to thank my family, friends, colleagues, and students who interrupt my concentration but light up my life. Financial support for this project has come from the University of New Orleans Liberal Arts Organized Research for a summer stipend and teaching-load reduction. Their support in this undertaking is gratefully acknowledged.

Martha C. Ward

1

More Folklore
than Folk Care

Men and women have always longed for both fertility and sterility, each in its appointed time and in its chosen circumstances.
—Norman Himes, 1970

*There was an old woman
Who lived in a shoe.
She had so many children.
She didn't know what to do.*
—Nursery rhyme

*There was an old woman
Who lived in a shoe.
She had few children.
She knew what to do.*
—Anonymous

Here is a story of a trial balloon that flew high and then burst. It chronicles the efforts of young idealists to provide comprehensive health care for the deprived families of Louisiana and ultimately for the rest of the world. As with most social movements, the story began with personal tales of hardships and triumph that give meaning where statistics fail. In the following case, a black woman, age twenty-four, was living in a housing project with her four children. Her husband had abandoned the family. She describes what she considers the fate of women like her.

If you're poor, you got no safety. Anything can drop you back in the pit. You get pregnant, you're back in the pit. You get sick, you got no job. But the hardest poor is being poor with too many children. It not only affects your physical health, but your mental health. You are despondent, living in the project. You are blaming your kids for just being there. You are looking at them and thinking of all the things you could have been if they weren't there.

This emotion goes to the child. You have a kid five years old setting fires in the kitchen and pushing his sister out the window. You say he is a bad child, but it is his mama putting her frustrations on him that makes him

1

bad. Those children were conceived in love with your husband, but it just wasn't time for them to be here.

I was as dumb as the gulls. I had four babies and my life seemed already used up. Living in the project. Frustrated. Going to church and spending hours on my knees praying: "Why did this happen to me? Why can't I be this? Why can't I be that?"

I knew hundreds like me, all locked in by being poor and having babies. Women who could have been doctors. Who could have been lawyers. Who could have been *something*. And my babies? It didn't look no better for them.

Of course, I had had help. I had been to Charity Hospital. I had gotten welfare. I had been to OEO. But it didn't mean anything. It didn't get me out of the pit.[1]

She credits the introduction of family planning to Louisiana with taking her and other women like her out of the pit.

In 1964, when our story starts, Louisiana resembled an underdeveloped country. On all the classic scales—illiteracy, illegitimacy, high infant and maternal mortality, welfare dependency, poverty, family pathologies, and the blighted lives of children—the state ranked consistently at or near the bottom.

Some have joked that Louisiana is the northernmost banana republic. The state is largely supported by the petrochemical industry, agriculture, and the products of the wild, fish and furs. New Orleans and the quietly beautiful bayou region draw tourists. The state is famous for flamboyant politicians, colorful scandals, and episodic public corruption, some of which play a part in this account. Southern Louisiana is dominated by Catholic traditions that go back to the settlement of the state over 200 years ago. Northern Louisiana and the legislature are largely in the hands of rural Protestant conservatives.

Class and color overshadowed all the health and welfare statistics, as well as the programs that purported to help. Racial prejudice was rampant in 1964. Per capita income was low for whites, lower yet for blacks. The same was true for educational levels. Black babies and mothers died at about twice the rate of white babies and mothers. Only bleaker data from states like Alabama and Mississippi saved Louisiana from being in last place in discouraging statistics.

To be poor in Louisiana was generally to be black. Thirty percent of the state's population was black; more than half of the black families had incomes below the poverty level; and a fourth received public welfare assistance, according to the 1960 census. Between 1960 and 1970, the median annual income for black families was less than $8,000 per year. The average level of education fell between the tenth and eleventh grades.[2] Although other racial and ethnic groups lived in Louisiana, public perceptions focused on the black-white dichotomy.

Health Care and Birth Control in the 1960s

In the 1960s entrenched institutions and attitudes perpetuated poverty and poor health throughout the state. Disinterest in public family planning programs and other forms of preventive medicine stemmed in part from the dual health care system with its public and private sectors, selected according to the patient's ability to pay. Preventive medicine, public health measures, and what is now called primary health care were largely unavailable to certain segments of the population.

Today birth control, or the more comprehensive family planning, has come to be regarded as a key to the prevention of disease and death and as a public health measure to cure many of the ills of society. But Louisiana in the 1960s had no mechanisms for the democratization of birth control. Traditions against contraception were rooted in the law, the church, the state, the medical establishment, and above all the mores and cultural traditions in the state. There were no birth control clinics in Louisiana, private or public, and no intentions to provide such a service.

Birth control was a dirty word. It conjured up images of sex, feminism, communism, or repressive social control. Furthermore, Section 14:88 of the Louisiana Criminal Code made it a felony to disseminate information about contraceptives or any birth control measure. Although no one had ever been tried, much less sentenced, under the statute, it served as a deterrent to public discussion and organized action (McCoy 1963). Legislative efforts to authorize the State Board of Health to begin community education programs for family planning had been killed in committee. In fact, the slant of proposed legislation was toward sterilization as a solution to the problem of women on welfare having babies. To judge from the record in other states, heavy Catholic and fundamentalist religious opposition to birth control programs could be anticipated. According to the Archdiocese figures, approximately one-third of the state's inhabitants were Catholic.

Women who could afford to pay and had educated themselves about contraception probably never knew that a visit to their doctor was technically illegal. They knew only that one must be extremely careful to find a doctor whose ideas coincided with their own. They avoided Catholic doctors. Such women, middle class by definition, developed informal networks of information about private doctors who could be relied on to provide contraceptive care. Assuming a minimum of two visits and no complications, the cost was roughly $40 to $75 per year. Of course, to make an appointment with a private doctor a woman had to be already familiar with family planning.

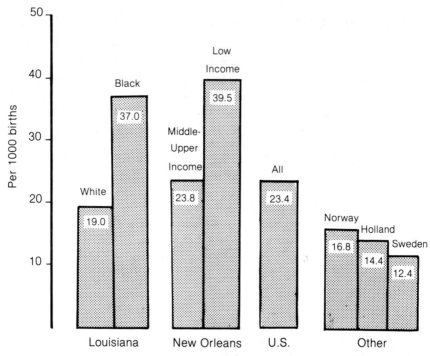

Figure 1.1 Infant mortality rates, 1965 (Source: Louisiana Family Planning, Inc.)

Poor women, who are the real focus of this story, enjoyed far fewer options. Within the state hospitals, little or nothing in the way of preventive medicine and especially family planning was available. Planned Parenthood had no chapters in Louisiana, and no sex education was offered at any level of the state's public or parochial schools. Some women did sneak through the net, educate themselves about birth control, and find a private doctor willing to help, but studies showed a striking difference in both availability and use of contraceptives between middle-class and lower-class women (Jaffe 1973; Westoff and Ryder 1970).

Infant mortality rates are frequently considered the single best indicator of a nation's health status. Statistics on infant deaths reflect a constellation of inadequacies in such areas as nutrition both during and after pregnancy, the availability and quality of medical care, and above all the societal commitment to human life. The infant mortality rates for the United States as a whole, compared with those for European countries, were embarrassingly high (Shapiro et al. 1968) (see Figure 1.1). In some places or for some groups, such as black families in New Orleans, the rates approached or equaled the infant mortality rates of Third World countries such as India or Egypt.

Blame for the poor rates of infant and maternal mortality is often placed on the sizable racial, ethnic, or immigrant groups with high fertility rates. But many researchers who have studied the figures know that different patterns of access to health care as well as poor diet, prenatal care, and education are directly reflected in the infant mortality figures (Hendricks 1967). They also point out the equally disturbing figures on morbidity (illness), prematurity, and retardation that result from the same causes as infant deaths. Babies with special health problems require a heavy commitment of resources from their family and from society.

Another tragic statistic is that for maternal mortality, the death of women in childbirth or from pregnancy-related complications. Before the introduction of family planning, septic abortions were the leading cause of maternal mortality. Inadequate prenatal care has also been directly correlated with both infant and maternal mortality (Dott and Fort 1975a, 1975b). Although the unflattering figures on deaths and illness were available in Louisiana, public health officials did not seem to regard preventive medical programs such as family planning as related to the solution.

Although the great birth control crusades of the twentieth century were fought for women's rights in fertility management, their successes were incomplete and had never been democraticized to the extent of reaching women in poverty. Virtually none of the reforms instituted by Margaret Sanger after a long series of legal and political battles had permeated such underdeveloped regions as Louisiana. Nonetheless, the shape of the battles fought and the victories won is instructive as background for the subsequent developments in the national family planning movement of the 1960s and the introduction of radical solutions in Louisiana.

The Woman Rebel

The mother of the birth control movement[3] was Margaret Sanger. Although much has been written about the effects of her crusade on U.S. life, I shall mention only the aspects of her work relevant to developments in family planning in Louisiana.

Margaret Sanger was a socialist, a mother, a midwife, and the sixth of eleven children from a poor Catholic family in New York. Her reforming zeal arose from what we would now call consciousness-raising experiences: the refusals of the labor movement to include family hygiene in their platforms, the death of her patient Sadie Sachs from a botched abortion after her appeals for birth control were rejected, and a deeply stimulating friendship with Havelock Ellis, the father of the study of normal human sexuality. Ultimately she wrote a number of books, delivered thousands of speeches around the world, and was jailed nine times in defense of her beliefs.[4] Small, beautiful, and charismatic, she traveled throughout the world meeting with such influential people as Eleanor Roosevelt and Mahatma Gandhi, some of whom she converted to her cause. Sanger coined the term "birth control" and published a journal called *The Woman Rebel*, which had the motto "No Gods, No Masters." She was the inspiration for the formation of several journals and organizations, including the National Birth Control League, a forerunner of the prestigious International Planned Parenthood Federation.

The Comstock Laws

Sanger instigated definitive battles in the legal and political arenas of the United States. In 1914, the issue of women's right to information about contraception ran into its first legal barrier. In 1883, Anthony Comstock, a postal employee, compiled the infamous Comstock laws (actually Section 211 of the Federal Statutes for the U.S. Post Office). The laws, designed to preserve the purity of late Victorian life in the United States, prohibited the use of the federal mails for the dissemination of foul literature. Mailing information about contraception, much less the equipment for it, left the sender liable for fines and a stiff jail sentence for pornography. (This is why prudish censorship is called Comstockery.) Moreover, many state statutes stated that no one could give out contraceptive information to anyone for any reason. Some left a loophole permitting physicians to give information to men to prevent venereal disease carried by women other than their wives. Sanger openly defied the Comstock laws, inviting prosecution. But she would have preferred to justify her violations on the basis of the First Amendment and freedom of speech and to avoid legal proceedings against her as a pornographer. To escape the latter, at one point she fled the country under an assumed name, having defiantly mailed a copy of her pamphlet, *Family Limitation*, to the judge in her case.

With the death of Comstock and as a result of a post–World War I retreat from prudery and the concerted efforts of social reformers in England and the United States, the majority of federal Comstock laws were struck down. The final victory came with a decision of the Supreme Court in 1936 that permitted one package of Japanese contraceptives to enter the country. The "One Package" decision removed the federal barriers but left standing many state laws prohibiting the dissemination of contraception information. These remaining statutes chilled state and local initiatives to offer family planning to any but private patients. Such was the case in New York, Connecticut, Massachusetts, and Louisiana well into the 1960s. Meanwhile, these laws did not prevent middle-class women from privately obtaining diaphragms or other aid. The laws were only instrumental in stifling contraception programs in public clinics, hospitals, or other agencies serving poor women.

Medical Endorsement

In her visits to Europe, Margaret Sanger began to realize that her visions of a brave new world for "mothers whose miseries are vast as the sky" would require conventional medical support. Doctors in the postwar era were just beginning to talk about the medical correlation of poverty, rising costs of welfare, infant and maternal deaths, illegal abortions, and related social problems. But U.S. physicians had only tenuously established their professional integrity; they feared quackery and amateur reformers more than disease. Although they worried about legions of women treating themselves, using folk remedies or dangerous nostrums, they also feared the dilution of medical authority by social reformers who openly discussed sex and expected them to do likewise.

Endorsement of birth control by some physicians may have arisen more from circumstances than from convictions (Reed 1978); they were concerned about a Sanger takeover of the medical prerogatives. Although most doctors gave qualified approval to contraception in cases involving pathology, they were distressed by a tendency they saw in the movement to blur therapeutic birth control (as they defined it) with a type of birth control on demand. They were reluctant to accept nonmedical reasons for its use. In contrast, the advocates of birth control related it to the happiness, health, and marital sexuality of normal women and, beyond that, saw it as a solution to many of the social and economic evils of society. Doctors criticized Sanger for not checking marriage licenses and for permitting women to seek birth control for personal reasons. (These same arguments are frequently heard in the abortion controversy today.)

But Sanger preached that marital or familial circumstances dictated the use of birth control. She insisted that contraception was a normal part of happy, marital sexuality as was the desire to limit or space children. Although these provisions were radical at the time—more often for the medical profession than for patients—we now regard the regulation of family size, child spacing, and fertility as conventional middle-class wisdom. In fact, Sanger's conservative emphasis on marriage and adult responsibilities appears old fashioned when compared with contemporary feminist philosophy of reproductive freedom and women's control of their bodies, both inside and outside of marriage.

In 1937, after two decades of aggressive crusading by Sanger, the American Medical Association agreed to support birth control and public education in the field, affirming the right of a woman to contraceptive assistance within the privacy of a doctor-patient relationship. The endorsement also backed Sanger's call for research to develop efficient contraceptive technology and studies to collect accurate information on women's fertility histories.

Catholic Opposition

The major Protestant and Jewish religious bodies had earlier been enlisted in the cause; by the early 1930s they had endorsed birth control and urged repeal of federal and state legislation that interfered with the free flow of information. With these symbolic victories behind her, Margaret Sanger tackled the Catholic hierarchy, but to no avail. Both sides proved intransigent and entered into fruitless battles that prevented compromise or reconciliation. In retrospect many Catholic clergy, doctors, and women appear to have had more open views on birth control than did the politically visible church fathers. But "politicians and bureaucrats feared that their public support of birth control would be profoundly provocative to their Catholic constituents. The threat, whether real or exaggerated, of Catholic political reprisals served as the most effective obstacle to governmental action on birth control" (Kennedy 1970:269). The myths that Catholic solidarity would prevent public action persisted until birth control became a national issue in the 1960s. Eventually the Catholic hierarchy in the United States was forced to recognize that it could not impose its views on non-Catholics. By the time the family planning movement started, the Catholic opposition had loosened its hold, not in response to Sanger-style persuasion or the intrinsic rightness of the cause but in response to political realities.

A Middle-Class Movement

Margaret Sanger's movement did not address the challenge of delivering services for birth control to large numbers of women. Her campaign had succeeded for middle-class women because it concentrated on legal rights and public advocacy. Middle-class families had understood the connection between fertility control and social mobility, and their incomes permitted private care. The poor, including immigrants, had limited access to medical treatment or organized services in preventive medicine, particularly for maternal and infant health.

One of the ironies of the birth control movement is the ideological shift from the view that women should be given control over their fertility as a step to a better quality of life to the conservative stand that birth control should be used for racist ends. The idea that birth control can be used punitively for supposed undesirables has continued to haunt the family planning movement. Many critics of lower-class fecundity rates persist in believing that birth control is available to all women. If they do not use it, then the only conclusion is that they do not want to. This attitude of blaming the victim was the last frontier of the birth control movement in the 1960s when the family planning movement attacked the issues of dual health care systems, poverty, and fertility on a national level.

Mother Charity

When family planning was eventually introduced into Louisiana in 1964, it came as a radical alternative to medical systems that provided care to poor people in the state. The story of how these health services were irrevocably altered by a birth control program can only be understood against the history of these peculiar institutions.

Louisiana's unique public health system began as a private philanthropic hospital founded by a sailor, Jean Louis, in 1735. It was consolidated under state control during the Depression as the populist legacy of Governor Huey Long, who vowed that every poor person in the state, including blacks, should have state-supported medical care. Today, this unusual system is the only one of its kind left in the United States.

A statewide system of ten Charity hospitals was capped by a flagship hospital in New Orleans. Over the course of nearly 250 years, "Big C," "Mother Charity," or just "Charity," has survived "five permanent buildings, four flags, three languages, the scourge of summer plagues, Civil Service, Huey Long, and one enemy occupation" (Arrowsmith 1979:33). Charity Hospital in New Orleans is frequently called the largest of its kind in the world, although what "its kind" means is not clear. It is billed as the largest hospital in continuous usage in the United States and one of the four biggest in the world (Grayson 1981:49).

In the 1960s neither the Charity hospitals nor other institutions in Louisiana offered birth control services or the broader programs of family planning because of the Comstock law and the perceived Catholic influence. The order of the Sisters of Charity dominated the nursing staff and its training. Although some doctors said that they assumed that this prevented birth control instruction, the sisters say that they would never have stood in the way of a medical decision or the doctor-patient relationship. Whatever the reasons, preventive medicine through family planning had been placed low on the priorities of Mother Charity and her daughters.

Most of the education of medical students and nurses was conducted through Charity where future doctors practiced on the poor. The hospital was the cornerstone of the dual health care system, with one style for the rich and one for the poor.

> For an enormous population, Charity is the high tribunal of medical care. The claim has been made that there have been more babies born in Charity than in any other hospital in the world. . . . In its history it has been the best, the biggest, the most mismanaged, the least responsive to its patients; it has been near the extremes of whatever one might look at in such an institution. (Arrowsmith 1979:1)

Charity Hospital was widely believed to provide the best services for gunshot wounds or emergency care. It also offered excellent treatment for such challenges as premature infants, contagious diseases, and trauma care (the medical inheritance of the indigent). But doctors and nurses who have trained there admit that services in obstetrics, gynecology, and pediatrics were, in most respects, a failure. The high rates of infant mortality and morbidity in the state were no credit to the system, certainly compared with conditions in the rest of the country.

Care Without Choice

Alternatives to Charity did not exist. The parish (county) health departments disbanded the few prenatal and postnatal programs in this period because of administrative complexity. In Orleans Parish, where the need was greatest, a survey explained that

> The New Orleans Health Department does not operate such a clinic service. The reason is clear and specific. If Charity Hospital eligible patients from our prenatal clinic were sent to Charity Hospital for their last month of observation, preparatory to delivery at the hospital, neither patients nor their records would be accepted by the hospital. If the procedure were varied and patients sent to the Charity Hospital early in pregnancy for registration with the hope that this would facilitate their acceptance later for delivery, this would also be unacceptable to the hospital. (New Orleans Department of Health 1968:17)

Many low-income patients could not participate in prenatal programs at private hospitals but had incomes too high to qualify for prenatal care at Charity. They learned that they would be accepted if they presented themselves as emergency cases at Charity. Deprived of adequate prenatal care, mothers and children often fell through the cracks of the health bureaucracy.

Care Without Courtesy

The issue of courtesy to patients at Charity Hospital has long been a sore point, particularly for minorities and women, despite occasional attempts to bring reform.

> Until the advent of federal health insurance programs, the only medical facilities for the indigent were the charity hospitals. The patient had to be willing to undergo a tedious and often degrading admission procedure; accept rude and sometimes irresponsible treatment from hospital staff, interns and residents; be confined in a multi-bed ward with no privacy, accept minimal facilities and services. (Gulf South Research Institute 1968:104)

Acute observers can still note the architectural reminders of racism, the years when the hospitals were divided into white or black wards and admission facilities. Linguistic traditions reflected the heyday of segregation and older customs of slavery. Women who were pregnant or had children were routinely called "mother," and elderly blacks were addressed as "aunt" or "uncle." All patients were assigned numbers that were changed from visit to visit. Personal names were never used.

Both patients and doctors have reported examples of callous treatment, including disrespectful language.

> "O.K. gal, get your black ass up here." "What are you so afraid of, it's just a finger this time." (in reference to examinations)
>
> "Mother, your roses come down yet?" (in reference to menstruation)
>
> "Mother, you didn't yell that way when you got like that." (to a woman in labor)

At Charity, women allegedly had no place to change clothes for an examination and were supposed to come to the hospital in skirts without underclothes. Sometimes women were examined in the hallways and other public areas. Conditions in other hospitals and clinics that served the poor were often no better. Many scandalous stories of the treatment of women were publicized for the first time when the family planning clinics were opened in 1964. Improving the mode of treatment for women was one of the major motivations.

To go to Charity, patients often had to skip work, arrange child care, find transportation or take buses with several transfers, and then wait all day to see a doctor. For these reasons they often declined the available care. Educational programs to back up public health services were a luxury Charity could not afford. With barely enough staff for the acute cases, the subacute cases and preventive medicine were neglected.

Care Without Communication

Even with programs such as the prenatal clinic that concentrated on cases of toxemia or other troubled pregnancies, Charity suffered from endemic problems of communicating across cultural, racial, and sexual barriers. As a mother of four children who attended these clinics recalls,

> I had been sent to the toxemia clinic at Charity. But I never knew what it was for. I didn't know I had high blood pressure. I didn't know that was dangerous for a pregnant woman or that you could die from it. They told us about diet, but I thought that was for the baby. They didn't tell us about salt. The doctors yelled, fussed and got angry about weight gain. They acted just like a Daddy! "No more than 20 pounds," they would scream; but they never explained how weight was related to toxemia. In the clinic or the maternity classes I attended, the women were resentful of the treatment or afraid that they were being used as guinea pigs. I saw women share this belief with each other but not with the staff. So they skipped meetings a lot and did what they thought was important for the baby, but that wasn't what Charity had told them to do. So they didn't go back until serious trouble developed or labor had started.

The doctors at Charity were incredulous at this attitude. They knew how important prenatal visits were and that 20 percent of the women delivering at Charity had not come in for an examination before the eighth month of pregnancy. One-third of the women delivering at the Charity hospitals averaged less than three prenatal visits; more than half skipped their postpartum checkup.

Among its other problems, the system was gradually resegregating itself during the 1960s as the white population seeking free medical assistance declined relative to the black population (Gulf South Research Institute 1968:103). Indigent patients fell increasingly under the provisions of Medicaid and Medicare or other federally funded health care programs and could choose where to go. Until recently, 95 percent of all babies born to poor mothers entered life at Charity. For the peak years of Charity, the figure often topped 9,000 babies per year. Today only about half of that number are born at Charity because mothers are being served elsewhere.[5]

Despite criticisms, for all practical purposes Charity was the primary institution for poor people, and the hospital struggled with largely intransigent problems not of its own making.[6] The nutritional status of many patients is an example. The relationship of good nutrition to healthy babies may be complex, but it is incontrovertible. That poor people have substandard diets is also well known. While conducting research in rural Louisiana and in the waiting rooms of Charity, I have interviewed women who told of practicing what anthropologists call pica (obsessive eating of nonnutritional substances; Lackey 1978:121). One local favorite substance is Arco starch, a brand of laundry starch that is eaten as a cheap form of caloric intake. Certain types of clay are reportedly consumed in Mississippi and Louisiana. Chronic malnutrition, less a case of too little food than the wrong kinds of food, contributes to serious health problems in poor families.

The Folklore of Fertility

If a poor woman has little recourse to organized medicine for assistance in fertility management, what are her alternatives? A black woman who had discovered birth control after five children said, "We were always afraid. Five days late and BOOM! We watched that calendar every month." According to accounts from many sources, one clear but drastic choice is folk medicine passed verbally through many generations and shared secretly in networks of friends and relatives. Folklore flourishes in traditional societies in which systems of modern medicine are inadequate. Louisiana has been known as a fertile field for folk practices such as herbal treatment, voodoo, gris-gris, and black magic (Brandon 1976). Within this broad tradition, beliefs and practices about fertility management are easy to collect by asking, "How can women stop having babies?" or "What makes the blood come down?"[7]

Use of folk methods of birth control or abortion has generally been regarded as a sin. Nevertheless, women discuss them and pass on information. This folk knowledge blurs the distinction between control and abortion. Women mention using or hearing of remedies that serve either purpose. For example, a douche made of boiled rusty nails is reported as a contraceptive and an abortafacient. The same is true for taking quinine tablets or potash pills or using turpentine as a drink or douche. One woman said, "Take all the laxatives you can think of." Another told of drinking a mixture of a half of a cup of pepper and plenty of salt in hot water. Such concoctions are reputed to bring on severe cramps and contractions that mimic giving birth.

Most of my informants thought that plant compounds were effective even when they did not know the recipes. In rural areas, plants like pennyroyal were often cited. In urban areas, the folk remedies included vitamin C or B-17, Laetrile, papaya seeds, mescaline, or an entire pack of birth control pills taken at once. Credit for the success of these methods was in excess of probability: Women may spontaneously miscarry or may not have been pregnant, but they credit home remedies for terminating their condition. They also confuse home remedies for birth control with those for self-induced abortion. Jumping up and down or drinking certain concoctions is believed to both prevent conception and end a pregnancy.

Beyond naive beliefs and ineffective abortafacients is induced abortion. What has been inserted into the vagina or uterus to abort unplanned pregnancies is limited only by imagination and physiology. Doctors and nurses are often appalled by the sticks, rocks, chopsticks, rubber or plastic tubes, gauze or cotton packing, ballpoint pens, coat hangers, or knitting needles. Douches believed effective in inducing abortions are made from detergents, orange juice, vinegar, bleach, disinfectant, lye, potassium pomegranate, or colas. The gaseous explosion of soft drinks is said to cause a miscarriage; some teenagers consider them spermicidal and use them for birth control. Informants also credited enemas or violent exercise with ending a pregnancy.

The persistence of folklore in the absence of standard medical alternatives attested to the dictum that

> contraception, as the only form of population control, is a social practice of much greater historical antiquity, greater cultural and geographical universality than commonly supposed even by medical and social historians. Contraception has existed in some form throughout the entire range of social evolution. . . . The desire for, as distinct from the achievement of, reliable contraception has been characteristic of many societies widely removed in time and place. Moreover, this desire for controlled reproduction characterized even those societies dominated by mores and religious codes demanding that people "increase and multiply." (Himes 1970:xii)

Women through the ages have been willing to discuss and use in secret assorted noxious compounds, recipes, and life-threatening solutions to achieve a measure of control over reproduction. They have been willing to face the wrath of spouses, church, and secular authorities. Abortion and harsh folk remedies persist when other choices are unavailable. The extraordinary determination of women to risk their lives provided motivation for advocates of family planning.

Abortion and Sterilization

Abortion was illegal in Louisiana until 1974. It could be obtained illegally by using folk methods or employing unauthorized practitioners.[8] Middle-class women could sometimes persuade their physicians to arrange one discreetly or to refer them to an abortionist. In the decade before abortions were legalized, a price of $500 was common in New Orleans. Women of means could go to Puerto Rico, Mexico, New York, or Europe.

In contrast, poor women had unplanned children or went to "the lady down the street" or "the woman downstairs." Neighborhood practicioners sometimes had been trained at Charity as licensed practical nurses or nurses aides. Their fee for abortions was between $50 and $75. This was expensive considering that a pregnant woman might earn $10 a day. If complications developed, she would have to be taken to a "drugstore physician" who operated in the poor sections of the community. This visit cost about $3. Relatives, some of whom may have had similar experiences, cared for the woman in their homes. Only in the most dire circumstances would a woman in difficulty from an inept abortion go to Charity. Consequently, the rate of septic abortions reported by the hospital was very low. Sometimes white women, who did not have access to the same networks as black women, went into black neighborhoods seeking abortions. Many who were not even pregnant sought abortionists' services (Harter and Beasley 1967).

Ironically, birth control by hysterectomy was available at the Charity hospitals. A story that circulates in the local medical community is that more hysterectomies are now performed at Charity than any other hospital in the country. According to one doctor, "if we're not first then I don't know who is." Supposedly when a patient exclaimed, "Lord have mercy, no more babies," she was scheduled for surgery.

In the decades before birth control methods became available women discussed the operation among themselves. Such surgery removed guilt over contraception, especially if a medical authority had recommended it. Women learned how to present the correct symptoms. Some, for whom standard English was an alien dialect, heard that a hysterectomy would be ordered if they reported "stress urinary incontinence." Lessened bladder control and repeated pregnancies were sufficient indications. Sometimes the doctors reputedly entered into a conspiracy with their patients. She would say, "I don't want any more babies." If she could answer yes to the question "Do you have pain, backaches, or heavy bleeding?" then the diagnosis was uterine prolapse and the cure was surgery. If she answered no, she was told to return and report heavy bleeding, backaches, and pain. On her return visit she was scheduled for the operation.

Doctors report that women in large numbers begged and pleaded for the operation. They themselves urged it for any patient who had had frequent or complicated pregnancies or any other serious health problem. The hospital staff was overworked and had large numbers of high-risk patients and eager residents grateful for operating room experience.

Their philosophy supposedly was "When you've got them, do it right." Doing it right meant a hysterectomy. They also justified the practice for its prophylactic value. Since comprehensive Pap tests and cancer or VD screening programs were not feasible on any regular basis, medical policy reputedly was to regard hysterectomies as a major form of prevention not only for pregnancies but also for cancer of the uterus or asymptomatic gonorrhea.

Feminists argue that hysterectomies are one of the most common unnecessary, even exploitive, surgeries on women. Where the cultural patterns are different or where coercion is possible, this may be true. Under the circumstances described and in the absence of organized birth control services, however, a hysterectomy was regarded by doctors and patients as the treatment of choice for women who wanted a socially justifiable control over their fertility and family size. The full spectrum of reproductive rights, as the feminist movement calls them, was unavailable in Louisiana, so women adapted themselves to limited choices.

Because of strict rules and review committees at Charity and other hospitals, sterilization was used very infrequently as a birth control option for poor and middle-class women alike. An essentially conservative institution in a largely Catholic community could justify hysterectomies as life-saving or reparative surgery in a way that it could never explain sterilization. Women learned not to bother asking.

From Myths to Informed Views

Louisiana traditions of reproduction and social class discouraged assertiveness on the part of the patients as well as open-mindedness from the medical establishment. The highly personal subject of birth control provoked contradictory ideals and subjective value systems masquerading as legislative or medical fiat.

Common attitudes about birth control ran the gamut from the commonplace religious one ("It's a sin and against God's will to prevent pregnancy") to the uninformed frightened one (that contraceptives reduce sexual drives or damage health). Those who questioned the necessity for repeated pregnancies were told, "God doesn't send more burdens than one can bear," or "If you can find food for one mouth, you can find food for two or three more." Some of the anxieties centered on traditional definitions of sex roles. A man might wish to exert control over his wife's or girlfriend's fertility: "She's not a whole woman if she uses birth control. It takes away her nature." Men might dwell on the conflicting fears that women with access to birth control would become promiscuous or lose interest in sex altogether. Some bragged about the number of children they had fathered and resented women's abilities to deprive them of such trophies. As a result, women often kept secret their sterilizations, abortions, or contraceptive practices.

Beyond these fears are general attitudes about the moral decay and promiscuity that may result from birth control and sex education. Conservatives favoring social control maintain that some groups have too many babies for the collective good and should be compelled to limit their reproduction. These alleged undesirable groups include the criminally insane, the retarded, and the very large group of women who receive public assistance (a euphemism for blacks in Louisiana). On the opposite extreme, low-income, racial, or ethnic groups fear government policies that may be intended to control their reproductive rate without their consent.

Physicians also espoused myths about birth control. Their rationalizations about fertility and family structure (particularly about blacks) helped account for the unavailability of family planning systems. Many charged that black women wanted to be pregnant and have all those children and that even if they did not want repeated pregnancies, they could not possibly understand the principles of birth control because they were not bright enough and lacked behavioral control. Thus, they perpetuated a self-fulfilling prophesy.

Because these myths were so pervasive, early family planners had to spend considerable time and money on motivational and opinion surveys to prove that lower-class women would embrace birth control with the same fervor as middle-class women did. The major issue in the 1960s (and it still persists in some circles) was whether family planning services would be acceptable to poor women. The debate centered on accessibility versus the culture and motivation approach (Jaffe and Polgar 1968). Anthropologists such as Oscar Lewis and Charles Valentine had popularized the term "culture of poverty," which is characterized by low economic status and a set of values differing from those of the wealthier classes of the same society. The poor do not postpone gratification or plan for the future. They are impulsive and live for the moment. Even if birth control were available, the lower classes would make little use of it because of their life-style patterns of apathy, fatalism, poor marital adjustment, excessive sex, machismo, and fears about masculinity on the part of males and the hungry womb or pronatalist syndrome for women (Rainwater 1960). As a subset of the culture of poverty, blacks were believed to produce disintegrating families in which illegitimacy carried no stigma and women were economically and psychologically dominant.

If poor women acted from different cultural and psychological values, then family planning services would be senseless without extensive programs to alter their perceptions of the world and to orient them to middle-class mores. Proponents of the culture-motivational approach failed to see that one problem of the poor is adjusting to the life-style of the middle-class providers. For example, welfare rules may jeopardize the recipient's eligibility for public assistance if she attends a family planning clinic. Sometimes clinics are not open at convenient times and have long waiting lines or hostile personnel (Jaffe and Polgar 1968). The accessibility argument was simple: When barriers to utilization are removed, poor women would be as eager as anyone else. "Despite the persistence of such unfavorable institutional factors and the relationship of family planning to deeply internalized attitudes about sex, even a modest improvement in the opportunity structure thus seems capable of bringing about substantial behavioral change" (Jaffe and Polgar 1968:230).

Nationwide fertility studies have shown a chronic inverse relationship between income and family size; that is, the more children in a family, the greater the likelihood of poverty. Poorer families desired an average of fewer than three children but had more. Families that used contraception relied on ineffective, nonmedical methods (Whelpton et al. 1966; Freedman et al. 1959). When coitus-independent methods (the pill, IUD, or sterilizations) were made available, enthusiasm for controlling fertility among the poor began to match established patterns in the middle class and racial-ethnic differences disappeared (Beasley and Frankowski 1970; Hellman 1971). To those who argued that the opportunity structure was the issue, the culture of poverty stance was an excuse for not providing family planning to those in need.

Introducing opportunities for family planning required a massive reordering of health and welfare priorities. Money and staff, already stressed by too many needs, had to be reallocated. The pressure for reform came largely from the outside, from segments of the professional and liberal political community. State health bureaucracies and the medical community only grudgingly facilitated the efforts (Black 1972). In Chapter 2 we shall see how an innovative family planning program was introduced into the state and attacked Comstockery, the Charity hospitals, and the culture of poverty to offer an alternative to abortion, folk medicine, and the consequences of unwanted pregnancies.

2

Margaret Sanger
Comes to Louisiana

Many women in poverty areas would like to limit the size of their families and are simply unaware of existing birth control methods, or do not have such methods available to them. Government at all levels—and particularly the Federal—should underwrite broader programs to provide family planning information.
—U.S. Commission on Population, 1972

Perhaps a century from now, when historians record the major events of our time, they will place high on the list the night when the power failed in a little Louisiana community and three humble women came through the rain seeking a better way of life and they found it.
—Arthur Gordon, 1970

The first article of the first issue of a new journal, *Family Planning Perspectives* (Beasley 1969b), reported the achievements of an innovative program. On the cover, Margaret Sanger, jaunty and triumphant, stood towering over a map of Louisiana (Figure 2.1). Family planning had arrived in Louisiana against great odds. The barriers of church, state, law, and public opinion had been breached. A successful program for birth control for poor women had been inaugurated. The story in retelling often assumes mythical proportions. People at later times would refer to the growth and climax of the program as those of a family planning empire; today they still tell grandiose tales of its founder.

Joseph Diehl Beasley, the hero of the family planning legend, was a pediatrician. From a small town in rural Georgia, he worked his way through medical school and then found private practice too confining. Restless, he searched his soul, cashed in his assets, and took his family to the London School of Hygiene and Tropical Medicine to study the health problems of underdeveloped countries, particularly those related to nutrition. His search led him to a semitropical and somewhat

19

FAMILY PLANNING

Perspectives

VOLUME 1, NUMBER 1, SPRING 1969

View from Louisiana
View from Washington: Reorganization, Consolidation-or Both?
Birth Control, Teenagers and the Law

Figure 2.1 Cover of first issue of *Perspectives*. Drawing of Margaret Sanger is by David Levine. Reprinted by permission.

underdeveloped land, Louisiana, and to the Tulane University medical school and School of Public Health and Tropical Medicine with their strong ties to Latin America, Africa, and Asia. His first appointment was in the Department of Pediatrics; he then became professor and chairman of the Department of Family Health and Population Dynamics, the Department of Applied Health Sciences, and other departments or institutes created during internal reorganization, some of it sparked by his family planning activity. Eventually he would hold an astonishing array of positions both inside and outside the university. But his initial base of support was this academic position.

Descriptions of Joe Beasley's personality and his personal relationships are rampant in Louisiana. Those who knew and "loved him like a brother" or as "my best friend in all the world" and who pay homage to his drive, ambition, and ability also admit that "he is crazy too." As one journalist put it, "The social turmoil of those years spawned many social engineers like Joe Beasley, but not many with quite so much ego-driven determination, far-down-the-road vision, organizational talent, promotional zeal, and political daring" (Littlewood 1977:88).

Supporters have compared him to Will Rogers, or social reformers martyred for their causes, like Martin Luther King, Jr., Gandhi, or John F. Kennedy. But his detractors reply, "He could sell snake oil to a snake." He has been called an overzealous saint, a con artist, a savior for women, a rogue, and a scoundrel. Joe Beasley has what biographers are fond of calling fatal flaws: He is a poor judge of character, hot tempered, driven, and too stubborn to compromise. He has high expectations for himself and others, and not even his detractors have denied his charm and charisma, even when they ran afoul of him. As one coworker remarked, "He was like an evangelist, and all of us got caught up in the excitement." "He was a man with an idea and we were privileged to help," said another.

The Growth of the Vision

Beasley and other doctors who have worked at Charity Hospital tell a story about removing a doll from the arms of a twelve-year-old girl to replace it with her newborn baby. Although probably apocryphal, this story illustrates the human tragedy that the nascent family planners hoped to combat. When tracing the growth of this program, particularly in light of the power and money it later generated, it is important to remember that its first impetus was idealism[1] and a gut reaction to child abuse, battering, unwanted children, and, above all, infant mortality.

Beasley's initial objective was promulgation of birth control; his plan grew to include control of population size and alleviation of global health problems. He wanted to move beyond Margaret Sanger's original definition of birth control by concentrating on the health benefits for families and babies as well as those for mothers. As he defined the concept of family planning to a medical audience, "Family planning is a positive concept which involves giving the individuals the information, the advice and the service necessary to plan the conception of a child under circumstances that will give the product of that conception an optimal opportunity to develop his physical, intellectual and emotional potential as a human being" (Beasley 1969a:98).

The Objectives

With the concerns of a pediatrician, Beasley interpreted the 1959 UN Declaration of the Rights of a Child to say that these rights applied to children only after birth. But he believed that certain rights of conception are owed to children even before birth:

> the right to parents who are reasonably certain their marriage will last; the right to be wanted and not an unwanted accident; the right to freedom from genetic defects; the right of adequate maternal care for the mother; the right of an adequate delivery and birth in which every effort is made to sustain life during birth adaptation; and the right to have emotional, intellectual and physical needs met as the child matures. (Coyle 1968:19)

Beasley could move easily from these concepts, which he called "defining the worth of a child," into the population problems that appear to endanger the world.

The logical bridge between these two extremes is family planning— "a health measure [that] may or may not be an instrument for population control. It must be a part of population policy. Regardless of its population policy, a nation must concern itself with certain major obstacles which prevent the attainment of family health and stability necessary to foster the optimum development of the child" (Beasley, 1969a:98).

Although present in all social strata, the major obstacles of which he spoke most often impede members of the lower class and minorities and prevent the delivery of adequate health care. The immediate problems that family planning should address include the unwanted child, the unplanned pregnancy, and the criminal or medically unsupervised abortion.[2] In this period the medical complications of abortions were the leading cause of maternal mortality.

> The other thing we saw was tremendous problems of induced abortion, with the highest predominance in the lower socio-economic group, and the middle and the upper getting more expensive abortions. So we see women very

literally carved up—very crude abortions—knitting needles, cloth tacking. And we see them coming in highly febrile, puerperal discharge in the vagina, germs in their blood, blood poisoning, septicemia, and those who survive have a very high probability of being reproductive cripples. . . . Then when we looked at it, there was a very low pattern of contraception in the lower socio-economic group, in spite of what seemed to be a very strong desire not to have unwanted children. . . . *I mean, if a woman will risk her very life with a criminal abortion, that's pretty damn strong motivation.*

At the other end of the spectrum, we were studying what was happening to that large number of young girls who were having babies, literally, babies making babies. They were bright kids in school, but the fact that they could get pregnant was alien to them—it's almost inconceivable how alien it was. And the fact that it could happen to them because of sexual intercourse was a revelation. . . . We've seen one girl who at age 15 had her fourth delivery— and was never told in the hospital or anywhere else how to prevent this. (Beasley 1973:n.p.; emphasis in original)

Beasley and his associates believed that they could offer hope to many who suffered unnecessarily: women in poor health, whose infants were most likely to die; teenagers, many unmarried, whose children were born retarded or premature; and battered or neglected children, whose mothers lacked emotional strength and community support. Inadequate nutrition could not be addressed by family planning directly but could become the target of broader health services. They also believed that unstable marriages could develop when a couple had more children than it could support. They espoused the rights of a woman to control her own body and choose her own conditions for reproduction.

The inability of a woman to control her fertility deprives her of a real right and a real power. I believe in the concept of voluntarism—that human beings can learn, that they can take the knowledge they gain and apply it to the solution of their problems, and that they have a right to do this, for they are involved in their own freedom. I think it's absurd to try to coerce a woman to do something she probably wants to do anyway. (Lelyveld 1970)

To the family planners, the lack of personal freedom to choose indicated society's lack of commitment to all its children.

The Groundwork

Through 1964 and into 1965, a concrete plan began to take shape. The events leading to the first publicly supported family planning clinic in Louisiana occurred simultaneously rather than sequentially. A great deal of groundwork had to be laid in the areas of politics, religion, medicine, and racial sensitivity.

From the first, Beasley attracted a cadre of unusually talented researchers whose disciplines included sociology, anthropology, epidemiology, biostatistics, economics, and management. During the mid and late 1960s—when the civil rights movement was at its peak and the antipoverty campaigns were growing rapidly—these researchers found applying primary research data to develop a program that would change people's lives a heady experience. These dedicated professionals produced an amazing variety of papers, reports, manuals, and research results. Their association with Tulane University legitimized their activities in the community and provided specialized services and a recognized conduit for research funds. The core of professionals and academicians conducted attitudinal studies to find out how much people knew about birth control and reproduction to determine whether they would favor family planning programs for themselves or for others. They intended to confront the myths of fertility and the poor, to organize hard data for the legislature and funding agencies, and to investigate the feasibility of starting a birth control program. They needed research results to provide an argument for family planning on medical, economic, and humanitarian, as well as political, grounds.

The initial set of statistics came from residents of Lincoln Parish, where, it was hoped, the first clinic would open. The researchers discovered that the people of the parish needed and wanted family planning services. Forty-three percent of the women in Lincoln Parish were in the lowest income group, but they accounted for 94 percent of illegitimate births, 70 percent of the unplanned pregnancies, and 50 to 60 percent of miscarriages, abortions, and stillbirths, and 59 percent of all live births. Unwed mothers faced four times the mortality rate of married mothers, and their babies were twice as likely to die at birth or as infants (Parrish 1973:239; Parrish et al. 1965).

Over 90 percent of the people interviewed (everyone who might qualify for aid) regardless of religious affiliation, race, or income level, believed that couples had the right to determine their family size, and they endorsed the concept of publicly supported aid to the indigent. In the lower socioeconomic groups more than 80 percent wanted more information for themselves about family planning (Beasley and Harter 1967:190).

One of the most persuasive arguments for family planning, especially with politicians, was the potential reduction in health and welfare costs. In public speeches, Beasley reiterated that for every dollar spent in family planning, the state would save $13.50. In truth, this was a wild guess because no reliable data existed to back up such a claim. Interestingly, the state published statistics much later that corroborated Beasley's off-the-cuff estimate: "For each dollar of the state general fund expended for family planning services, the state saves $14.60 in unwanted pregnancy costs" (Louisiana, Division of Policy, Planning and Evaluation 1981:39).

Beasley knew that white policymakers in the Bible Belt would be receptive to a program that would reduce the birth rate of blacks. So he assured legislators and other policymakers that family planning was an alternative to rising welfare costs. This approach appealed to them: They would no longer have to debate controversial and expensive laws on involuntary sterilization or proposals to jail the parents of illegitimate children. Family planning could be represented as a class- and color-oriented form of social control.

Beasley and the family planners contacted the Surgeon General, the National Council of Pediatrics, and other agencies that were concerned and had the money to support a project. The first grant came from the Children's Bureau of Health, Education and Welfare. This initial grant and the subsequent ones, increasingly more generous, were unusual because the bureau had a reputation for not contributing to experimental programs. Providing a grant for attitudinal studies in a controversial and unproved area was a significant deviation. Bureau members were convinced for the first time that family planning was a key element in maternal and child health: better to prevent retardation than to try to cure it.

Beyond the intrinsic worth of the research, Beasley had a rare gift for getting money from the government. He favored dramatic presentations with the right amount of statistics on charts. His cause was just. Not even bureaucrats could harden their hearts against the ghosts of children and the hope for healthy families. On the average, Beasley traveled to Washington once a month. He wined and dined the right people and learned the ropes of grantsmanship. Washington is not immune to charisma.

Demographers believed that the "toughest nut to crack" for family planning would be the Southern, rural, conservative counties with a significant nonwhite or ethnic population (Freedman et al. 1959; Beasley and Parrish 1967). To show any progress at all, providers had to reach most of the eligible women while coping with conservative opposition. As a result, family planning programs were in large urban centers at this time.

The Prototype

Lincoln Parish was selected as the first place to try out the new programs because it met the proposed statistical criteria (Beasley and Parrish 1967:29; 1969:169). The planners wanted a governmental unit with a population no greater than 50,000 and with a nonwhite population making up between 30 and 50 percent of the total. If the crude birthrate was above 20 per 1,000, then the fertility and family planning problems would be similar to those in other parishes or counties in the South. Furthermore, the composition of medical personnel, facilities, and support services should be consistent with those in other rural areas. Adjacent parishes would act as controls for statistical comparisons. People's needs for family planning would have to be demonstrated and the eligible women contacted within a short time. Two years was the period initially projected.

In fact, the selection of Lincoln Parish as a site for a "research laboratory for population and family planning studies in a rural setting" (Beasley and Parrish 1967:29) was largely a case of serendipity. Ruston, the seat of Lincoln Parish, had an integrated and well-respected community medical facility called the Green Clinic and a dynamic pediatrician, Dr. Bruce Everist, who recalled:

> There were three pediatricians at the Green Clinic and we were working like the devil to reduce infant mortality. We did everything we knew how to do, but it still stayed too high. The black rate was about twice as high as the white rate (about 28–30 per thousand for blacks and 16–17 per thousand for whites). Why should this difference persist? We were committed to providing equal care for all women. Finally I realized that something else was going on. *Even if they had been born on the steps of the Mayo Clinic, those babies would still have died.* (Personal communication, April 8, 1982; emphasis added)

So Everist took his problem to the two medical schools in New Orleans, and surrounded by boxes in a beat-up old building, he found Joe Beasley, who had some statistics from an infant mortality study then under way and a burning idea. They talked all night and by morning had an outline. Beasley thought that he could borrow $600; the money, the facilities in Ruston, and a pediatrition like Everist would permit a beginning.

With the money and an old Ford to make the 600-mile round-trip, the collaborators began the effort to open the first clinic in Lincoln Parish. They had decided against a passive program; instead, they would go to recruit patients as aggressively as possible. They intended to test new methods that included searches for records and vital statistics, home visits, and follow-up visits for missed appointments, and they planned to create a welcoming atmosphere at the clinic.

They actively sought approval and support from many agencies and individuals.[3] If the governor, attorney general, Catholic archbishop, the president of Tulane, and other leaders gave their endorsements, the rest of the state would follow. Before granting endorsements, these leaders raised a number of political questions. Would the program influence costs for tax-supported agencies? What were the attitudes of racial and religious groups? Would the program be medically sound? Would indigent families accept it? Would people who could afford private doctors be eligible? Would the practices and policies of the program be acceptable to the politicians and the medical establishment? These concerns indicated a need

> to avoid basic disagreements between established agencies and various vested interest groups. Years later, after the success of the Lincoln Parish Program had received national and international recognition and the more inclusive Louisiana State Family Planning Program was being developed, it became possible to obtain cooperation from other groups because of their likelihood of receiving funds or other forms of direct reward. These inducements did not exist at the outset; rather, convincing answers to the questions raised had to be provided. (Parrish 1973:242)

The Guidelines

Through compromise and with surprising harmony, a set of guidelines was gradually established between the family planners and the establishment. Financial eligibility requirements would be designed for the poor. The program would be racially integrated. Adequate medical supervision would be provided and current medical practices used. To satisfy the conservative and religious constituency, only the "ever married, ever pregnant" women would be served: Only women who already had children or were married could receive family planning assistance. Liberal proponents of family planning wished to record marital status as part of data collected but found checking marital status as a criterion for services repugnant. They simply could not turn away unmarried women who were otherwise eligible and in need. Eventually, this requirement fell into disuse, although it continued to be an aspect of official program policy.

At the grass-roots level, questions of genocide and coercion surfaced. Would women be forced to use birth control as a condition for receiving welfare benefits? The confidentiality of records would have to be guaranteed. Would such a program condone promiscuity, open the doors to legalized abortion, or permit a choice of contraceptives? Many people, already feeling threatened by racial integration, questioned the wisdom of letting women have control over their fertility.

The family planners met regularly with leaders in the black community, who were aware of the statistics on births and deaths. After numerous private consultations, they decided to have a meeting in one of the local Baptist churches. As Beasley later described the meeting to an audience at Harvard University,

> It was full of old people, young people, women with children. I was properly introduced, and what have you, by the minister, and then I gave a talk on what we were going to do—what we were going to teach everybody about contraceptives. When I pulled out the first pill and condom up there in the church, I swear it was like the first violinist in the New York Philharmonic breaking out into a boogie-woogie in the middle of Bach. It was the quietest moment I have ever seen. Everybody, even the children, just shut up because they sensed there was something big going on. And then this old fellow in the first row said, "Amen," and everybody started talking. (Beasley 1973:n.p.; Littlewood 1977:92)

The Catholic Connection and Other Obstacles

Unless it diffused the opposition of the Catholic hierarchy in Louisiana (which has the second largest diocese in the country), the family planning movement would be facing a long struggle for acceptance. The history of Catholic dogma and political action against birth control is well known.[4] Only months before the opening of Louisiana's first clinic, the city of Chicago and the state of Illinois had won a long and enervating battle with the Catholic Church to start, even on a small scale, a family planning program for poor women in that state. Catholic opposition could mean the defeat of the movement's hopes.

Beasley and his associates did not battle the issue in public forum as others had done. Rather, they chose to meet quietly with a representative of the bishops of the diocese and a member of the Family Life Apostolate to negotiate a set of compromises that would not publicly betray Catholic concerns but would permit tax-supported services. As the story goes, they had their meetings as gentlemen should, over bottles of old wine in some of New Orleans' finest restaurants. There the skeleton of rapprochement was reached. The church's position would be that "We will not endorse, but we will not oppose." One of the church's leaders who had participated in the negotiations was later quoted as saying:

> The issue with us is basically freedom of conscience. Most of the clients are non-Catholic. We can't tell them how to run their lives. The real problem being attacked here is not birth control or family planning. It is better health care. This is why we see no reason for an official position to be developed by the Church. (Father Joseph Bourgeois in *U.S. News and World Report* 1969:56)

At no time did Dr. Beasley actually meet with the archbishop, thus allowing the archbishop the option of remaining neutral. Negotiations were always conducted through the liberal Jesuits, who were willing to discuss the health issues of family planning.

Major conditions to Catholic silence, however, were made final just before the opening of the first clinic. No mass communications or advertising was to be used. The project was to remain out of the southern part of the state until the officials of the church had reviewed the procedures. The clinic could not offer abortions or give referrals for abortions. Natural family planning—the rhythm method—must be offered as an option, and any woman who elected it had to receive complete instruction. (The rhythm method had an understandably bad press with family planners; the joke circulated that people who practiced it were called "parents.") The agreement was honored, and every woman who came to the clinic was asked about her religious affiliation and her awareness of her church's position on birth control. She was referred to a priest if necessary. If she elected the rhythm method, she received the full, expensive instruction. If a woman did not care about the church's teachings on contraception and elected another method, she received assistance as would a non-Catholic.

A number of reasons have been suggested for the church's easy acquiescence to a long-taboo subject. Clearly, a program sponsored by a university was preferable to one led by the archenemy, Planned Parenthood. This international organization, heir of Margaret Sanger, had no chapters in Louisiana but had engaged the Catholic establishment in heated battles elsewhere. Planned Parenthood included abortion and sterilization reforms in its public agenda. As part of the negotiations, Beasley promised the Catholic Church that Planned Parenthood would be excluded from any activities in Louisiana for at least ten years (Beasley 1973). It was.

Some observers have suggested that in the period after the Second Vatican Council in 1962, when a new ecumenical spirit seemed to ease the strictures on birth control, Catholic bishops were responsive to change. Hopes for reforms were dashed in 1968 when Pope Paul VI issued the encyclical *Humanae Vitae*. Others contend that the more liberal Mediterranean Catholic influence in Louisiana (in contrast to that of the Irish and north European Catholics in the northeast) was responsible for the flexibility on this issue. The official explanation from the family planners is that the Catholic hierarchy was convinced by the studies linking the lack of contraception with high infant mortality, illegitimacy, retardation, and family pathology. Perhaps. But these statistics had long been available and had not mellowed Catholic opposition. For whatever combination of reasons, Joe Beasley found the key to unlocking what he euphemistically called "widespread community support." In Louisiana, the Catholic Church was no longer perceived as a monolithic institution that could intimidate secular political authorities on matters of repro-ductive freedom.

The next step was to overcome the state's version of the old Comstock law. One possibility was to ignore the law, open a clinic, and await prosecution. Another route was to seek legislative action. But legislators took seriously the anticontraception statute; previous attempts to au-thorize and finance the distribution of family planning information had failed in committee without a single dissenting vote. Forty-five percent of the members of the state legislature were Roman Catholics (Louisiana, State Legislature 1965). Both options would have been time consuming, would have seriously decreased the clinic's value as an experiment, and would have opened the doors to confrontation. Church-state connections were deeply entrenched and might have provoked the kind of legal battles over the right to provide birth control services and legislative folly that Connecticut and other states were experiencing.

The third alternative was to seek a reinterpretation of the law from the state's attorney general. But Beasley was an outsider with no inheritance of the overlapping familial and school ties that characterize state politics. Through a fortuitous contact in the state board of health and Tulane University, he managed to approach the attorney general as a medical professional armed with the preliminary survey results showing the extent of the health problems in the state. Convinced by this approach, the attorney general issued the reinterpretation in August 1965, just a month before the first clinic was scheduled to open.

Beasley had also been meeting with Governor John McKeithen, who was extremely surprised that the Catholic Church appeared so docile. The governor's permission was necessary because federal funds were to be used. He was willing to allow an experimental program funded from outside, but he did not want the state government identified with it because of possible controversies. Beasley warned the governor of the dangers of discussing the issue as one of population policy or control.

I told him that, in my opinion, the greatest danger to the program at this time lay in the accusations by racist extremists and especially Mr. Joseph Singelmann and Judge Leander Perez. The reason for this statement was that both Singelmann and Perez are advocating birth control as a way to decrease the number of Negroes. Governor McKeithen agreed with this and assured me that he would speak with Singelmann and Perez and encourage them to discontinue their current activities and to refrain from making any statement on the nature of birth control in Louisiana.[5]

Singelmann and the late Perez, powerful white politicians of the States' Rights party, were not alone in advocating repressive measures to control minority reproduction. The late Leander Perez, legendary czar of Plaquemines Parish, had already linked birth control and racism in a widely quoted statement, "The best way to hate a nigger is to hate him before he is born." Their spirited defense of birth control for racist reasons would have inflamed already tense feelings and given black community leaders a chance to withdraw support pledged to the program.

The First Clinic Opens

The clinic opened on September 10, 1965, and seven appointments were scheduled for that evening. But on that day Hurricane Betsy struck. The high winds, heavy rain, and power outages reached as far north as Lincoln Parish. No one believed that the women scheduled for appointments would keep them. Three struggled through Betsy's rain and winds to the clinic, and the doctor and nurse, using flashlights and candles for light, went through the prepared drill. In a movie made later about the program, *To Hunt with a Cat*, Hugh Downs said that as the eye of the hurricane passed the first IUD in Louisiana was inserted. Although IUDs had been used before, this instance may have been the first time that a *free* IUD was used in Louisiana with the sanction of state, church, and law.

During the six months after the dramatic night of Hurricane Betsy, the clinic restricted its services largely to postpartum mothers who had been contacted through the local hospitals in which they delivered. At the same time in Lincoln and in Orleans Parishes, the KAP surveys (questionnaires about knowledge, attitudes, and practices that served as feasibility studies) were under way. As data, clinical experience, and community support increased, staff members began to search the health department's vital records to identify women who would be at high risk if they were to have another pregnancy. High risk at this point depended only on demographic variables gleaned from vital records: age, problems with previous births, or number of children already born (parity). Sixty-two percent of the medically indigent women were in a high-risk category (Beasley and Parrish 1967). Each of them was contacted personally and given an appointment.

The program was then opened to all medically indigent (but still married) women, and eligibility was gradually broadened. Medically indigent means qualifying under one or more standards for free health care. The program's search procedures were aggressive and sophisticated, allowing direct personal contact between family planning staff and potential patients. Figure 2.2 shows the rationale of patient identification.

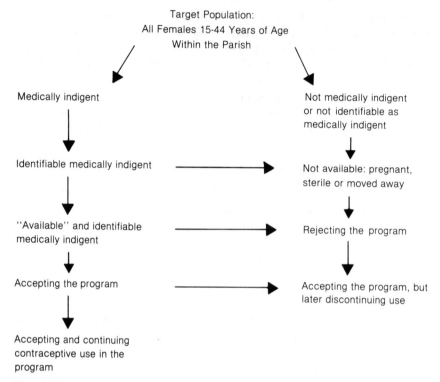

Figure 2.2 Strategy for identifying patients (adapted from Joseph D. Beasley and Vestal W. Parrish, Jr., A progress report on a Southern rural planning research program conducted in Lincoln Parish, Louisiana, Advances in Planned Parenthood, *Proceedings of the Excerpta Medica Foundation*, New York, 1967, vol. 3, p. 31).

Once contacted, the majority of eligible patients kept their appointments. For those who did not, a follow-up system tracked them down. When the first appointment was missed, a telephone call or postcard was used to set up another appointment. After the second missed appointment, a staff member visited the patient's home. At any stage, a women could choose not to participate. The type of contraception chosen might also dictate different follow-up strategies. Patients could call in at any time for an appointment (itself a novelty for poor women).

New training systems for the staff had to be designed. Teaching the nonmedical staff (including the clerk) about reproductive physiology and contraceptives was only the first step. The staff had to communicate with patients who were often embarrassed or sensitive about sex and the most intimate parts of their bodies. "A specific goal of the training was for the nurse to learn to be able to hold each type of contraceptive in her hand and to discuss it with a patient without embarrassment or distaste or projecting the impression that she regarded it as dirty, bad, or unladylike" (Parrish 1973:242).

Training sessions encouraged the nurses and staff (all of whom were female except for researchers) to augment their professional skills with open female-to-female communication. Once they learned to articulate and accept their own knowledge and attitudes about sexuality, they were better able to convey respect for patients and the family planning process.

> For health professionals to act as if they conceive the patients as objects without sex, feelings, or a mental capacity to understand does not mean the patient agrees. The patient does not forget the examiner, nor does she necessarily believe that the person doing the examination forgets it either. A desexualized view of the patient can, of course, act as a defense mechanism for the health professional to protect her or him from personal fears or insecurity. . . . This may make it impossible to lead the patient toward a higher respect for herself or to help her become an effective user of medical services. (Parrish 1973:243)

The training provided a basis for seeing how women's attitudes toward childbirth, pregnancy, and sexuality operated and how their life experiences might influence their decisions.

The clinic staff members also had to alter traditional attitudes toward sex roles and responsibility among themselves. The doctors, program coordinators, and director were male; all patients and the support staff (nurses, LPNs, clerks) were female. If doctors acted haughty and treated patients as objects or if nurses were caught between their joint roles as women and professionals, family planning programs would acquire an unsavory reputation. To break down the prevalent doctor-nurse-patient hierarchy, the program gave nurses more responsibilities and more room to assert themselves. The female staff members served as role models and, if necessary, as buffers between patient and doctor. Some nurses have reported chastising doctors who patronized or were rough with patients. Doctors who worked for the program were said to be socialized by their female colleagues.

The experiments in Lincoln Parish were a test case for an emerging model of patient-centered medicine. Because participation was voluntary and the patients were not sick in the usual sense of the word, the organizers had to learn to be unusually sensitive and to develop mechanisms that increased rather than hampered communication.

Successes in Lincoln Parish

Under the circumstances that prevailed in Louisiana, the mere existence of the family planning program in a rural area was a measure of success. Since the parish did not suffer from overpopulation, the question became how to evaluate and judge the accomplishments of the clinic. It is difficult to find verifiable indices of achievement in family planning programs. One measure of success would be a change in what the literature calls out-of-wedlock births. Among social scientists the stigma of having babies without benefit of clergy mattered less than the high statistical correlation between illegitimacy and maternal deaths, stillbirths, infant deaths, and prematurity. Beyond the immediate health problems, early child bearing brought negative socioeconomic consequences for a woman and her family throughout her life. The younger a woman was during her first pregnancy, the less education she would receive and the less likely she was ever to marry (Beasley and Frankowski 1970:256). Children born into these circumstances were more likely to have handicaps in physical and emotional development and to require greater public expenditures for remedial care.

After the first two years of the program in Lincoln Parish, several indices related to indigent or illegitimate births appeared to diverge strikingly from those for surrounding parishes without organized efforts. Surveys showed that the total number of births to women who were medically indigent decreased. In Lincoln Parish it declined 32 percent, whereas in the nearby control parishes the decrease was only 6 percent. The number of out-of-wedlock births and the number of such births to medically indigent women in Lincoln Parish fell more than in any other parish. A drop of this magnitude confirmed one of the program's goals. "Lincoln Parish is the only parish in the state to experience a decrease of this size in the illegitimacy ratio" (Beasley and Parrish 1969:176).

In testimony before a U.S. congressional committee on family planning, Beasley added these statistics:

In the three years of operation of the program, the number of indigent births in Lincoln Parish showed a decline of 44 percent; in the surrounding parishes, 25 percent. The number of illegitimate births among the poor dropped by 11 percent in the other parishes, but 34 percent in Lincoln Parish. Perhaps most significantly, all illegitimate births to women who have had at least one previous pregnancy declined 12 percent in the surrounding parishes and 50 percent in Lincoln Parish. The percentage change was even higher when only illegitimate births occurring among the poor were considered: in four years—1964 to 1968—the number of such births declined by 55 percent (and by 24 percent in the control parishes). (U.S. Congress, House, Committee on Ways and Means 1969:922)

It is extremely rare for any program to claim a restructuring of complicated rates such as illegitimacy in three years of operation. Later these statistics—or the interpretations of them—were questioned for this reason. Meanwhile the findings from Lincoln Parish were used with striking effect in professional papers, testimony to the U.S. Senate, and grant applications. However, the program's researchers had moved into the troublesome arena of public health and vital statistics, the interpretation of which is open to debate.

It must be noted that trends toward decreased fertility and illegitimacy were evident in records for the state as a whole at this time; also, the statistics for any parish in any one year may be fortuitous or random. Furthermore, given the constraints on the program, the only group in which changes could be observed was that made up of women who had already borne children. For this group, the birth rate remained constant through the first year but decreased markedly from 1966 to 1967 and continued to decline in subsequent years (Beasley and Parrish 1969). These trends are the first indications that experienced women are receptive to and are practicing family planning.

Although there is no statistical proof that exposure to the ideas of family planning contributes to its success, certainly common sense suggests that the more public discussion and sensitive treatment by health professionals, the more easily adoption is accomplished. At the outset, response to the family planning program was cautious: Only 12 percent of the women came into the program on their own initiative or through recommendations. However, these figures validate the intensely systematic approach to identifying and contacting the eligible people. Without the outreach and follow-up mechanisms, little response would have been generated.

Family planning projects such as this can be judged by a general response rate (the number of people who accept an appointment); another rate for women who elect to remain in the program is also used. The initial acceptance rate was 57 percent. Judged by higher rates later generated by the program, this figure is low. Judged by rates of acceptance in other rural programs in the United States and underdeveloped countries, this rate is high.

Most of the research and program evaluation was directed at a specialized audience outside the state who was also beginning to experiment with the delivery of new ideas in family planning. For example, Beasley's group calculated the cost of the Lincoln Parish program, since "despite their importance, cost studies in planning and administration of population programs are quite scarce. Actually, we do not know of any elaborated with the detail used here" (Correa et al. 1972:1657). Treating each patient cost $58.51 during the first year; this figure declined to $42.03 by the third year. Nevertheless, the costs for the program as a whole continued to increase as new patients were added and old ones continued. Beasley's group used these figures to show that the public programs were more efficient than private doctors.

Some of the major achievements during this period were less tangible than figures on costs or trends. Within the community, residents began to refer to the program as "ours." Despite its initial suspicions, the community had been won over. Furthermore, the model worked: It had proved possible to enlist significant levels of participation through personalized contact. Although demonstrably ignorant about family planning, couples exhibited strong motivation. Patients with little formal education were successfully using the IUD and birth control pills. Staff morale was extremely high. "It is amazing how much a professional can learn about life and how better to do her job, when she listens to the lay wisdom of the patients" (Parrish 1973:244).

Personnel development was a significant breakthrough. Before 1965 no local people had been trained in birth control services. One of the two obstetrician-gynecologists on the staff was ignorant of the IUD. He was flown to a training course given by a leading manufacturer of the device. To allay fears of coercion in the use of IUDs, the staff developed a consent form, which was later adopted nationally. Paraprofessionals were paid on the basis of the task they were hired to do rather than their previous levels of education or job experience, and a plan for job and geographic mobility offered additional motivation.

Each category of tasks was delineated, and each received elaborate attention: analysis of the problems, goal setting, monitoring, training, financing, community relations, and outreach. But this effort was not aimed simply at correcting the health problems of indigent women through family planning. Beasley's hope was to create a delivery system that could be applied to other medical-social problems. The original plan was to build a comprehensive maternal and child care program in which family planning was only a component. Funding restrictions prevented the full realization of this dream.

No Better Mousetrap

Family planning, contrary to appearances, is one of the most complicated health services for any population. A patient must know something about her body. Decisionmaking is not a one-time or a one-person matter. The decision to use a contraception method is made repeatedly and within changing family contexts. Continued contacts between the program personnel and the patient are needed over a long period of time, particularly if she is pregnant or in poor health. The agency that provides contraceptive care to women becomes their general practitioner as well.

Contraceptive technology was crude and unsuitable for mass public health campaigns until the arrival of the IUD and the pill in the early 1960s. It was widely believed that poor women could use only methods that were removed from the sex act and did not require elaborate equipment. In Louisiana as elsewhere, the pill and the IUD promised to be such methods. Specialists assumed that the IUD would be the more popular choice; it was certainly the cheapest. But the IUD had an initially high failure rate, and the pill, which was the more expensive method to deliver, was far more popular. Older women or those with marginal health were counseled against the adoption of the pill, although some programs in the country pushed the pill to the exclusion of other methods. For IUD users, the risks of pregnancy were higher than for pill users. Infections, perforations of the uterus, pain, excessive bleeding, and expulsion of the device have been frequently reported. The IUD is generally unsuited for women who have never borne children. In subcultures such as that of southern blacks, in which heavy bleeding is a poorly tolerated symptom of pathology and folk beliefs about intrusive objects in the body are strong, the IUD is not a popular choice.

Contraceptive technology, despite its billing as one of the great liberating forces in the twentieth century, is primitive. But no other methods are available for wide-spread use: There is still no better mousetrap. Although sterilizations for males and females are the major advances, they are not appropriate for all people. The major improvements have been made in the administration of services—a different delivery system. Family planning requires continual monitoring and medical supervision for each patient—an essential but expensive approach. In part because of the lack of adequate research moneys,[6] government and health care professionals have had to focus on new approaches in preventive medicine in lieu of new technology. The difficulties of dispensing and using the present-day technology add to the unsolved problems of the psychological and social factors in acceptance.

Uncle Sam's Growing Interest in His Poor Nieces

The Louisiana program, with stupendous foresight or luck, rode the crest of the federal funding waves from the start. The years from 1964 to 1974 were the boom period in Louisiana and the nation as family planning and its benefits grew into a national priority. Much of the policy formation at the federal level came from Louisiana.

Even before the entry of the government into the family planning business, many obstacles to public-supported birth control were removed. In 1958 a long-standing ban on contraceptive prescriptions in New York City municipal hospitals was challenged and defeated. In 1965, the U.S. Supreme Court struck down a Connecticut statute penalizing the users of contraceptives (*Griswold* vs. *Connecticut*). This landmark case established the right of couples to plan their families without state interference. Other states removed their Comstock-inspired restrictions and even liberalized laws on abortion (as in Colorado). In 1963, former president Dwight D. Eisenhower recanted an earlier statement that population control programs were none of the government's affair and endorsed the concept. President Lyndon B. Johnson, in his 1965 State of the Union message, vowed to seek new ways to deal with the population explosion. He singled out family planning as one of the four most critical health problems in the nation and pledged to give it special attention.

Simultaneously, professional associations made or renewed commitments to the philosophy of family planning (McCalister et al. 1973). The American Medical Association came out for the first time in favor of the dispersal of birth control information at tax-supported institutions and recommended coordinated teaching programs in human reproduction and sexuality. The American Public Health Association, which includes professionals in many fields, supported contraceptive services including sterilizations for men and women, safe and legal abortions, and universal public education. Following suit, the American Nurses Association and the National Association of Social Workers endorsed family planning and related it to the broadest imperatives of social policy and welfare. Many other voluntary and professional organizations were including the problems of overpopulation, the rights of women to choose, and the reduction of poverty-caused illnesses on their agendas.

By 1964, the oral contraceptive and the IUD were out of the test phases and into mass markets. The civil rights movements, the war on poverty, and civil disorders gave rise to a rhetoric of "breaking the cycle of dependency." The government was asked to switch sides, cease prohibitions on birth control, and become the major funder and proponent of these services. Even those who had not succumbed to the idea of a governmental role in a population crisis were still left with the relationship between family size and poverty, particularly among minorities. The costs of welfare programs were rising and family planning saved money; $20 to $70 for each pregnancy averted was a frequently quoted cost-benefit ratio (Dienes 1972:259).

In 1964, the federal government offered family planning only to other countries and to military personnel and their dependents. Only thirteen states had rudimentary programs. Although that figure grew to forty states by 1966, none attempted a statewide system of services. The District of Columbia, Maryland, North Carolina, and New York City had instituted programs through maternity clinics and hospitals. The first federal interest came from the venerable Children's Bureau, which, with its large grant to Louisiana, had begun to support family planning training for professionals and basic research on people's attitudes (U.S. Department of Health, Education and Welfare 1966, 1968).

The Office of Economic Opportunity (OEO), as part of the war on poverty, was gearing up to channel funds directly into targeted neighborhoods for projects to alleviate poverty. It too was convinced that family planning and maternal-child health were promises too long denied. By 1966, Community Action Programs (CAP) included family planning as a health service, and in 1967, Congress directed OEO to give "special emphasis" to birth control delivery systems. At OEO, officials were keen on community-based advisory and advocacy boards and offered funds to train aides or paraprofessionals from the impoverished communities they served. Agreements between the states and the federal bureaucracy paralleled promises already made in Louisiana: Health services were for poor people; there was to be no coercion, no mass media campaigns; and proper medical supervision and spending limits were required. At the national level, however, the guidelines for abortion and sterilization were less rigid than in Louisiana.

In 1965, amendments to the Social Security Act required state health departments to extend services, including family planning, to all areas of the country within ten years. Grants were available for rural poverty pockets and distressed urban areas. In 1967, the Child Health Act specified that at least 6 percent of all maternal-child health grants to public health agencies had to be set aside for family planning. Further amendments to the Social Security Act that year required states to offer family planning to all poor women receiving assistance through Families with Dependent Children (AFDC or ADC). These were coups for family planners, because this law stated that federal funds could be used to pay for services to any woman who had in the past or might in the future need welfare payments. Family planners could exploit this extended eligibility to offer a wide range of maternal and child care services. Coupled with older legislation—some dating back to the original Social Security Act of 1935 or the public health acts for research and training— these new provisions allowed state and private agencies to create whole new programs and to finance them extensively from outside the state

(Hellman 1971). This approach was nicknamed "Congress's blank check for birth control."

The Department of Health, Education and Welfare, as the lead agency, designated family planning a priority program in 1968 and established a unit on population and family planning. It estimated that over 5 million women in the United States were in need (fertile and poor), but less than a half million were receiving services.

The greatest potential support to states, voluntary organizations, and private physicians came from the Medicaid programs (Title XIX of the Social Security Act). If states chose to offer family planning under Medicaid, the costs of drugs, contraceptives, physicians' fees, and inpatient and outpatient care would be paid by the government. States with the lowest per capita incomes received the highest percentages of funds. Any state with excessive infant deaths (above 18.3 per 1,000) would receive special consideration. Thus in Medicaid states, or states like Louisiana with poor health statistics, any agency that offered family planning to eligible women could be reimbursed.

Family planning was rapidly expanding as a health service for reproductive-age women who had little access to crucial services like postpartum examinations and prenatal or well-baby care (Landman 1968). The role of the government grew dramatically as new legislation offered both money and a mandate to serve poor families, particularly those within the welfare and AFDC systems.[7] If states like Louisiana were not to start their own bureaucracies for birth control, they would have to contract with other organizations. Large sums of money through the liberal initiatives against poverty and its side-effects were available for the first time to address these health needs. That not enough money was ever allocated or that national priorities changed is another part of the story (Polgar 1975).

The View from Louisiana

The Lincoln Parish demonstration model, buttressed by research experience and growing federal largess, was ready for export from a quiet rural parish into the more raucous and culturally heterogenous atmosphere of New Orleans. The family planners were stymied by the inefficiencies of the state health department, and they chose to become a private, nonprofit organization.

We set up a corporation to run the Louisiana Family Planning Program, because I tried to run the program out of the state, and I couldn't do it. I couldn't get the nurses and the doctors and the people and the supplies and the penicillin—and I couldn't get them occurring all at the same time. I couldn't hire the kind of people I wanted because of Civil Service. And because of the budget, if there was somebody I needed to compete for and go outside, I couldn't hire him. So I decided I'd do it out of the university, and I got paid by the university—and that was worse. So I got permission from both the state and the university and the powers that be to start my own non-profit corporation. And so we did that. (Beasley 1973:n.p.)

This status freed them from Civil Service, anemic funding, and competition with other health agencies. It spared them the unpleasant alternatives of fighting or cooperating with the state legislature. Although a few other states chose to use private foundations, none enjoyed the flexibility or rapid growth that characterized the Louisiana experience.

The family planners were beginning to articulate their vision. Although the facets of their dream varied according to their audience, it grew more rapidly as the triumphs mounted. Reporters were struck by a motto prominently displayed in Beasley's offices: "In tinkering with society, good will is not enough" (J. C. Furnas). A skeptic told me that the next line should have read, "but money will help." The quotation expressed the relationship between the ideals of family planning and organizational zeal. The family planners proposed to translate their good intentions into "cold logic, keen attention to detail, thoroughness of plan, and the precision of execution of a military campaign. An analogous medical project, in terms of organization, would be the yellow fever program of the Rockefeller Foundation during the early twentieth century" (Coyle 1968:10). A complicated plan to put their hopes and experiences into action was reaching fruition.

3

Building the Model

What caught my fancy was the idea of offering services to indigent women the same as private doctors were giving. Nobody, and I mean nobody, was talking then about treating poor women with dignity. We said we'd do it and we did.
—Joan Smith, personal communication, 1981

An example of how family planning can be made to work in this country is exemplified by the story of what happened in New Orleans.
—Westoff and Westoff, 1971

Buoyed by the initial successes of the Lincoln Parish pilot project and the increasingly lucrative sources of funding, the family planners moved into the metropolitan area of Louisiana, Orleans Parish. For the tourist, New Orleans is a city of splendid architecture, unsurpassed cooking, jazz, Mardi Gras, and a rich ethnic blend of people. It is magnolia trees, Creole mysteries, and wrought-iron balconies. It is "the city that care forgot." For many inhabitants, however, New Orleans is the city that forgot to care. Its atmosphere of bread and circuses for the masses cloaks poverty in significantly greater shadows than in other Southern cities like Atlanta, Dallas, or Houston. In 1975, University of New Orleans economist James R. Bobo published an economic study that dovetailed with the grim health statistics. Few analytical studies of the local economy existed; Bobo's report laid bare the dismal state of the local economy and sent shock waves through the complacent sectors of the community. The elite had suppressed, ignored, or denied the fact that "metropolitan New Orleans simply has a high (disproportionately high) percentage of the disadvantaged—the subemployed; and this is a drag on economic development" (Bobo 1975:62).

According to Bobo, being poor (at or below the officially defined poverty line; impoverished, underemployed) was almost the same as being black. In the greater metropolitan area "about 65 percent of all impoverished persons were black . . . and 38.9 percent of all black

42

families were below poverty" (Bobo 1975:63). Moreover, the poor in New Orleans constituted a larger percentage of the population than in the rest of the nation. Blacks in some neighboring parishes fared better but only marginally. Black women continued to earn less, suffer more discrimination, have less education, and bear more family responsibilities. Despite these deterrents, black females had been in the labor force in higher percentages than white women had and were free from the elitist taboos against employment. But they had fewer opportunities for advancement and social mobility through marriage than had white women.

By 1980, the number of people in New Orleans receiving public assistance, including food stamps, was approaching 100,000. Although the city contains nearly a dozen colleges and universities and a struggling public school system, 38 percent of the people over twenty-five had not completed more than eight years of formal schooling (New Orleans Area/Bayou River Health Systems Agency 1980:218).

Within city government, the problems of poverty and race were not being addressed by the overwhelmingly white and often hostile administrations. Although New Orleans was becoming a black-majority city, no black had served on the city council since Reconstruction. In the late 1960s, as the civil rights movement grew nationally, leaders within the effectively disenfranchised black community of New Orleans organized a new power base in historic neighborhoods. Two groups, in particular, gained recognition: the Southern Organization for United Leadership (SOUL) was centered in the Lower Ninth Ward and Desire Project, and the Community Organization for Urban Politics (COUP) represented the Seventh Ward, a traditional Creole neighborhood. COUP and SOUL endorsed political candidates in city and state elections. Both Governor Edwin Edwards and Mayor Moon Landrieu are said to have been elected in 1970 because of the solid block of black votes delivered by these groups.

> As a result of Landrieu's mayoral victory in 1970, SOUL struck some deals that most people feel were beneficial to the New Orleans black community. It is generally believed that in return for their support, Landrieu agreed to black control of federal community action and model cities programs; in addition many blacks gained prominent city jobs including, near the end of Landrieu's term, the Chief Administrative Office. (Dent 1979:67)

Black influence in local politics continued to grow and was strengthened as blacks gained control of federal money for the war on poverty. The family planners' concerns for the health consequences of poverty, their own federal funds, and the deepening ties to the black community involved them increasingly in these grass-roots political development and community organizations.

Involving the Community

Just as in Lincoln Parish, a massive public relations campaign had to be waged in Orleans Parish before the opening of the first clinic. Many agencies were expected to provide financial, moral, or tactical support; others were to be persuaded that new concepts in family planning did not run counter to their already vested interests.[1]

The Catholic Church had agreed to support and monitor the basic health programs and to assist with natural family planning instruction. Protestants, through the Federation of Churches and the Ministerial Alliance (black ministers), agreed to advise on the moral-religious questions of sex education and premarital pregnancies. The Ministerial Alliance was particularly sensitive to the needs of black families and was easily enlisted in a public relations effort; its members had been preaching about these problems without a practical platform for many years.

Pharmacists and the Louisiana Pharmaceutical Society were dismayed. After all, the pill was the most profitable prescription drug during the 1960s and early 1970s, and pharmacists feared the economic repercussions of free distribution of pills to so many women. But the family planners argued that poor women were not buying them anyway and that when they were no longer economically strapped by frequent child bearing, these women would be better customers for drugstores. This rationale seemed to satisfy the pharmacists, who raised no further questions about free pharmaceuticals.

The Board of Education of the Orleans Parish Schools agreed to drop the policy of expelling pregnant teenagers and to operate a special high school in which they could complete their education. The Louisiana Family Planning agreed to provide prenatal care and financial, educational, and sexual counseling for these teenagers. The School Board agreed to phase in a program of family life and sex education but only on a very limited scale.

The ties between the Louisiana Family Planning Program, Inc. (Family Planning)—Beasley's New Orleans–based corporation—Tulane University, and the two nearby medical schools were extensive. Physicians from both medical schools were contracted to staff the clinics. Family Planning helped to train medical and nursing students and provided money, data, and patients for a wide variety of action-oriented research. They also trained health professionals from other universities in town (three of them for black students). They invented a joint record system and referred patients back and forth to Charity as needed. The parish and state health departments were similarly involved with the advanced record system, reciprocal staffing, and referrals. This level of cooperation for health care delivery systems was new in New Orleans, and its central focus was birth control.

Local medical societies were promised nothing although they were consulted about the medical policies of the clinics. In the beginning, some members of the medical societies expressed resistance, even antipathy. One doctor who was involved in the Lincoln Parish project was booed off the stage of the state Academy of Pediatrics when he discussed family planning. Later the Louisiana Medical Society endorsed the concept. As time went on, local medical societies increased their support for the health and demographic aspects of family planning, although the financing of services remained a prickly issue for many doctors.

Within Orleans Parish, a number of official boards, such as the New Orleans Health Corporation and the New Orleans Area Health Planning Council (NOAHPC), had to be involved in the effort. These boards proliferated, particularly in response to a new influx of funding from the Office of Economic Opportunity (OEO). OEO community action agencies (under a variety of acronyms) screened patient complaints, referred patients, helped recruit paraprofessionals, and advised on related policies. Later, the hidden agendas of these agencies proved to be especially troublesome as the conflicts between state and federal bureaucracies and within competing ethnic groups surfaced (Krause 1977; Wolfe 1970).

On all possible occasions, as in Lincoln Parish, the family planners contacted community groups to offer speakers, seminars, and training sessions. They spoke to Head Start mothers and teachers, the Neighborhood Youth Corps, city recreational staffs and patrons, labor unions, veterans groups, parent-teacher associations, churches—anyone who would listen. The goals of the Louisiana Family Planning Program, Inc., being discussed in public were sweeping:

> to organize, operate and administer an effective community program in family planning, a program of such value that it would reduce significantly the recorded rates of perinatal and infant mortality, maternal mortality, prematurity, and illegitimacy. This program would provide family planning information and services which promote the dignity and integrity of the family, foster an environment which enhances the ability of the family to develop the potential of each child and improve community health. (Applied Health Sciences Department 1972:2)

Every community agency that heard these goals also heard the program's survey results and the solutions proposed. The share of health

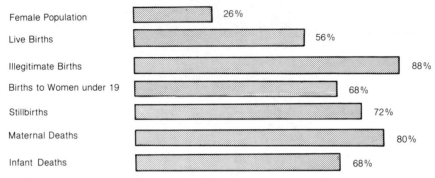

Figure 3.1 Contributions of the indigent to selected health problems, Orleans Parish, 1970 (Source: Louisiana Family Planning, Inc.)

problems attributable to the indigent was out of proportion to their numbers in the community (see Figure 3.1). The family planners in the program would attempt to locate, educate, and help the women represented by these rates through a massive public health campaign.

Four groups of women were targeted as potential participants in the family planning program. The first group was composed of the women who had just had a child at Charity Hospital (immediately postpartum). Between 8,000 and 9,000 babies were born to indigent women each year at Charity Hospital in New Orleans alone. These numbers represent 95 percent of all indigent births in the parish. But less than 40 percent of patients received any examination after their baby was born.

A clever compromise between the obstetrical departments of the Tulane and Louisiana State University (LSU) medical schools and the family planning demonstration project was implemented. Charity medical services could not handle a double postpartum caseload as well as the additional family planning services, even if they had wanted to. They agreed to let the new family planning clinics provide all postpartum patients with both their routine six-weeks' checkup and contraceptive counseling.

The second group of priority patients included those who were high risk but not necessarily postpartum. These were women (1) who had given birth to six or more offspring; (2) who had had children when they were under 16 or over 40 years or who began childbearing after 35; (3) who had had one or more stillbirths or premature infants (defined as weighing 2,492 grams or 5 pounds 8 ounces or less) or had had other history of infant deaths; or (4) whose last child was born out of wedlock. The names of women in this group were taken from Charity Hospital records.

The third group to be served through a family planning program had had deliveries at Charity during the three-year period from 1964 to 1966. The fourth group included the balance of indigent women who might need family planning services but who did not fall into any category. The planners anticipated a patient load of 50,000 to 70,000 women per year when initial visits and revisits were calculated (Beasley 1967b:6). No other metropolitan area in the country had a program that matched these ambitions.

About the Birds and the Bees

A common question asked anthropologists is whether in some primitive societies people fail to make the connection between intercourse and pregnancy. Do they understand what causes babies? The answer is that in all human societies people know that intercourse may cause babies but not how. Also, in most human societies a rudimentary knowledge of how to prevent pregnancy exists, even if it is ineffective. Coupled with these is substantial folklore on how to make babies when they are deeply valued. Another question frequently asked is why some people (minorities, Catholics, blacks, the poor) have so many children. Don't they know?

New Orleans Metropolitan Family Survey

The family planners needed research to show that families might indeed be ignorant of the facts (but not stupid) and favor birth control if it were available. A number of remarkable and as yet unduplicated studies grew out of this research project, the largest of which was the New Orleans Metropolitan Family Survey (NOMFS).[2] The research team studied the developmental cycle of families, particularly black ones, because they would constitute the bulk of the patient population.[3] In the surveys, men and women were asked about how their family was composed and their household structured through time, how their families started, and how authority was distributed. In addition, they were quizzed about their knowledge of reproductive physiology, the ovulation cycle, contraceptive usage, desired family size, and feelings about family planning. The striking results easily lent themselves to a pro-family-planning interpretation.

The respondents' ignorance about reproduction was extreme. They knew that sexual relations and babies were related but not why. Only half had any knowledge of the union of sperm and ovum. The other half lacked essential information altogether. Respondents were asked, "Do you think a woman is just as likely to become pregnant at one

time as another? Why? When is it?" Eighty-seven percent of the respondents knew nothing about the ovulation cycle. The following were
typical answers to the questions about ovulation:

> I think anytime you sleep with a breathing man you've had it. (age 37, five
> pregnancies) (Beasley, Harter, and Fischer 1966:1849)

> Because it just happens with the nature of God. If He wants to bless us,
> we shouldn't complain. (age 34, six pregnancies) (Beasley, Harter, and Fischer
> 1966:1899)

> Anytime. I know that eggs come down and stays there just waiting to be
> fertilized. (age 28, five pregnancies) (Beasley, Harter, and Fischer 1966:1849)

> There is a certain time of month. I don't know how to count it. It looks to
> me like you feel more loving at certain times of the month. This is the time
> you can get pregnant. (age 37, eight pregnancies) (Beasley, Harter, and Fischer
> 1966:1849)

> One of the freaks of nature, I guess. It is nature itself. If nature want you
> to have it, you will. (age 26, four pregnancies) (Beasley, Harter, and McCalister
> 1966:199)

> I don't know. I think it is that the blood mixes up. (age 33, six pregnancies)
> (Beasley, Harter, and McCalister 1966:199)

> It all depends on how long you have been without a sex relation. If you
> are away from a man and then go back to having sex relations again you
> get pregnant right away. (age 25, four pregnancies) (Beasley, Harter, and
> McCalister 1966:199)

> Avoid relations three days before and three days after your period stops.
> (age 29, nine pregnancies) (Beasley, Harter, and McCalister 1966:199)

The respondents were then asked to name all the precautions they knew
to prevent pregnancy. About 30 percent knew of no methods at all, and
of those who could name at least one technique, one-third mentioned
folk remedies such as cola or potash pills. If they could name only one
method, it was usually the condom.

The following questions were designed to justify to the community
that respondents desired family planning services (Beasley, Harter, and
Fischer 1966).

	YES
1. Do you feel that couples have the right to decide for themselves when to stop having children?	90%

2. Do you think New Orleans couples who cannot afford to go to private doctors should have an office or clinic where they can go to find out how couples can keep from having more children than they want or can care for?   94%

3. At the present time, would you like to know more about precautions or family planning methods that either you or your spouse can use so that you can have marital relations without becoming pregnant?   68%

4. Would you want your sons and daughters to be informed on methods of family planning or on the use of precautions?   90%

Opinions about the provision of family planning services to the medically indigent were positive. Only 11 percent of the Catholic respondents even knew the church policy on family planning. The more children and the more education that a woman had the more she wanted her children to have access to family planning information.

On a question about desired family size versus the actual fertility to date, the family members interviewed responded emphatically.

> One of the most revealing figures in all these data is that 72 percent of these women of reproductive age do not want any more children. That is, they not only do not want to become pregnant this year or next, they never want to be pregnant again. Another way of looking at it is that 83 percent of these women do not want any more children or at least no more than a total of three. (Beasley, Harter, and Fischer 1966:1853)

Sixty-eight percent of the women with some grade-school education had already reached or exceeded the family size they had thought desirable when first married or pregnant, but they were still in their early reproductive years.

Low-income, high-risk mothers with infant mortality greater than that for the rest of the population were a particular concern.[4] These women, still in their midtwenties, had an average of five pregnancies with at least one infant death. Their response to the idea of contraception was the most enthusiastic in all the subsamples. Although they had the least functional knowledge of the reproductive processes, 100 percent believed that poor people and their children should have access to family planning. The majority wished never to be pregnant again.

The Interpretation

The results of the New Orleans Metropolitan Family Survey shed considerable light on black family structure, which was beginning to be an obsessive issue in academic circles. Social scientists theorized that black family structure reflected matriarchal patterns brought from Africa or that it was a social pathology stemming from the harsh conditions of slavery or from adapting to urban culture.[5] Most researchers assumed that the ideal or at least average family type in the United States was the nuclear family. Certainly their data showed that this was the pattern to strive for, begging the question of whether it worked for everyone. The majority of families in the New Orleans study, black or white, approximated the norm of the nuclear family: husband, wife, and their children. The statistically most important difference between black and white family structures was for black unmarried mothers and their offspring: Black women more frequently conceived and delivered their first child without a husband than did white women and stood out as a group when the statistics were analyzed. Young white girls who found themselves pregnant might give up the baby for adoption, seek an abortion, or enter into a "shotgun marriage." Young black girls and their babies more often remained with their family. The custom of raising children within the extended family networks remains a very significant part of black family life.

To establish a nuclear family a couple needs economic independence or solvent parents to support them and a new baby. For poor couples, particularly black ones, neither condition exists. Marriage is a less viable alternative for a girl if the male has little or no economic security.

> There are far-reaching consequences of beginning a family early in life with the delivery of an illegitimate child. The age at which a stable nuclear family can be formed is delayed. Prospective husbands must be able to support a child as well as the mother in these cases. An economic drain on the parental family usually continues for some time after these illicit conceptions. . . . The family, with such a rapid generational turnover, hardly had time to recover from the economic drain of raising one generation before it must turn to the problem of supporting a growing set of grandchildren followed by the problems of supporting declining parents. (Fischer, Beasley, and Harter 1968:299)

In the groups surveyed, the lowest fertility was among black or white women who married before conceiving. Reproductive rates were highest among black women who conceived while unwed but married before delivery. The child-bearing pattern for black and white women who had their first child out of wedlock was fascinating. There was a noticeable pause in pregnancies following the first birth; most of the women never had another. But after a long interval, succeeding births (if they occurred at all) followed each other at shorter intervals than with other women.[6]

The moral could not be missed. In addition to preventing or postponing initial pregnancies, postpartum counseling for women who had already borne a child was essential.

Unfortunately, few of these insights were publicized in the community. Here was evidence that, despite the stereotype, only a small number of black women produced numerous illegitimate children. Other than the extensions begun by young unwed mothers and their offspring, the majority of families followed the nuclear model.

The hypothesis that "many women are unable to plan the size of their families because they lack sufficient knowledge of reproductive physiology, of the ovulatory cycle, or of effective family planning technics" (Beasley, Harter, and Fischer 1966:1847) but would favor planning services were they available was proved valid. The hypothesis that random fertility resulting from this lack of knowledge is a contributing factor to family disruption—a golden thread running through the history of family planning—probably cannot be convincingly demonstrated.

Preaching the Gospel

As the survey results accumulated, the key question was how to reach substantial numbers of women. Advertising and media exploitation were prohibited. Because the entire welfare department staff carried an average caseload of 120 clients (more than twice the national average), it could provide little assistance in making referrals to the clinics.

Previous studies had shown that a clinic would have higher rates of attendance, particularly for controversial services like birth control, when a system of neighborhood visitation by indigenous personnel was used (Moore 1968; Polgar 1966). This approach meant finding and training workers from the community to be served. The program administrators recognized that they needed down-home native speakers of local dialects, who knew the tricks of community organizing such as voter registration drives or church membership crusades. These outreach workers each had to act as what anthropologists call a cultural broker, that is, as an intermediary or bridge between two cultures.[7]

Initially, there was opposition in Louisiana to taking women directly from the community and training them for tasks that were viewed as the province of doctors, nurses, social workers, or other professionals. But family planning is an anomalous area that crosscuts the standard divisions of labor. Professionals are not successful agents of change because they are, by definition, members of an alien subculture. Reducing the medical mystique and rigid hierarchies by using outreach workers was the core of democratizing birth control. At first, because the system was innovative and therefore open to criticism if not failure, the program leaders overrationalized and overtrained the outreach workers. But experience substantiated their novel assumptions that the more similarities between the frontline family planning worker and the women they recruited, the better the performance of the program.

The Outreach Workers

Indigenous personnel bore titles like family health counselor, auxiliary home visitor, or health worker. The title that became popular in Louisiana was outreach worker, which carries a flavor of missionization and salvation. The first recruitment, circumventing potential problems of hiring from the patient community, was unorthodox and brilliant. An imaginative social worker contacted women with whom she had previously worked in Head Start or other community action programs. Initially five women were hired directly from the housing projects or welfare rolls. Several of the women were the sole supporters of their families, which averaged more than five children. All were intelligent and assertive, although not well-educated, black women.

Annie Joseph, a Baptist, did not initially believe in birth control. When recruited into the program from Total Community Action and Project Enable, she was living in a housing project with her four offspring. The family planning organizers explained the principles, converted her, hired her, and sent her out to convince others. Women asked her, "Why did you wait to tell me about this?" She answered, "I didn't know myself, but now we've come to help you." As Annie Joseph said, "They were my neighbors, my friends. I know their problems. I speak their language. I was effective because I could tell them that I sat where you sit." She handed out appointments cards on streetcars or busses or in Krauss's department store. She called women or dropped by their houses to remind them of appointments. She kept them on schedule by repeating the message of salvation through family planning. When food was distributed as part of a nutritional program, she invented recipes for preparing milk, peanut butter, cream of wheat, or other foodstuffs into nourishing meals. "I'd know who needed carfare. I'd just give it to them and get reimbursed out of petty cash." She and the other staff members started bringing in clothes to be redistributed: a party dress, a winter coat, a boy's outgrown suit. She had an answer, a choice, and health care to offer the woman who confessed, "I'm ready to give up. I can't work. Just baby after baby. If I have another one, I have to quit my job. How can we live?" Because of her commitment, Annie Joseph was awarded the Charles E. Dunbar Medal for Public Service (given by the state Civil Service department).

Gloria Favorite had had nine babies in seven years before she heard about the Louisiana Family Planning Program. She said, "My husband

and I were so afraid of making a baby that we were scared to talk to each other" (Lelyveld 1970). She broke her first appointment, suspicious of anything that sounded too good to be true. Finally convinced, she went to a clinic, made her own fertility decisions, and started work as a member of the first outreach team. She amassed a stunning record for persuading women in situations like her own to make and keep appointments.

Another of the original five outreach workers, Jacqueline Harvey, said, "At Family Planning, I was selling a free health insurance policy, a policy based on a woman understanding her body, deciding about how many children she wanted, and controlling her reproduction. We were crusaders for the cause." She and the others worked 10 to 14 hours a day and gave out appointments on Saturdays and Sundays to contact mothers who worked or could not come in during the week. They were evangelists spreading the word, the gospel of birth control. "I would have worked without the money. I saw so many mothers desperate enough to try illegal abortions. The problems were hunger and child abuse. Family Planning was a helping hand. Otherwise, we'd all still be caught up."

Training the Recruits

Said the social worker who began the word-of-mouth recruiting and training system for the outreach workers, "We changed their lives. First the lives of the women who worked there and then the lives of the women who came as patients. We taught them a vigorous pursuit of health and an alternative to passivity." The original role envisioned for the outreach workers was simply recruitment and follow-up of patients. Soon their role expanded into activities more like those of social or case work (Lipscomb 1969). They became skilled at recognizing obstacles to long-range planning for their new converts. The paraprofessionals helped families use community resources to alleviate problems with health (both mental and physical), employment, housing, or conflicts with the law. When the outreach workers reported the inconveniences of clinic hours, a night clinic was opened. Because of the transportation problems into the central city, a clinic across the river was inaugurated.

The supervisors and researchers who were training the outreach workers developed an entirely new system which was widely copied when the program attracted international attention (Moore 1968; Barrentine 1969; Beasley and Frankowski 1970). Review and retraining were constant as responses to reports from outreach workers about patients' beliefs, folklore (even voodoo), and criticisms. Problem-solving and role enactment techniques, formal lectures on reproductive physiology and contraception methodology, and field trips into the medical complexes proved highly effective (Lipscomb 1969).

The outreach workers were driven by the knowledge that they were truly saving lives as well as controlling fertility. Some of them discovered during their own physical examination, which was part of the training, that they had dangerous untreated health conditions. One had an undiagnosed cervical cancer and underwent a live-saving operation. With these experiences in mind, they assigned high priority to reaching any woman with a positive Pap smear, venereal disease, diabetes, or other threatening medical condition. Tracking down these women often involved considerable detective work. The outreach workers made home visits and even accompanied women to special clinics for referral.

A complex system of evaluating the performances of the outreach workers substantiated the success of the indigenous worker system, and the cadre expanded to as many as fifty at any time. Soon they were training counterparts for other states and many foreign countries. Other programs wishing to duplicate the achievements in Louisiana looked first at these paraprofessionals. The astonishing "kept rate" (women who accepted and met appointments) that made this program famous reflects the evangelical fervor of the outreach workers.

The motto of the program became, "Value the individual patient's privacy, dignity, and right to choose."

> Poor patients receiving care under tax-supported auspices frequently have their privacy, dignity or right to choose disregarded. If those rendering service believe that their patients are "too dumb to learn," "not interested," "poor protoplasm or they would not be poor," then it is unlikely that patients will maintain a sustained relationship with the program. (Beasley 1969b:12)

Learning from the negative models of Charity Hospital or the welfare department, the staff called all patients by title and last name. Numbers were not used in the clinics to identify patients. Patronage, harrassment, discussion of patients as if they were not there, and failure to explain health conditions and medical decisions were all forbidden. Anyone who could not accept these restrictions was not hired; as some medical students learned, anyone violating them in the clinics was fired or returned to Charity. The clean, modern, well-lighted waiting rooms and private examination rooms became an expression of the value system of the new program.

Headway and Headaches

Accounts of the formative years of the program emphasize the electric atmosphere of creativity and social service and the attitude of "let's do something about it." Even the dullest reports shine with the hope that the knowledge gained would be instrumental in solving serious problems. The staff members were encouraged to return to school with the financial assistance of the program. Some employees rose from welfare recipients to supervisors. Others were writing, speaking, and consulting in public forums from Washington to the World Health Organization.

The first clinic in Orleans Parish had opened in June 1967. By the end of that year, three satellite clinics within the parish also opened in neighborhoods with housing projects and large concentrations of poor families (the Desire, Algiers-Fischer, and Sara Mayo area clinics). The plan was to decentralize the family planning services and eventually to extend services into a broader range of maternal and child health care activities.

With two years of the opening of the Orleans Parish Demonstration Project, 17,459 families were active participants. The number of patients who remained active for at least 18 months increased to 85 percent. "We set a goal of reaching all of the post-partum, high risk and low risk population identifiable through vital records within two years of the commencement of operations. We actually identified, educated and offered family planning services to all of this group within the first 18 months" (Beasley 1969b:5).

Humane Service

Increasing numbers of women kept their appointments (Beasley and Frankowski 1970). Black women were still six times more likely to accept an appointment and sign up for contraception than were white women. The greatest level of acceptance was among women from ages 20 to 24; these readily perceived the need for spacing children.[8] Older women, whose families were at or near the desired family size, had the option of sterilization through the referral system.

The wisdom of having outreach workers visit mothers fresh from the delivery room soon became evident. Often the hospital visitor arrived before the baby was brought in to the mother. Without any follow-up stimulus, over three-fourths of these women kept their appointments. "Since this percentage is considerably higher than is typically reported for return on postpartum appointments in programs serving the medically indigent, it is noteworthy" (Moore et al. 1974:364). Concentrating on hospital contacts first was a new way of thinking for family planners (McCalister, Hawkins, and Beasley 1970).

The intensive follow-up system was also working. Sixty-two percent of the patients kept appointments without being reminded. But the number of women who kept their appointments increased by 22 percent when they received a note, a phone call, or a home visit. This rate of participation (85 percent of those contacted) was the highest reported from any voluntary program in the country (Beasley, Frankowski, and Hawkins 1969:237).

Extraordinary attention was dedicated to keeping the waiting time to minutes. This characteristic was a revelation to new clients because the waiting time at Charity could range from 6 to 12 hours. If patients who dropped in could not be accommodated, they were given an appointment. All women received contraception counseling, sex educational classes, and other services, including annual breast and pelvic examinations and a screening for cervical cancer. If problems or questions arose before the two-month follow-up appointment, the patient was urged to contact the clinic. When a special health problem not under the usual category of fertility management services was diagnosed, the woman was referred. By offering an annual physical examination—a novel preventive health measure for most of the women—the family planning clinic acted as a family doctor.

Innumerable small but humane services began to surface. Transportation funds were provided to a few women who might not otherwise have been able to use the clinic service. Infertile women who asked for help in planning a family were referred to the best infertility specialists in the state; the program paid for the medical services of couples who had difficulty in conceiving. Baby-sitting services for patients were developed.

Noticing that some of the women in the clinic for prenatal checkups were eating pickles, potato chips, and soft drinks, the staff arranged with the state health department for the specialist on nutrition to be assigned to the clinic. Later a Food Supplemental Program with federal financing was added. Although instructors stressed the relationship of good nutrition to healthy babies, what the clinic could do, apart from giving moral suasion and dispersing educational materials, to change the eating habits of pregnant women was never clear.

Confining Guidelines

The externally imposed eligibility requirements were always a burden. Guidelines from the federal government, state, or grant sources were tedious, lacked uniformity, and changed through time. Family Planning always used the broadest, most liberal limits to define the poor and near poor. Hating to turn away anyone, it stretched every guideline. If a woman had been eligible and enrolled in the past but her circumstances changed, she could continue as a patient. This practice strained staff members' discretionary abilities and hampered the cost-accounting system.

The liberal conscience behind the Family Planning program was pained by the federal guidelines and by the agreements made with the Catholic Church prohibiting provision of birth control services to those under 21 who had not been married or pregnant. In Louisiana, these girls could receive sex education and physical examinations but not the contraceptive service. Although the national Planned Parenthood board of directors had voted unanimously to offer the full range of services regardless of government policy, the Louisiana planners had to refuse services. Sometimes teenagers and their parents tried to circumvent regulations.

> There were some 13 or 14 year old girls who came into the clinic as a group and gave false information regarding the ever-married, ever-pregnant history which made them eligible for the service. They were given appointments. However, the nurse sensed they did not stick to their original stories on questioning them further and was able to determine from further questioning that they were not telling the truth and had given false history to meet our criteria.[9]

Even when parents gave permission, teens could not receive direct aid. This restrictive policy was lifted in 1972 and services for teenagers added. Exceptions for the mentally retarded were made by referrals.

No one on the staff was enthusiastic about the rhythm method. Although the medical staff expended considerable energy to present it as a legitimate choice, only 0.3 percent of all patients elected to use this method (Beasley, Frankowski, and Hawkins 1969:247). Because of the educational effort involved for so few patients, the rhythm clinic was one of the most expensive parts of the program. However, it was an essential element to ensure the neutrality of the Catholic Church, so the usual cost-effectiveness rules did not apply.

The unsuspected health problems that appeared when large numbers of women were examined were shocking to Family Planning personnel. Fifty-eight percent of all patients seen during the first year had serious health conditions—high blood pressure, diabetes, cardiovascular problems, toxemia during previous pregnancies, or other undiagnosed organic conditions—that made pregnancy or even the use of birth control inadvisable. Many of these women were having their first routine physical examination as an adult. The referral system and the definition of high risk had to be extended. Outreach workers redoubled their efforts to contact women.

A woman who is unhealthy, whose family has already reached or exceeded the desired size, or who emphatically wishes to avoid more pregnancies is not a suitable candidate for birth control. She needs access to the option of legal, medically safe abortion or sterilization. Dr. Beasley had spoken out nationally in favor of abortion.[10] When questioned about this view locally, he blandly maintained that abortion would be less an issue if birth control was available to women (*New Orleans States-Item*, April 4, 1966). To judge from the comments that I have collected, it is likely that some staff members, informally and secretly, referred selected patients to safe but illegal networks of abortion services rather than see them go to "butchers" in desperation.

In public, the family planners stuck to their dictum that "abortion is not a form of birth control." This was their official policy. Sometimes, however, the intrauterine devices failed, and a woman became pregnant despite her commitment to birth control. This dilemma was resolved by running an "underground abortion railroad." (Beasley, personal communication, July 21, 1983). A program official made an appointment at the Margaret Sanger Research Bureau in New York, paid the patient's airfare out of untraceable discretionary funds, and even provided transportation to the airport if necessary. As Beasley observed, "The way we saw it, it was not the woman's fault. It was our responsibility." He had often said, "I never met a woman who wanted to die from an illegal abortion." No one had statistics on how many women in the program were treated to abortions. Later when government investigators turned the program inside out looking for abuses of funding, they uncovered no evidence of this practice. The potential for public scandal was great if the practice had been known.

The state health department had to be persuaded to help on the delicate question of patients at Charity Hospital who were recovering from illegal abortions. These women needed family planning and were an untapped source of referrals. The department agreed that Charity could release their names so they could be treated as ordinary postpartum patients. Since abortions were illegal, without the push from Family Planning these women could have been treated as criminals.

Black-White Differential

Another painful surprise was the differential response rate between the races in New Orleans.

> Many lower socioeconomic white patients, because of their racial prejudice, are not receiving family planning services. For example, the clinic receives frequent requests from women to be seen in either segregated clinics, or to be seen under special circumstances. Because these requests are not honored . . . it creates hostility and rejection of the program. The problem of how to reach this population and simultaneously operate a truly integrated clinic has proven to be perplexing. (Beasley, Frankowski, and Hawkins 1969:240)

During the first year of operation, 96 percent of the patients were black. Although the proportion of white participation increased, it never topped 15 percent in Orleans Parish. Several professionals noted the difficulty: "Whites perceived the Family Planning was for blackfolks. In fact, some blacks thought so too. It was a concept inherent in the times." White women were believed to have more access to private doctors and were not accustomed to black professionals. Although some private doctors had black patients (paying or otherwise), their appointment schedules were rigidly segregated by time. White patients might be sharing the same facilities and the same doctor with black patients, but they did not know it.

A more compelling reason for the different rates of success by race is the support networks that had been so masterfully tapped in starting the program. The black community was united by the racial stigmas, a common history of segregation, the civil rights movement, and the New Left reforms. Blacks had long been active in neighborhood associations or other institutions that defined the black community; whites had few counterparts to these. Middle-class whites felt little responsibility to provide improved health care services for lower-class whites. A major strength of the black networks was the dynamic, articulate, and aggressive women whose informal, but very real, influence was behind the family planning movement. Women who had no need of birth control for themselves were activists in the cause of better health care. They constituted the single largest bloc of support for Family Planning and were so visible that politicians began to see them as a potential political force.

Another reason for the black-white differential—which could not be openly discussed—was the postpartum referral system at Charity. Although indigent black women had little choice but delivery at Charity, poor white women often could give birth at private hospitals because of discrete financial arrangements. The postpartum hospital visitors could not contact them there because interference with the private practice of medicine was tacitly forbidden. Eligible women could voluntarily come to family planning clinics but could not be recruited. Because most women using the program's contraceptive service were black, it was vulnerable to suspicions ranging from racism to genocide.

Almost a year after the opening, outreach workers began to report a sudden increase in evasion and refusals in certain neighborhoods. An investigation showed that Black Muslim and black power influences were strong in these areas. The genocide issue, in the throes of heated national debate, had reared its head for the first time in New Orleans. Prominent black leaders and some of the militants were contacted by Family Planning personnel. To improve public relations, the clinic staff was reminded that "emphasis on birth control should be taboo. Emphasis on family planning and health maintenance would be better. This is a teaching job."[11]

It is a tribute to the program's professionals that they were able to tap the support of the black community leadership and to diffuse many of the controversies linked to race. But the program was identified by many in the community as another social service for blacks. Although they had diffused the problem, it reappeared in 1971 with far more dramatic consequences for family planning.

It is impossible to measure the positive changes that resulted from the opening of public dialogue about birth control and women's health. Control, planning, dignity, and choice were lauded from church pulpits, in newspapers, and through networks of friends and relatives. Reluctant at first to attend the clinic—remembering treatment at other free institutions—the women soon came to regard the program as their family doctor. They asked to deliver babies there rather than at Charity. Through the years, I have frequently heard moving accounts of women who believe that the Family Planning program saved their lives.

4

From the Possible to the Impossible

A neglect of effective birth control policy is a never failing source of poverty, which is in turn the parent of revolution and crime.
—Aristotle, *Politics*, Book 1, chap. 6, pg. 1265-B.

The number one success story in the history of the United States' birth control movement.
—Alan Guttmacher (Gordon 1970:87)

I'm hell-bent on making the system work.
—Joe Beasley, 1973

A story is told of a visitor from Korea who was flying to the famed Lincoln Parish Project. Looking down on hundreds of miles of rice fields and pine forests, he commented on what seemed to him the low population density of Louisiana in contrast to Asia. "Why would you need a family planning program when you obviously do not have an overpopulation problem such as we have?" he queried.

The answer centered on the poor women of Charity, some too young or too unhealthy to have babies. If the connection seems obscure, think of it the way the family planners did. They had moved from high-risk mothers, infant mortality, and the quality of life to questions of public health and the prevention of social problems through birth control and medical services. They believed they were developing practical models in Louisiana that could be exported into countries where overpopulation was an immediate threat.

Although there were many population experts, few had frontline experience in the mass delivery of contraceptives. The Louisiana family planners had moved squarely into the middle of the population debates with a tailormade plan. It is, however, a leap of faith to move from the more carefully structured world of family planning to the dilemmas of international population control.

The growth of the program from 1967, when it opened in Orleans Parish, until 1970, when services were made available to all medically indigent in the state, was exponential. Since no other statewide programs were extant in the United States at that time, it is difficult to compare the Louisiana Family Planning, Inc., with other efforts. It was sui generis.

The Statewide Drive

In autumn 1968, the Department of Health, Education and Welfare approved a grant of $1.75 million for Family Planning to be expanded into all parishes of Louisiana. By this time, the strategies of staffing, record keeping, and community involvement were so efficient that internal reports sound like a military campaign.

Anticipating that the quality of services to patients might slip because of poor management during a growth period, the family planning staff added modern management, evaluation, and monitoring techniques. They made long lists of specific detailed tasks, the person assigned, and the projected date of completion. The tasks ranged from contacts with each police jury (parish government) to the date of delivery of contraceptives to remote parishes. "Because of the crucial timing factor, the success of such a program design depends upon meeting tight deadlines. This can be done with realistic planning, continuous review and good communication. We seldom missed a critical date, and when we did we almost never took more than a week to pick up on it" (Beasley and Wells 1971:73).

As the tasks became more complex, computers were assimilated into the operation. Former employees insist that data processing and record keeping techniques at Family Planning were the most sophisticated in the state. "That would not be a difficult record to surpass," one said, "since some state health agencies were keeping records of patient visits with chalk marks on the wall. For all I know, they still are."

Program leaders worried about opposition from the heavily Catholic Cajun parishes of southern Louisiana, but no incidents were reported. In Monroe in northeastern Louisiana, however, the Protestant fundamentalists saw red. There the "hard-shell" Baptists, claiming that birth control was against God's will, tried to run the clinic organizers out of town. They used an all-purpose accusation: Family planning was a Communist plot and family planners were Communists (Wells 1972:118). (They did not care for sex education or integration either.) Although Monroe had proved to be a tougher town than neighboring Ruston in

Lincoln Parish, the Baptist antagonism was diffused by public relations efforts similar to those successful strategies in Orleans Parish.

In the rural clinics the policy of assigning nurses, aides, LPNs, or technicians to tasks previously done by physicians met with resistance. Although the patients and staff were pleased with this innovation, the rural physicians were not (Britanek 1972). In metropolitan areas doctors were willing to relinquish their traditional roles; task sharing reduced the time needed for physicians to see patients without jeopardizing their access to education and counseling. In New Orleans because of elaborate scheduling and deemphasis of the physicians' role, doctors' services were limited to giving pelvic examinations or providing diagnoses in unusual cases. In the rural areas there was antipathy and resistance to this team approach. The nurses trained in New Orleans had to provide counseling and encouragement to change the doctors' attitudes.

Monthly narrative reports (Health Education Reports) allowed the central bureaucracy to keep track of its far-flung empire and to see problems quickly. For example, the Ouachita Parish clinic wrote

> the new class is going well, and is probably operational in all parishes in the area now. The last I heard, the residents had really improved their behavior so this is good news. It will take a while for our image in the community to improve likewise, but with auxiliaries beginning to do active community education in group settings and develop volunteers to support the program, prospects should be good. (Wells 1972:118)

Workers in Monroe reported progress after their troubles with fundamentalists. From Alexandria in Rapides Parish, the report stated: "Classes going well. Nurses very enthusiastic about increased IUD acceptance rate." In the heart of French Cajun Louisiana (Calcasieu Parish), the nurses took the initiative of changing their prepared materials and speeches to fit local customs. The supervisor remarked, "Contrary to my predictions, they seem to be very comfortable telling it like it is to patients and seem to do an excellent job. We're finding that language and phrasing appropriate to most of the rest of the state needs modification over here."

In the monthly narrative reports the dry statistics were enlivened with details about staffing problems and interagency cooperation. "Nurse Administrator X was quite upset after attending the meeting at the [community center]; however, after talking to you on the phone, she felt much better. I would like to say that is not the first time that Family Planning personnel have been insulted or embarrassed by OEO personnel in Rapides Parish" (Wells 1972:165).

Baton Rouge is still significantly behind other areas. Bridge-building between nurses and auxiliaries is essential to the life of the program and will be difficult because of a long history of animosity and distrust on both sides. . . . I have gotten them involved in some specific "research" on how to explain IUD insertions to patients and they seemed pleased that I have confidence in them. (Wells 1972:118)

By the end of 1970, the Family Planning program's detailed organization and its idealism had reached thousands of patients, hundreds of health care professionals, dozens of community agencies, significant parts of the federal bureaucracy, private foundations, and the scientific-intellectual community. Adequate funds were available, and the cost-effective areas of education, training, and counseling were expanded. The highly individualized attention to patients was exceptional and probably accounted for the high rates of participation.[1]

Money Matters

Despite the organization's success in expanding statewide, it continued to face peculiar problems, some with serious consequences. One was the cost-accounting system. The objective of the primary accounting system was simple on the surface: to keep expenditures within the budgeted limit for each category and total expenditures within the limit of each grant. In retrospect, a cost-accounting system should have been established earlier, but patient records, facilities, the supply system, and managerial structure seemed more pressing than the fine tuning of internal administration from which patients derived no benefits.

Without an adequate cost-accounting system, costs varied widely between clinics. In 1970 the average payroll cost per patient visit was $10.72 over the entire state but ranged from $15.90 to $7.75 in different areas (Wells 1972:95). Costs also fluctuated according to the requirements of the granting agencies and the eligibility conditions of the patients.

Balancing Inflow and Outflow

Government grants, state contracts, and the largess of private foundations permitted Family Planning, Inc., a nonprofit corporation, to meet obligations for salaries, employee benefits, utilities, and other fixed costs. Surviving on grants ("soft money") is usually feast or famine. Since the corporation could not use grant funds for investments or capital expansion, sources had to be steady as well as flexible. New sources of funding were continually needed to allow for expansion rather than just maintenance.

Many federal grants required matching funds, but the guidelines for matching funds varied according to the source of the grant.[2] A minimum of 10 percent was required for a research demonstration, whereas outside sources had to supply up to 25 percent of some HEW grants. The most significant variation for the family planners was the difference between HEW and OEO grant requirements. OEO was more flexible and permitted in-kind contributions, but HEW matching funds had to actually be derived from some other source such as the state health department, Charity hospitals, Tulane University, and private foundations such as Ford and Rockefeller. As the program grew, however, it encountered increasing difficulties in finding funds for matching the HEW grants. The chronic tensions of meeting these requirements and of keeping the money flowing became evident after 1972. "The uncertain and unpredictable aspects of grant funding played a major role in the budgeting practices" (Wells 1972:183). From 1967 to 1970 the program administered fifty-five grants from diverse public and private sources. Federal moneys for the statewide operation amounted to about $14 million. Keeping track of money and the rules for its management grew more complex.

The number of patients in the program increased by 400 percent. New patients averaged five visits per year. Birth control was only one of the many health services they received. Each increase in the patient load increased the total cost geometrically. The costs for maintaining the women continued to increase. No agency in the United States had enough experience to predict whether private doctors or the publicly supported providers cared for patients more efficiently. The family planners in Louisiana often said that their costs averaged between $8 and $10 per patient per year (Wells 1972:95; Correa et al. 1972). But this estimate depends on what is included in the final accounting.

Providing Facilities

The corporation had opened 148 clinics. But in a state with bad roads, the administrative personnel needed better mobility. A 1969 management study showed that travel costs had been mounting steadily but could be reduced by leasing an aircraft. Although the aircraft leasing saved $61,000 in 1970, it was related in the public mind more to political favors than to antipoverty agencies. Airplanes later surfaced as an issue not of efficiency but of corruption.

Most of the space for clinic facilities came in the form of donations (matching and in-kind contributions) from state health agencies. The free clinic space had an estimated annual rental value of $600,000 by 1970. Chronic shortages of space still existed in some areas, and approximately a fourth of the facilities needed major or minor renovations.

One family planning unit met in a mental health clinic, two in churches, and two in federal housing units. Sometimes prefabricated storage buildings were purchased (Beasley and Wells 1971:73). Because these facilities were not sufficient, Family Planning decided to build a fleet of mobile clinics. This clever innovation was encouraged by granting agencies, but the mobile clinics became a "smoking gun" by the end of the story.

By the end of 1970, the organization had 533 employees and an average monthly payroll of $260,000. Sixty percent of the staff was classified as paraprofessionals so the training programs still required a large commitment of time and money. Grants financed the training of administrators and personnel from other states and foreign countries. Forty-seven countries sent government officials, medical personnel, or program administrators to see how a family planning program worked in a developing state. Their counterparts in the United States were also invited to Louisiana to view the program, attend special seminars, and adopt the model.

Justifying Expenditures

The family planners were also struggling to justify that the money spent produced results. The achievements had to be measured in some way, but "Family Planning Program Evaluation is not a well-developed art, much less an exact science. The evaluation of the performance of such programs has received a good deal of attention but the methodologies are still controversial and the results inconclusive" (Reynolds 1972:69). The easiest and least effective way was to measure changes in people's attitudes about contraception (the KAP [knowledge-attitude-practice] studies). Although these studies have cross-cultural validity, they do not demonstrate a cause-and-effect relationship. A second solution was to chart changes in behavior, for example, to determine how many women accepted the service. But no standard definitions existed, and many programs failed to distinguish among women entering the program, using contraceptives, and continuing to use them throughout the reproductive span (Bogue 1970; Petersen 1981).

The ultimate effect of family planning is a demographic change, a decrease in birth and death rates. But no one can prove conclusively that a specific program deserves credit for fertility declines. These rates have decreased in the past and within certain groups without interventionist programs like family planning. In this field as in most of preventive medicine, no one can prove that an accident was avoided. An event that simply did not happen is hard to quantify.

So evaluators are left with middle-range statistical measures, such as changes in fertility patterns within one group, trends in actual versus expected rates or indirect calculations of effects on fertility (Reynolds 1972). Alternatively, the program could collapse its statistics into gross estimates of impact on the whole population. These simplified statistics have the most appeal to funding agencies. The same can be said for cost-for-patient figures, which seem to offer some comparability between programs. Economists have been intrigued by complex cost-benefit analysis, which demonstrates how much money has been saved for each birth averted. Because of the different values placed on a human life, the estimates of dollars spent to dollars saved range from 1:3 to 1:30 (U.S. Congress, Senate, Committee on Finances 1973:387).

Despite these difficulties, the Louisiana Family Planning program needed to justify its existence quantitatively. Many of the data it published were used to answer just these questions, and most of the professional criticism directed later toward the program was based on its claims that it had altered birth rates in the state. But one demographer praised the published material from Louisiana: "One should not ignore the large amount of valuable work being conducted in such places as Korea, Taiwan and Louisiana" (Reynolds 1972:83).

Is Family Planning Population Control?

In the 1960s, the U.S. government began a decade of serious discussions on the problems of overpopulation. The central theme that emerged from the population debates was that a government-subsidized birth control program for the poor could be equated with a national population policy.

The pinnacle of the national family planning movement was the Family Planning Services and Population Research Act of December 1970. Congressional discussions of the population problem began in 1965.[3] During these and subsequent hearings, the legislature concluded that domestic family planning was an area to which the government could contribute without adopting coercive measures to control the population. Controversial topics such as abortion, aid to minors, sex education, mass propaganda, or sterilization (voluntary or otherwise) were not considered for action.

The widely acclaimed Title X of the Public Health Service Act authorized up to $382 million to expand services nationwide during the next two years (the upper spending limit was never reached). This legislation was the first to state that the United States had a population problem within its borders. A vague connection was made between world population problems and family planning. The act did not spell out any long-range goals of population management nor specified means of attack. Small amounts of money were allocated for population research, but the bulk of funding went directly to family planning for the poor. This act was essentially ambivalent. In July 1970, Richard M. Nixon, in the first presidential speech on population policy, observed that "by the year 2000, or shortly thereafter, there will be more than 300 million Americans. This growth will produce serious challenges for our society" (American Enterprise Institute 1970:5). Nixon went on to ask how all these new Americans would be housed, educated, or provided with medical care. How would this growth strain the environment, natural resources, political processes, and social institutions? But to a problem of these dimensions, his answer was

It is my view that no American woman should be denied access to family planning assistance because of her economic condition. I believe, therefore, that *we should establish as a national goal the provision of adequate family planning services within the next five years to all those who want them but cannot afford them.* (American Enterprise Institute 1970:7; emphasis in original)

Nixon emphasized that no action by the government would infringe on religious convictions or private conscience. The goals of family planning as government policy were roughly the same as those in the Louisiana program. Borrowing figures from Planned Parenthood, the Ford Foundation, and the Louisiana model, the president reiterated that 5 million medically indigent women needed subsidized services, although only one in four was receiving them. The government was serious about family planning, but the quotation from Nixon's address is the ultimate statement of government policy on the population problem.

Policymakers had not suggested a causal link between the world's population explosion and a woman's desire for fertility control. Few women attend birth control clinics with the motivation of allaying through personal action the growth of world populations. The government's only stated goal was to facilitate and pay for access to contraception while permitting complete freedom of choice.

One leading demographer, Kingsley Davis, criticized U.S. policymakers for making personal planning synonymous with government policy: "I call it collective gold displacement. The Federal Government is spending millions of dollars under the illusion it is getting population control. All it is getting is bad advice. . . . The basic motivation to have children is very strong" (*New York Times*, October 5, 1969). He went on to explain that people will continue to have children until subtle and adverse conditions necessitate a change in values. "The population problem does not lie in some group of blacks having more children than they want. You cannot brush it off on some particular group. It lays itself open to the claim of genocide" (*New York Times*, October 5, 1969). This broadside was aimed in part at the Louisiana model.

Davis (1967) and Judith Blake (1969) argued that the family planning programs only provided technological services and could not bring about fundamental changes in society or population control. Blake contended that the family planning movement was essentially conservative, notwithstanding the liberal rhetoric. Pressures for legislation had come from population lobbies and government bureaucracies, not from the kind of people who had crusaded earlier for birth control. The leadership included few women and was not tied to feminist agendas.

Oscar Harkavy, Frederick Jaffe, and Samuel Wishik (1969) swiftly refuted these criticisms in an article published in the prestigious journal, *Science*. Population policy proponents and family planners stressed that the government had not established population reduction or stability as a national goal. Rather, as Nixon had said, the hope was to offer family planning services to the poor as a public health measure. The Lincoln Parish program's achievements in reducing the rates of illegitimacy were singled out as the best example of the authors' major points (1969:372). Later, the fact that a journal as highly regarded as *Science* published an article praising Louisiana's program incited academic infighting and statistical battles that affected the entire course of family planning.

Population Control and the Entrepreneur

With worldwide attention focused on the need to control population growth, any person or program with an imaginative plan, practical experience, and articulate concerns took center stage. As the Lincoln Parish demonstration widened into Orleans Parish and then became the first state family planning program, it began to attract national attention.[4] Family planning was an end in itself and the logical first step or prototype for solving the world crisis. A problem so sweeping suited Joe Beasley's style. He had harbored visions of combining medical knowledge and managerial technology to save children in the Third World, and his rare practical experience became a model.

Beasley spoke dramatically of the national and international tragedies that were less the case of baby booms and too many people than the high birth and death rates in lower socioeconomic groups.

In New Orleans at this time we estimate that 39 percent of the families are in the lower socio-economic segment or medically indigent and they're producing over 53 percent of the births occurring in the city. The same is true in Philadelphia, Cleveland, Chicago. . . . If you happen to be poor in the city at this time and are born alive—you have an 85 percent higher

chance of dying before you reach one year of age than you do if you're in
the middle or upper socio-economic group. Or if you happen to be poor in
some of the counties of the Mississippi Delta, your chances of dying are on
the order of 150 to 200 percent higher if you happen to be indigent. Similar
things can be said about Harlem, or about census tracts in Chicago or Watts.
Talking about rural areas west of the Delta, some of our mortality rates
among the indigent children are approaching those of cities like Cairo, Egypt
or Sao Paulo, Brazil. (Coyle 1968:17)

As it became obvious that family planning services could be delivered
en masse to poor women and that the Louisiana model could be exported,
Beasley lectured more frequently about the population problem. He was
passionate and outspoken. He always talked about the causal chain that
ran from the rights of a single child, through freedom of choices for
women, to family stability and reductions in world population growth.
One of the key links in the chain he postulated was a faith in women
and strong advocacy of their rights to decide.

If you have a culture where the woman is not subservient to the male, but
is emancipated, and the woman is given a choice for her own welfare, she
is going to decrease the number of children voluntarily. She is aware of the
consequences, the risks and problems, and aware that she can actually control
her own reproduction—that is a very revolutionary concept to many women
of the world. (Coyle 1968:15)

Looking to Latin America

In 1972, Joe Beasley and the Family Health Foundation (the corporation's new name) were awarded a grant from the U.S. Agency for
International Development (USAID) to study the feasibility of instituting
family planning and maternal-child health programs in selected areas
of Latin America. This grant and those that followed permitted export
of the Louisiana model to countries suffering from endemic poverty
and rapidly increasing fertility rates.[5]

The plan called for limited pilot projects in four countries: Brazil,
Colombia, Mexico, and Venezuela. Each site was chosen because of
preexisting links to an academic or medical institution that acted as an
intermediary with government officials. Many of the professionals staffing
these projects had been trained at Family Health or had attended Tulane
University. The plan for attacking the seemingly insuperable problems
in Latin America combined most of the elements of the established
family planning programs with new thoughts on generic health care.
As usual, Beasley's team would train and utilize paraprofessionals. They
projected a triage system in which the less serious public health cases

were treated in local clinics and the regional or national teaching hospitals handled cases of increased complexity. The various facilities in the system would treat the causes, not just the symptoms, of the high mortality rates: untreated illness, environmental contagion, infectious diseases, poor sanitation, recourse to traditional cures or home remedies, and limited medical services. Nutrition played a key role, although the patterns of economic maldistribution linked to history, class, and value systems were not addressed.

Family Health's movie, *To Hunt with a Cat*, touted the achievements of the Louisiana program and presented in sentimental language what its staff hoped to accomplish in Latin America. The most poignant scene in the movie showed a cemetery in Cali, Colombia, where vultures gathered on the walls to watch processions carrying small plastic caskets to a long row of tiny graves. The narrator explained that 125 babies were born in a nearby hospital each day. With little or no prenatal care, more than half of them might die. In this area there were four times as many abortions as births. To Joe Beasley, the problems in Latin America were just the same as those in Louisiana magnified several times. He believed that Family Health could use the model and experience gained in Louisiana to help the ill-fated Latin American children while addressing the root causes of overpopulation.

When Tulane University and Family Health signed an agreement with the Ministry of Health in Mexico, they pledged technical assistance in the operation of a pilot community health program. The foundation officials vowed "to obtain a balanced reduction of death, sickness and fertility and improving nutritional status." Beasley explained that this was "the first such agreement, to our knowledge, to have been reached between a major nation of the world and an organization in order to bring a systematic methodological large scale approach to these major health problems" (*Times-Picayune*, May 6, 1973).

There were practical dilemmas in scientific paradigms. The pilot health programs were only a drop in the bucket of existing problems, and the dramatic, well-publicized Louisiana demonstrations had dealt with smaller and less stressed populations than those in Latin America. Although the Family Health planners were concerned with the quality of life, politicians in Washington, the Ford and Rockefeller foundations, and quasi-governmental agencies such as the Population Council or the UN Fund for Population Activities emphasized the quantitative aspects of population control and the strategic and military interests of the United States (Lelyveld 1970; Polgar 1972).

The population control issue linked Family Health and Beasley with the Central Intelligence Agency (CIA) and the Department of Defense. At a meeting with Nixon's top aides, Beasley implied that the CIA had a natural interest in international population control (*Vieux Carre Courier,* December 12, 1973). Beasley had been a member of the population control establishment for years and had always talked of extending the scope of the Louisiana model to encompass population problems. But the talk of population control, war, the CIA, and Latin America scared many Louisianans, and others believed that the wider schemes deflected energies that should be focused locally.

Despite the grants and the promises, the foundation's south-of-the-border programs were never fully completed. No systematic studies of their effects have ever been conducted. Although there are family planning programs in Latin America now, none is administered from a private foundation in Louisiana.

Jumping on the Population Bandwagon

From 1966 on, Beasley testified regularly before House and Senate committees on legislation or appropriation bills related to family planning or population.[6] In 1968, he was named director of the National Advisory Council for the newly organized Center for Family Planning Program Development. Three months later the Department of Health, Education and Welfare announced his appointment to the National Advisory Health Council (an appointed twelve-member body that advised HEW on national health issues). Warm relationships between Planned Parenthood–World Population and the Louisiana family planners resulted in considerable exchange of services. Frederick Jaffe, Alan Guttmacher, and other leaders in the population movement often testified with Beasley in Washington and cited the Louisiana program as an example of success. In 1966, Beasley was elected to the Board of Planned Parenthood, then chairman of its Executive Committee, and in 1970 chairman of the Board of Directors.

Late in 1968, Harvard University announced that it had created an endowed chair of population and public health and that Dr. Joseph Beasley was appointed to it. For several years Beasley commuted to Cambridge as a visiting professor in the School of Public Health and as medical director of the universitywide Center for Population Studies. At Harvard, public health and political science students analyzed Louisiana's family planning success as part of the case-study methods in advanced classes. Beasley also served as a consultant on the applicability of the Louisiana model to similar problems in the urban-industrial hub of the Northeast.

In mid-1970, President Nixon named Beasley to the National Commission on Population Growth and the American Future, chaired by John D. Rockefeller, Jr. In January 1971, the commission, including

Rockefeller and some of the most prominent people in population control research and development in the United States, visited New Orleans to see a functioning and successful family planning program firsthand. As Senator Robert Packwood of Oregon testified,

> I can say in all fairness that Joe Beasley, as much as any single person on that Commission [the National Commission on Population Growth and the American Future], was the driving force in its recommendations. . . . In my estimation he has the most successful statewide family planning program in the United States and he is an extraordinary leader in any capacity, medical or otherwise. (U.S. Congress, Senate, Committee on Finance 1973:375)

A golden stream of honors, awards, and job offers poured in for Beasley and the program. The Millbank Memorial Fund gave him a grant of $40,000 to spend on population dynamics. Ford, Rockefeller, and Lilly foundations, among others, made conspicuous grants for family planning research and demonstration projects through Tulane University. Beasley won awards for public health service in Louisiana. During this period, he was director of Louisiana Family Planning, Inc., and of the Institute of Health Services, chairman of the Department of Family Health and Population Dynamics of the School of Public Health and Tropical Medicine, visiting professor at Harvard, and chairman of the Board of Planned Parenthood. In addition, Beasley acted as consultant to the World Health Organization, the State Department, the Agency for International Development, and the World Bank.[7] He brought new meaning to the term *overachievement*.

Later, detractors scoffed at Beasley's idealism and called it raw ambition, a doomed "save the world" obsession, or a cynical ploy to manipulate government and private funding sources. They charged that the population bandwagon was lucrative and more spectacular than the prosaic elements of family planning.

The press referred to Joe Beasley as "the dynamic young doctor," "one of the leading experts in the field of population control," and "Mr. Family Planning." He and his program were reaping national honors and international recognition. There was talk of a Nobel Peace Prize.

5
The Peak Is Reached

We're going to make Louisiana a utopia, the kind of state nobody had dreamed of. Then, after I become President, we'll use Louisiana as a pattern.
—Huey Long, campaign speech, 1934

The family planning system has developed into a major system for the delivery of preventive health care to women of low or marginal incomes and may be the largest such health care system in the nation today.
—Frederick Jaffe, president, Planned Parenthood, 1973

Family planning has finite limits. It is, after all, primarily for fertile women. But there are no limits to the broader concepts of family health or community medicine. After 1970, with the statewide plan in full operation and receiving exhilarating international attention, the drama shifted to other stages.

If the key word had been *planning*, now it was *replication*. The concepts that had proved workable for the organization of family planning were now to be transplanted (replicated) not only into other geographical areas but also into other types of health care and research-development projects. The growing foundation in Louisiana saw its role as generic health care and human services, as well as family planning. The bounty of the government and private foundation largess was greater than ever before.

By March 1972 after several intermediate name changes, the former Louisiana Family Planning, Inc., had been incorporated within a broader structure called the Family Health Foundation. The organizational charts changed radically to reflect the added dimensions. Beasley had expanded the New Orleans–based private corporation and had taken a new title as president. Although the family planning services were still central, this expansion and name change announced the corporation's movement beyond birth control into new forms of health care. In the first organizational chart published for Family Planning (Beasley 1969b), individual tasks, clinic organization, and birth control support were paramount. The last chart published (Figure 5.1) outlined broad conceptual areas rather than administrative lines. Family Health Foundation was a broad umbrella comprising five subdivisions: (1) Louisiana Family Planning, (2) the Parent-Child Development Center, (3) the Model Cities Neighborhood Health Clinics, (4) the International Division, and (5) the Research Division. The Parent-Child Development Center was established by the Office of Economic Opportunity to investigate the effect of changes in child-rearing patterns on the culture of poverty. To expand the resources and techniques employed in family planning clinics to the field of community medicine, Beasley and his associates planned the Model Cities clinics. They were simultaneously expanding their research and demonstration projects in four countries in Latin America.

The term *community medicine* seems to sum up much of the new direction and visionary drive in this period.[1]

> This strategy will encompass day care, adult education, nutrition, transportation, housing, manpower development, care for the aged, environmental sanitation, legal support, drug rehabilitation, ecological coordination, and the provision of a positive framework for industrial development in the areas of the Neighborhood Health Centers. The most unique aspect of this strategy is its potential to demonstrate the use of an academic/non-profit foundation complex as the mechanism through which a major city can expand and improve its health and human development. (U.S. Congress, House, Committee on Appropriations 1973:1646)

The long-term projections of Family Health involved much more than family planning. The outreach workers had met the challenges of recruiting and retaining patients. In 1972, national legislation offered a new nine-to-one match of federal to state funds; however, states failing to provide family planning services to recipients of Aid to Dependent Children lost a percentage of that money. This arrangement provided an incentive for other states to adopt the Louisiana model.

The system so well established in Louisiana was replicated in Illinois, where Catholic conservatives who opposed state-funded birth control for unmarried women had delayed programs for some years (Littlewood 1977; Dienes 1972). Now that the religious issues were resolved, Illinois moved rapidly to implement a family planning program on the Louisiana model.

> A statewide family planning program was put into operation in Illinois in fifteen months compared to the five years it had taken to implement the program throughout the state of Louisiana. The Illinois program is now the

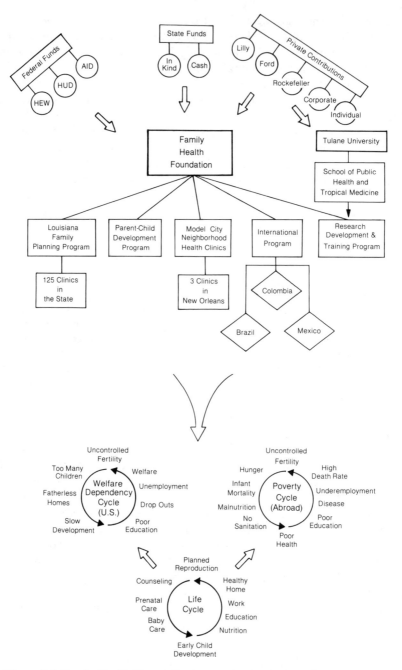

Figure 5.1 Family Health Foundation's organizational chart (Source: Family Health Foundation)

second largest program in the United States and has achieved levels of success similar to those in Louisiana. (U.S. Congress, House, Committee on Appropriations 1973:1650)

Meanwhile, students in public health were trained at the foundation to replicate the Louisiana formula in foreign countries.[2] Students from abroad planned to return home with the blueprints for family planning.

A Mania for Management

Beasley's team exhaustively experimented, researched, and appraised the growing sophistication in management systems. Because of their flexible private foundation and interdisciplinary expertise, the family planners could move rapidly in replicating their system while simultaneously evaluating its progress. The operations research techniques were designed to spot day-to-day problems in departments or areas of service. Managerial concern was particularly evident for such areas as patient response and activity, cost for patient services, and the outreach worker system (Correa and Beasley 1971, 1974). Some of these measures included

utilizing data curve fitting and linear regression for trend analysis, systematic review of program costs as measure of efficiency versus future funding requirements, and Gantt charting of future program factors such as agency reporting, both progress and financial, proposed preparation activity and key milestones event indicators. (Applied Health Sciences Department 1972:9)

(The jargon became overly self-conscious, but the granting agencies loved it.) Grant applications, reports to funders, internal reports, professional papers, theses, and dissertations contained thousands of pages of statistical data and elaborate descriptions of systems analysis and management by objective.

At the main offices in New Orleans was a room especially designed for processing grants. With its large staff, sophisticated organization, and modern technology, the foundation could prepare a grant application overnight if necessary. The same apparatus produced reports and provided an awesome source of data for researchers. Certainly nothing in the state health bureaucracies, universities, city government, or few businesses could duplicate the technical capabilities that the Family Health Foundation mustered. For the first time in Louisiana, the record-keeping system could follow a patient through the maze of eligibility forms, referrals, hospitalization, laboratories, and other bureaucracies.

Marketing Family Planning

Modern marketing techniques reformed the publicity for birth control. The references to suppressed women, battered children, unstable families, or mental retardation were gone. In their place, family planning aims were discussed as a marketplace in which professionals use consumer research to create a demand for goods, services, and information in contraception. The concepts of business, economics, and management were increasingly substituted for the medical and social services model.

The Louisiana family planners gradually came to view their efforts as "the perceptive application of marketing concepts and technology in the field of family planning" (El-Ansary and Kramer 1973:2) and to rely more heavily on the marketplace terminology and viewpoint (Dunbar 1973). Target markets and the special characteristics of customer subgroups (rural-urban, north-south, postpartum–never pregnant) could be identified; adapting new strategies to meet their particular needs resulted in higher rates of "selling." They already had a philosophy of "take the service to the customer" with home visits, hospital visits, follow-up, and computer-generated letters. In effect, the outreach workers were salespeople whose selling performance could be monitored.

Cost-benefit analysis, cost control, and management information systems enabled the researchers "to collect continuous information about customer characteristics, customer behavior, and other marketing participant characteristics and attitudes" (El-Ansary and Kramer 1973:4). They applied break-even and cost-benefit analyses to individual work performance and used employee incentives to increase recruitment of new customers. By studying the monthly management reports, researchers could isolate any problem area (personnel, service, supplies) and reorient their resources for greater productivity.

Family Health researchers' urge to include business and industrial techniques in health care delivery is nowhere more evident than in their elaborate production of media presentations. Although they had reviewed commercial packages, none used imagery, actors, or music that was likely to appeal to black women—the largest sector of the audience in Louisiana (Beasley, Durel, and Jones 1973). With typical verve, they decided to produce their own media software. They started with a slide lecture on the six fundamental methods of contraception. Over the years they added printed materials, brochures, pamphlets, posters, and audio and video cassettes. Teenagers saw a color film, *A Three-Letter Word for Love*, or the five-screen panoramic slide-sound show, *A Time to be Born*. Eventually the researchers made their own movies about the program, to be shown to wider audiences than clinic participants. This tendency to aggrandize the program culminated in a documentary for national television. Narrated by Hugh Downs, the film was called *To Hunt with a Cat*. This unusual title, derived from a Brazilian proverb, "If you don't have a dog, then hunt with a cat," expressed one of the dominant motifs of innovation and ingenuity in the program.

Audiences of patients in the waiting rooms of Charity Hospital, the neighborhood clinics, and the family planning clinics saw films on such topics as nutrition, sickle-cell anemia, obesity, breast cancer self-examinations, venereal disease, accidents, and even oral hygiene. The foundation also prepared media sets explaining the infrastructure of health—what services were available and how to navigate through the system.

Foundation personnel investigated the possibility of using mobile projection units to reach segments of the needy population beyond clinic waiting rooms. Although this plan never materialized, it raised concern among politicians that the foundation had the money and populist ideals to reach large numbers of poor people and could influence political as well as health behavior.

The activities of the communication division show the rationalist philosophies of the program:

> People will make rational decisions about their health if they have the basic health education and information on which to base their decisions. The ability to bring such health education and information to patients and the public, and to train health practitioners, plays a large part in the effectiveness of any health delivery system. (Beasley, Durel, and Jones 1973:18)

Foundation personnel truly believed that when people are educated to the consequences of their actions (such as sexual activity), they can take rational responsibility for their lives and health.

Mysticism, Charisma, and Money

The attention to management and business styles within the foundation was overtly self-conscious. Internal reports from this period reflect a belief that management was a mystical or superorganic entity, even an end in itself.

> It is through efficient and effective management of resources with a focus on stated goals that any program derives coherence. The role of management is often overlooked or underestimated in medical and social programs. As a critical process involving specialized sophisticated skills, it must be consciously and systematically included in program design. (U.S. Congress, House, Committee on Appropriations 1973:1675)

The contradictions between the written accounts of foundation policy and the internal atmosphere at the foundation, however, were striking. Despite the mania for management and the torpid justifications, charisma was more important to leadership than bureaucracy. Initially, the personal intensity of Joe Beasley was omnipresent even when he was physically absent from New Orleans. The management system of generic health care could be replicated, but the cult of personality that surrounded such a dynamic individual did not transplant well. Although the literature from the foundation describes an ideal—albeit dull—world, the verbal accounts describe the mix of personal charm and bureaucracy in the management of the Family Health Foundation as anything but dull.

Management also became synonymous with allocation of money. When the Ford and Rockefeller foundations sent visitors to Family Health, they were treated less frequently to statistics on the amelioration of poverty through family planning than to explanations of how incoming money was spent and channeled through the maze. One director, who developed a reputation as a financial wizard, drew

complex blackboard diagrams while explaining to the Ford and Rockefeller men how cash flowed through the organization for purposes of reimbursement. The executives would all seem sure and excited by [his] figures . . . but afterward they could be seen taking other FHF officials aside, shaking their heads, and expressing their absolute bewilderment over what exactly happened to all those hundreds of thousands of dollars. (Mackintosh 1975:58)

The New Elite

As many of the new professional staff who worked for the foundation have told me, the management style took a different form from that of the years of Lincoln Parish and the opening of the New Orleans clinics. Beasley was deeply involved in his many other activities and no longer worked closely in daily decisionmaking. The composition of management began to change subtly. A new elite of administrators, all lawyers or trained business executives, was hired to implement the new management techniques. They were bright and glib and loved the complexities of grantsmanship, contract manipulation, dealing with government officials, and routing money through the corporation (Mackintosh 1975). They also relished the accouterments of power: salary raises, airplanes and limousine service, and dinners at New Orleans' finest restaurants. The original cadre of social scientists and researchers left for various reasons or continued their projects without direct involvement in the new management decisions.

A chasm within leadership began to grow, although it is difficult to pinpoint the moment at which the division began. The new executives appeared, from my viewpoint, to block leadership from middle management and to cut off the democratic flow of communication that might have alerted them to problems. Gone was the energetic exchange of ideas and tasks across racial, sexual, or class lines that had characterized the early years. The professionals and paraprofessionals, who had staked their careers in family planning, continued nevertheless to enroll new patients, add services, and maintain the program's principles. During the early 1970s, however, they gradually found themselves excluded from the halls of power and decisions of the inner sanctum.

Clap, Cancer, and Contraceptives

The Family Health Foundation clinics were booming. Rules for eligibility had been relaxed, so more women were brought into the program. The proportion of white patients had increased to 22 percent across the state. In 1971, 170,000 women kept appointments, mainly for return visits (checkups, resupply of contraceptives, or prenatal care). About 80,000 women had been initiated into the program across the state; one-third were from Orleans Parish. The ratio of new arrivals who had never been married or pregnant increased steadily.

Patient Profile

Statistical patterns, for which the family planners took credit, seemed apparent: New patients were younger and had fewer children. There was a noticeable reduction in family size in all age groups; two or three children were more the norm than were the seven or eight of past years. Older women were having far fewer children, and the crude birth and death rates declined. Although the family planners cited their program as having "a marked program impact" (Family Health Research Group 1971:11), it is hard to sort out just what factors influenced these rates.

Over 100 variables had been used to explain or predict whether women would continue to use birth control after its initial introduction (Sear 1973:80). Other studies conducted at Louisiana Family Planning (Hawkins 1969; McCalister and Thiessen 1970; and Mather 1975) contained little information about the patients' private motivations but described in detail the demographic characteristics of the patient population.

Patients with a grammar school education or less had a rate of accidental pregnancy three times as high as that for patients who had graduated from high school. Women living with a so-called husband had better records of continuing a method than did those living with no husband. Patients with any past experience in using contraceptives had twice as good a chance of averting an unwanted pregnancy as did women who had no previous experience. Age, however, was the most telling predictor. Women under 21 years were four and one-half times as likely to incur an accidental pregnancy and showed higher rates of quitting a method altogether than were older women (Hawkins 1969).

Researchers branched out into economic explanations of why women chose to participate in a family planning program. Did women's decisionmaking fit into the family planners' own rationalist philosophy that people would maximize their opportunities and reduce their costs? Economic variables that might affect the demand for contraceptives such as price, distance, and income were analyzed (Cook 1971). Then nineteen more were added, ranging from fertility and marital history to race, religion, education, and age. But this analysis still omitted variables such as a woman's support systems, self-esteem, body imagery, or sexual-marital prospects. In summary, understanding the decision to contracept proved to be as complex as offering the services.

Health Screening

From the start of the program, and certainly as the concept of family planning broadened into maternal and child health, it was obvious that screening for venereal diseases (VD) would be necessary. In New Orleans in 1968, one in every forty-five citizens was treated for infectious VD—a rate about three times the national average of 765 per 100,000. A sample of 1,129 postpartum women who came to the Family Planning clinic for their checkups revealed a 7.4 percent rate of previously undetected gonorrhea (Ahmad 1970:8). The results of undiagnosed and untreated gonorrhea in women can be permanent sterility, pelvic inflammatory diseases, blindness in infants, or stillbirths and miscarriages. A high proportion of women have no symptoms but can spread the infection to others.

As part of routine examinations, clinic physicians tested for venereal disease and referred the women with positive tests to appropriate agencies for treatment. Some of the former workers remarked, "Sometimes we got worried we'd be known as just a clap clinic." In the first three months of 1974, a total of 18,317 gonorrhea cultures were processed. The Center for Disease Control in Atlanta estimated that 17 percent of the women with undetected gonorrhea would develop pelvic inflammatory disease, which would cost an average of $615 per patient to treat. So family planning statisticians calculated that their screening procedures had saved the state and the Charity Hospital system $338,000 during those three months on one disease alone (Family Health Foundation 1974a).

Another part of the routine medical examination was a Pap smear. When an atypical, suspicious, or positive Pap smear came back from the laboratory, outreach workers immediately contacted the patient. Sometimes only periodic monitoring was needed. More threatening cases were referred to Charity for surgery or other treatment. In 1973, over 100,000 Pap smears were processed, and 497 necessitated follow-up measures. The Colposcopy Service of the foundation examined all these women.[3] Although most suffered from chronic infections, twenty-six had cancer. In a burst of bravado rare for bureaucratic reports, the head of the Colposcopy Service noted:

The Colposcopy Service has saved someone $93,395 as a very conservative estimate. The very minimal cost for usual evaluation of these patients, i.e. cold knife conization (extensive surgical sampling of cervix), in the New Orleans area is about $235.00 (three days in hospital, operating room fee, anesthesia and this does not include intravenous fluids, chest x-rays, blood work, etc.). The real savings however, is not in dollars and cents, but rather in the fact that 497 women did not have to be subjected to the surgical procedure of cold knife conization of the cervix with its attendant morbidity, complications secondary to anesthesia, infection, hemorrhage, etc. Plus the fact that these women did not have to be away from their families even one night. (Family Health Foundation 1974a:19)

Teenage Patients

As births in some categories declined rapidly, another problem began to attain frightening significance. The number of unwed teenage mothers was increasing epidemically. At Charity illegitimate first births to teenagers increased by 40 percent from 1967 to 1970 (Ktsanes 1977).

In the early 1970s, there was a national movement to liberalize eligibility requirements for adolescent girls and to organize programs that addressed their unique characteristics.[4] The legal rights of minors to many services, including contraception, were expanded. When the president's U.S. Commission on Population Growth and the American Future published its report, teenage pregnancies became a national priority.

The Commission recommends that birth control information and services be made available to teenagers in appropriate facilities sensitive to their needs and concerns. . . . The Commission recommends the development and implementation of an adequately financed program to develop appropriate family planning materials, to conduct training courses for teachers and school administrators, and to assist states and local communities in integrating information about family planning into school courses such as hygiene and sex education. (1972:143)

The first clinics for teenagers, both in Louisiana and in other parts of the country, were geared to provide both sex education and contraception before the first pregnancy regardless of parental consent or marital status. Louisiana's first such clinic opened in June 1972 in New Orleans and offered Saturday rap sessions on a walk-in basis in a building away from the clinic facilities. Teenagers attended the lectures and media presentations and were given an opportunity to talk with a sympathetic social worker. They were signed up for an appointment at the clinic if they wanted it.

The adolescents in the Louisiana program came largely from poor families and were mostly black, but their behavior in the program did not differ radically from groups in other states. The proportion of teenage girls who visited the clinics to their total number was smaller than that for older women. They tended not to remain steadfast in contraceptive usage. About 20 percent were crisis oriented: They were seeking counseling to alleviate immediate fears rather than to aid in long-range planning. The studies showed that these adolescent girls had little rapport or communication about sex with their male partners or with male peers in general. Indeed, their relationships with males were often the source of misinformation and value conflicts. The rap sessions at the clinics provided a place not only where the teenagers could receive sex education but also where they could air their confusions about sexual relationships (Ktsanes 1980).

Although there was no significant difference by race for time of contraceptive initiation (between 17 and 18 years of age), attendance at rap sessions revealed significant divergences by race in other areas. Over half of the black girls were more aware of the "sequential reality of intercourse and pregnancy than white girls" (Ktsanes 1980:100). Even for those who used contraception regularly, however, the motivation to prevent pregnancy appears to have been incompletely internalized. The studies showed that these girls did not understand the consequences of pregnancy. In one sample of black girls, only 60 percent believed that early pregnancy would inhibit their aspirations. Although they approved of both contraception and pregnancy, they often saw them in the reverse order; they wanted to discuss birth control only after the birth of their first child. Few perceived problems in being pregnant teenagers (Ktsanes 1977).

All the social workers and other professionals who worked with the teens reported that it was impossible to underestimate their ignorance of sexual functioning. Few girls had received any information prior to their first menses. At that time, their mothers might say only, "Now you're a woman. Stay away from boys, or you will get pregnant." Girls would think that this meant that they could get pregnant only during menstruation, so they should avoid sex during their periods.

A study by Andrew Dott and Arthur Fort (1976) showed the medical urgency of providing family planning information to adolescents before their first pregnancy. Although participation of teenagers increased both in Louisiana and nationally, the numbers were not sufficient to alter the plague of "babies making babies." The teen clinics were only a token. If the Family Health Foundation had put as much energy and money into the problems of adolescent pregnancies as it did into the other efforts described in this chapter, its teen program might well have become the prototype for combating the national crisis.

Federal Money and the War on Poverty

The Family Health Foundation (FHF) was riding high on the social liberalism of the war on poverty. Just as the family planning program had expanded dramatically beyond birth control, so had the maternal and child health schemes grown beyond innoculations or aid to crippled children. The Office of Economic Opportunity (OEO) idealistically directed a great deal of money toward reducing poverty. Two programs in particular—the neighborhood health clinics and the mother-infant development projects—were almost tailormade for the Family Health Foundation's goals and experience. The Louisiana Family Health Foundation was renowned for its family planning successes and was associated with a university medical school. Both the FHF and the OEO focused on the needs of the poor black community of New Orleans. The foundation wanted more money for capital projects and expanding programs, and Model Cities program needed a contractor with recognized experience.[5]

Project Head Start

The most visible example of the U.S. government's war on poverty programs was Project Head Start. Policymakers and the scientific establishment hoped to break the cycle of poverty for children of low-income families by offering compensatory education. But Head Start was a crash program and lacked carefully designed research to determine the validity of interventionist strategies to eliminate supposed cultural deficits. Head Start essentially offered a child preschool preparation that was not provided by parents, home environment, or cognitive development during infancy. As an experiment in experimentation, OEO first established thirty-six demonstration centers—Parent and Child Centers (PCCs)—to supplement Head Start. But even these centers emphasized direct services rather than research and demonstration that would prove what intervention—if any—altered the cognitive and social prospects of disadvantaged children. So in 1970 OEO expanded three of these PCCs into Parent-Child Development Centers (PCDCs). In New Orleans, the Family Health Foundation was picked as one of the PCDC sites. It had an established PCC, the research experience, and the ties to other OEO projects (Blumenthal et al. 1976).

The clientele of the new PCDC in New Orleans was composed exclusively of black people because they constituted more than 90 percent of the poor in the targeted neighborhoods (Blumenthal et al. 1976). In all three national sites mother-child pairs were randomly assigned to either a control group, which was subjected to periodic testing but not intervention, or a pilot group in which child-rearing behavior and intellectual development were supposed to improve. The center at each geographical site invented and systematically tested a different model. The New Orleans center was unique in using paraprofessionals. At least fifty women who had just given birth at Charity Hospital entered the center as participants and were then trained to create the curriculum and teach it to new recruits. This approach, of course, paralleled the outreach worker system in family planning.

If the pilot models had positive effects on mother-infant growth (and they did), then as a second phase the models would be replicated in three other locations. (The New Orleans model was to be transferred to Detroit.) This second phase was to demonstrate whether the system was cost effective, could be readily copied elsewhere, and had long-term effect on the participants. The third phase was to be nationwide dissemination of the successful models. Because of a changing socio-political climate, a new administration in Washington, and the inability to engage the interest of private foundations in longitudinal and ex-perimental research, however, the last phase was aborted. Even though they lasted only a decade and were not completed, the PCDCs were the only survivors of OEO, which collapsed in 1974.

Those who have worked with the PCDCs are very proud of their results, even if the original plans were never completed. Elaborate testing showed that the IQs of the pilot children increased over the control group; mothers were generally more sensitive to their children's needs and used more elaborated language with them. The program significantly affected children's intellectual performance and positively influenced the mother's socialization skills (Andrews et al. 1982:77).

But at what price? The PCDCs were very expensive. Each stage after Head Start served a smaller number of people and required more money.

Family planning client of the Family Health Foundation receiving instruction in child care. Photograph courtesy of Warren Gravois, University of New Orleans.

Like other segments of the Family Health Foundation, the PCDC in New Orleans offered a vast array of medical, social, and educational services otherwise available only in fragmented form. The direct annual cost for every mother-child pair was over $5,000; indirect costs were much more. The amount of money indirectly saved by obviating later remediation or other social services cannot be measured. As in birth control, an expense or disaster averted is not amenable to statistics.

Furthermore, the program was too small to effect social change for more than a few individuals. The combined participants for the three sites numbered just over 300 pairs. Those who worked hardest in the PCDCs admit that despite the money spent, the extensive battery of tests, the video taping, and the goals of their science, "available measures were insufficient to the evaluation task. The developmental processes that the programs were to strengthen in the mothers and the children were too rich for existing measure" (Andrews et al. 1982:67).

This decade-long, multimillion-dollar investment in parent education research was an attempt to find a way to change a lower-class culture by changing the child-rearing habits of poor mothers. Although the program administrators were culturally sensitive (and there is no reason to believe otherwise), they were middle-class white professionals, and their cultural bias toward methods of child raising was that of the middle class.[6] Unlike the dispensers of birth control, they did not offer instruments of immediate social or individual change.

Although structurally a part of Family Health, the New Orleans PCDC avoided local publicity and was located apart from the foundation. Most people in the community were unaware of the connection. As a result, the center escaped scandals involving the parent body and avoided some of the pressures attendant on federal antipoverty programs.

Model Cities Program

Through the Model Cities funding, OEO wanted to establish research demonstration health clinics in areas of severest poverty in the United States. The agency's philosophy paralleled that for many initiatives begun by the family planners. The Office of Economic Opportunity described a four-pronged strategy for these comprehensive health centers:

(1) a full range of ambulatory health centers; (2) close liaison with other community services; (3) close working relationships with a hospital, preferably one with a medical school affiliation; and (4) participation of the indigenous population in decision-making that affected the center and, where feasible, their employment in subprofessional and other positions. (Levitan 1969:194)

The agency realized that though the war on poverty had to include health care (that had been painfully evident in Head Start), the expense of revolutionizing the dual health care system would be prohibitive. So it could provide only limited funds for selected urban areas.

Although the family planning money had been channeled through the state, the clinics, or Tulane University, funds for the neighborhood clinics went through the Model Cities, the OEO superstructure, and highly politicized city agencies. Management problems were significantly different. The frustrated, action-oriented family planners had to spend hours meeting with representatives of Model City health committees, the major city health care agencies, and other planning groups to coordinate the new project.

By entering health care services as a means to fight poverty, the OEO assumed that existing health care institutions were not responsive to their clientele. If the programs were to serve the people, the people should have a major voice in defining their needs and supervising the providers: The OEO called this "maximum feasible participation of the poor." This new-wave idealism did not work.

> There would eventually be a conflict between the guideline calling for close working relationships with a university medical center teaching hospital, and the guideline requiring participation of the poor in decision making. . . . Soon struggles began to develop between town and gown over management of the center, who would hire whom with whose permission and approval, and who would have real power and control over the setting. (Krause 1977:161)

In New Orleans, despite the family planners' experience in working with the community, the problems were severe. The writer of a Model Cities report (1970:24) confessed that "the Policy Advisory Committee has functioned inefficiently due to the inherent conflict between professional delivery of services and community participation." Later, the former medical director of the New Orleans clinics, Andrew Dott, summarized his own experience with Model Cities and the requirement for "maximum feasible community participation" as "creating a management structure of inexperienced people under the control of community people knowing nothing of health who must hire and train inexperienced personnel to operate an underfinanced project in a neighborhood of high social discontent and high expectations. Another definition—political patronage" (Mackintosh 1978:256).

The health professionals wanted comprehensive, long-term health services. They emphasized treating inadequate nutrition, obesity, hypertension, and sickle-cell anemia and providing health education and social services on the family planning model. But the community wanted immediate benefits, such as ambulances, eyeglasses, free dental care, and jobs. They got them. The satellite clinics created new categories of jobs, and the steering committees demanded control over who was employed. In this respect, too, their wishes prevailed.

In establishing the Model Cities clinics, the Family Health Foundation increased its public relations problems. It referred to the Charity system as outmoded and "progressively degenerate" (Bechtel Corporation 1971:1) and proposed that the neighborhood clinics, with their modern diagnostic equipment, could absorb Charity's outpatient load, reduce the number of hospitalizations, and treat larger numbers of patients more efficiently than Charity did. The traditional medical establishment also felt threatened by claims that the OEO program would be a "prototype of a statewide network in support of the entire Charity Hospital system" or that "this far-reaching program can serve as a model not only for Louisiana, but for all the metropolitan areas of the United States" (Bechtel Corporation 1971:40).

The extravagant dreams for the Model Cities clinics were not fulfilled. Whereas the foundation planned eight outpatient clinics for New Orleans and the surrounding parishes to serve almost 300,000 people over a five-year period, only three satellite clinics opened (Desire, Central, and the Lower Ninth). Even with these, numerous political problems delayed the timetable. The expensive equipment and the newly trained staff— consisting of general practitioners, residents, interns, and paramedics— could not be moved into the clinics on schedule. One of the primary goals was attained: Emergency transportation services were provided to the neighborhoods served by the Model Cities. The ambulances bore the Family Health logo and the drivers—Vietnam veterans—were Family Health employees. In 1972 and 1973 the clinics treated 49,000 eligible outpatients for dental, optometric, or laboratory services, or provided twenty-four-hour emergency ambulance services.

The evidence indicated that Family Health was providing excellent medical services and comprehensive planning too long absent in Louisiana, but it was in over its head when health services became more political than medical (U.S. Comptroller General 1975). All the money came from the federal government and was subject to its accounting procedures. Model Cities provided only the loosest supervision, and guidelines from Washington changed regularly. Private doctors perceived a threat to their sources of income and did not support the neighborhood clinics (Chandler 1974; personal communications).

By 1970, the Office of Economic Opportunity had outlived its founding ideals and had little national impact on social policy. There were only forty-nine OEO comprehensive neighborhood health centers in the United

States, and they constituted a minor element in health care for the indigent despite the elaborate publicity and hopes (Krause 1977). In May 1974, the whole Model Cities program was terminated amid loud gnashing of teeth in New Orleans. The black community, which had the greatest stake in the clinics, regarded them as a major service as well as source of jobs for blacks (*Louisiana Weekly*, May 18, 1974; June 22, 1974). Editorials noted that courtesy and dignity had been the watchwords of the neighborhood clinics. This was the humane legacy of the ideals of family planning and of clinic practice.

The professional people whom I interviewed who were directly involved in those events usually claimed that association with the Model Cities program was the foundation's most serious mistake. Funding, always tenuous, did not even last a decade nationally, and it never approached the amounts necessary to establish satisfactory demonstration projects, much less to restructure the dual health care systems in the grand manner that Joe Beasley and others had envisioned. The mandated community participation was frustrating and abrasive and above all lacked the intrinsic gratifications of the successful birth control programs. The link to Model Cities opened Family Health to greater financial problems, patronage, graft, and political manipulation. Model Cities money was a magnet for a new group of politically mobile black elites in New Orleans whose machinations contributed to the collapse of the foundation (Mackintosh 1975; Chandler 1974b).

Genocide: The Achilles Heel

From the beginning, the family planners had feared the controversies that surrounded a class- and color-centered contraceptive drive. Politicians and bureaucrats with scarcely concealed prejudices liked to say, "Procreation is the poor man's recreation." By the late 1960s, those who were the targets of such sentiments were beginning to react.

> Long sensitive to this kind of anti-poor (and especially anti-black) "taxpayer" vigilantism, a counterforce is developing among some segments of the poor (and especially among some segments of the black poor) themselves, who are suspicious of governmental family planning programs as possibly concealing a hidden agenda to coerce the poor through such measures as punitive sterilization, deprivation of welfare, seizure of children and even jailing of unwed parents. (Beasley 1969b:15)

The rise of black militancy coincided with the emergence of birth control programs and sparked a resurgence of the spectre of genocide. "The charge that birth control and abortion are integral elements of a white genocidal conspiracy directed against Afro-Americans has been heard with increasing frequency and stridency in black communities" (Weisbord 1973:571).

After the spate of analyses, such as the Moynihan report (1965), on the real or imaginary pathology within black family structure, militants became sensitive to implied or blatant criticisms of black family life (Murray 1977). Because they differed from the white middle-class norm, the activists charged, black families were often viewed as deviant and thus as a legitimate target of federal remediation. The federally funded birth control clinics in poor or black neighborhoods were a convenient focus for protest. Some leaders preached that only by increasing the sheer numbers of blacks would progress be made; to voluntarily reduce birth rates would be politically maladaptive if not suicidal. The Family Planning and Population Act in 1970 only fueled these fears, as some blacks perceived more massive federal interest in birth control than in other health programs. The Black Muslim weekly criticized the Ford Foundation, then the leading private foundation funding population research; the paper ran cartoons showing birth control pills marked with a skull and crossbones or drawings of the graves of black infants whose potential achievements were lost (*Muhammed Speaks*, January 24, 1969). Some blacks saw poverty and racism, but not large families or the high infant mortality figures, as the root of their condition. They resented the faddism among white liberals, who were abandoning civil rights to champion environmental causes.

National opinion samples, however, indicated that only a small minority of blacks believed that increased population brought power or that birth control programs were a genocidal plot. That small minority was almost exclusively made up of young male militants (Weisbord 1973; Stycos 1977). Other groups either ignored the issue, had historically supported family planning (particularly the Urban League and the NAACP), or vociferously advocated free abortions, sterilizations, and contraception on demand (like the Black Panthers).

Racial Tensions

In 1968, bomb threats by black militants forced the temporary closing of family planning clinics in Pittsburgh. In Cleveland a family planning clinic was burned. The brothers exhorted black women to bear children for the revolution: "The pill is genocide. Do your duty. Blacks should never limit their family size." But the sisters in Pittsburgh and other places were having none of it: "The womb is not a weapon. Women run the risks. We have the choices." In Pittsburgh the women organized to force the reopening of the clinics. As Shirley Chisholm, the feisty black congresswoman from Brooklyn, pointed out, this was mostly male rhetoric for male ears (Littlewood 1977). In not one forum in the United States did these young male militants find female support. So the battle lines were drawn not only by class and color but also by sex.

Although black women constituted 30 percent of those in need of subsidized contraceptive services nationally, in Louisiana they made up the majority. There the racial tensions in health services had been diffused by the family planners. Perhaps because of this solid effort or because Louisiana often lags behind trends in other parts of the country, the genocide issue did not appear until 1971. Rather suddenly, just as the controversies appeared to be on the wane elsewhere, gatherings about family life, community development, abortion, or the environment were disrupted by dashiki-clad young black men wearing opaque sunglasses and Afro hairstyles. They also marched grimly through the halls of the Family Health Foundation. Outreach workers in project areas of Muslim activity reported intermittent harassment but did not curtail their home visits.[7]

One outreach worker heard of a meeting in the Magnolia Project and went without an invitation (or permission from Family Planning, which was unwilling to send employees into danger). As she remembers, "It was a brain-wracking experience." The meeting was conducted by middle-class males who did not even live in the project. They called her a "pill-pusher" and "a traitor to her race." She replied heatedly, "You can get numbers, if you want, in the cemetery, because that's where lots of mothers and black babies are."

On another occasion, outreach workers used their informal channels to discover that the wife of a prominent man preaching the conspiracy of genocide was using birth control to space their children. Just as in Pittsburgh and other places, the articulate and well-organized women held the line. They retorted, "When you men leave home and desert your kids, you're the one practicing genocide." They argued that the militants would retard progress for black females by depriving them of knowledge and power of their own bodies. Quoting from W.E.B. DuBois, a black historian and a founder of the National Association for the Advancement of Colored People (NAACP), they yelled, "We're not interested in the quantity of our race. We interested in the quality of it."

The black ministers in whose churches the first words of birth control had spread remained stalwart; no support for the militants came from that quarter. If votes had been taken in these public forums, women and the cause of birth control would have won. As another outreach worker recalled, "We converted a lot of the brothers."

But the women who publicly countered the militants' opposition and argued for family planning were not present as meetings between Family Health officials and the militants became more intense. The press reported after one of these meetings that "a reshuffling of the staff of Family Health, Inc., recently has precipitated an inquiry into the organization's structure and operation by some of its employees" (*Times-Picayune*, January 4, 1972). Lead by the director of the Central City Economic Opportunity Corporation, the black group presented a list of demands "in order to begin an evaluation of the organization's relevance to the black community." The demands took five minutes to read, and the group left refusing to hear the formatted lecture on family planning and the successes of the program.

Several years later, after accusations about the Family Health's affairs began to fly, these meetings and their consequences took on more sinister overtones. Many of the people present at these meetings were not employees of Family Health. The distribution of patronage and federal money—not genocide—was the issue. With OEO and Model Cities money, the neighborhood black political grass-roots organizations such as SOUL and COUP had become major forces to reckon with in New Orleans.

Mau-mau and Co-opting

In the only analysis published about what really happened during and as a result of these meetings, Douglas Mackintosh reported that "a small group of well-organized individuals in the New Orleans black community decide it's time to mau-mau the Family Health Foundation on the genocide issue. The time is right, the providers of the service are feeling anxious (read vulnerable), and black militancy still scares folks" (1975:55). *Mau-mau*, a term from the 1960s, refers to the generally superficial but intimidating tactics of black militants who claimed to represent the black community better than the white liberals who controlled the federal money.[8] Their show of ethnic solidarity sometimes won concessions leading to access to power, jobs, and money. Many poverty program administrators responded by putting more blacks in front-office or visible positions to diffuse their complaints. Beasley promoted one critic into top management and hired others for the clinics. Relatives of the black militants were employed by the foundation. But the demands for more black participation made a mockery of the favorable reputation for hiring, promotion, and pay scales that the foundation had legitimately earned. Hiring black males from out of state did not placate the militant's demands for patronage either. Sometimes the strategy of co-opting the opposition succeeds; in this case, it had complex and devastating consequences.

Black women were overwhelmingly supportive of the birth control programs; they had come to believe that through them they and their children were receiving excellent health care for the first time. The opposition came from black males (Beasley 1973; Mackintosh 1975). Largely from the middle class, they were stung by the criticisms of them in the family planning literature. The statements about family instability, black infant deaths, child abuse, and abandonment did not paint a pretty picture of male sexuality or social responsibility. They could politically support a birth control program only if it were part of a larger health care project that redounded to their credit. Beasley has since said that he believes that part of the pressure they brought to bear was reflected in the modification of the project's name, from Family Planning, Inc., to the broader and more euphemistic Family Health Foundation (personal communication, July 20, 1983). (There were other related reasons for the name change.) At this same time, the OEO-funded Neighborhood Health Clinics and the Parent-Child Development Center, geared to the black community, were opened. Ironically, they were controlled by some of the same men who had raised the genocide issue, pushed for patronage privileges, and objected to the association with contraception and health care for women.

Fearful of losing the black support that had brought his program to prominence and of giving credence to accusations of coercion or genocide and needing the money from OEO to keep the program afloat, Beasley allegedly made the decision to try to buy off his opponents. He could have chosen to fight them by enlisting the support of the mothers in the program. The mayor of Pittsburgh, after all, had crushed the militants in his city. Instead Beasley hired a young lawyer and militant, Don Hubbard, in a top administrative position. Others or their relatives were put on the payroll. Through a complicated intrigue that only later became apparent (see Chapter 6, section on Promised Revelations), another black politician, Sherman Copelin, was reputedly paid off to reduce the pressure: He had been appointed director of New Orleans' Model Cities Program, the contractor for the neighborhood health clinics. He was also a founder of a neighborhood association that had helped elect the mayor (Mackintosh 1975).

The genocide controversy in New Orleans was linked to a national issue when Senate committee testimony revealed that at least 2,000 involuntary sterilizations had been performed with OEO funds in other states during the 1972-1973 fiscal year.[9] These sterilizations had been performed on poor black women without their knowledge or consent. The Relf incident, in which two teenage black girls had been sterilized, became the landmark. The committee heard testimony that involuntary sterilization was performed frequently in the South for welfare mothers after several children. Coercion included threats of terminating welfare payments or other penalties. Those who equated family planning with genocide were confirmed in their beliefs that federal programs were underwriting eugenicists who wanted to impose their views about population quality on minorities and poor women (Littlewood 1977).

Although Family Health offered sterilization counseling and vasectomies with OEO funds, an investigation of its records found no evidence of involuntary sterilizations. Louisiana was the only Southern state in which no women complained of coercion in testifying about federally funded services (U.S. Congress, Senate, Committee on Labor and Public Welfare, 1973). In a program that depended on the assistance of blacks, offered them training and rapid promotion, and even hired black militants, there were no reasonable grounds for charges of genocide.

Distant Rumblings

As the foundation grew larger, so did its problems. Each new patient recruited meant an exponential growth in return visits for additional health services. New sources of funding had to be exploited. During the Nixon administration, family planners across the country lobbied for more stable government money. The social security legislation in 1969 tied family planning to entitlement programs that no politician could touch (the aged, disabled, blind, and handicapped). Beasley had worked with Planned Parenthood, legislators, and policymakers in the Nixon White House to pass the new laws that included a generous ceiling of $2.8 billion for family planning. Despite intensive political pressures, however, HEW never published rules and regulations to guide states in the use of these federal funds (called Title IV-A moneys), and some states decided not to use these moneys until clear instructions were issued.

Beasley made a portentious decision to use the Title IV-A money in Louisiana even without directions, and $12.4 million eventually came into the state (*American Medical News* 1974:1). From 1970 to 1974, the Family Health Foundation had to improvise amid the chaos of conflicting or nonexistent regulations. It hired lawyers both in Louisiana and in Washington, paid legal consultants, and directed its energies into mastering the technicalities of money management. Guidelines for Title IV-A funds stipulated that family planning services were among those to receive matching funds from the government (first at a 3:1 ratio, then at a liberalized 9:1). But the foundation still had to find the matching money, an increasingly difficult prospect. By 1973, the federal funders had pulled back from their broad-scale endorsement of family planning at any cost. The flow of money was limited, and the shock waves reached the heart of the foundation.

The exigencies of funding, the lack of clear guidelines, and the government's weakening commitment to family planning and the war on poverty were conspiring to produce trouble. At the same time, the genocide controversies were only the tip of the iceberg: Growing political problems in the state were beginning to threaten the very existence of family planning. The battle lines were being drawn.

6

The Great Family
Planning War

Only two men ever did anything to give good health care to the people of Louisiana: Huey Long and Joe Beasley. And they were both rogues and scoundrels.
—A former FHF administrator

The day of continuing federally funded categorical health programs administered from Washington is rapidly drawing to a close and rightly so.
—Caspar Weinberger, Secretary of HEW, 1974

Should Beasley be right and audits discover no wrongdoing, it is certain that he and those who agree with him will argue that the medical society was motivated to attack him out of jealousy and spite and a basic philosophical opposition to federally funded medical care for the poor.
—*States-Item*, December 29, 1972

Even as the development of Family Health Foundation was touted as a major national and international success story, the cracks began to show. Despite its seeming prosperity, the foundation was struggling financially. Under the Nixon administration, government agencies like HEW were dismantling the war on poverty and related social welfare programs. Eligibility requirements were tightened. The annual increases for projected expansions did not materialize (Weinberger 1974). Just as the funding stabilized, the foundation needed fresh funds. Although it had enough money to maintain family planning services at existing levels or to permit limited growth, the foundation had focused its budget and creative energy on new forms of expensive health care.

Medical Rivalry in the State

Relations between the Family Health Foundation and the Louisiana State Medical Society were increasingly strained. The medical society has been characterized by members and nonmembers as being an archconservative organization that played a heavy hand in state politics. In the early 1970s less than half of the state's doctors—and only one black physician—belonged to it.

The Louisiana State Medical Society had endorsed both the concept of family planning and the private program during the growth years of the statewide drive. But in July 1971, when the name was changed to Family Health, Inc., and then in March 1972, when it became the Family Health Foundation, doctors within the society began to question medical services and delivery systems that went beyond birth control. The foundation was taking on the appearance of a rival medical system. The medical society started to challenge the foundation's relationship to state-supported services. Was there unnecessary duplication? Was the state justified in retaining its basic $10 million contract with FHF? Why did FHF receive a two-year contract for $3 million from the state when during the same period it received $6 million in federal money for what seemed to be the same purposes? Were they the same purposes (*Times-Picayune*, December 28, 1972; *States-Item*, December 29, 1972)?

Some of the state health department officials were angered by the existence of a rival organization using federal money through state contracts to provide public health services. As correspondence shows, they maintained that

> There was never a *logical* reason for the creation of a duplicate *privately* administered health department, such as FHF appears to be, to give birth control in Louisiana. The whole matter was a folly from the very beginning in 1966. In practically all other states, these services are planned and rendered by the health departments. There is a sense of impropriety associated in supporting the luxury of the private State health department in Louisiana.[1] (Emphasis in original)

By this time, state health officials were convinced that they had always been in favor of contraceptive services and should have been the first vendor. Their new commitment to family planning did not date to the early demonstration clinics, the abrogation of the Comstock laws, the agreements with the Catholic Church, or the initial research but to the later federal mandate that states provide family planning for the poor and to the money consequently available (Louisiana, Health and Social and Rehabilitation Services 1973).

Even so, many people in the state bureaucracies remained confused about the exact nature of family planning. Was it a social service like welfare, a medical service, a public health measure, or just an educational device? Some in the state health department had been convinced of the value of family planning in preventing corollary health problems but appeared to believe that the service consisted of lining poor women up to distribute pills with perfunctory exhortation about their use.

A Cheaper System?

The state health establishment contended (as it still does) that it could do the job far more cheaply than the private foundation could and, in fact, that it should have been doing it all along. The budget of the FHF was as large as those for some divisions within the state bureaucracy and twice as large as that for the city health department (*States-Item,* December 29, 1972). State officials insisted that they could run a family planning program at one-fourth, one-third, one-fifth (estimates varied) of the costs at Family Health (Louisiana, Health and Social and Rehabilitation Services 1973). But the state had no interest in the wider programs: community medicine, overpopulation, Latin America, or research in innovative health care delivery.

Frustrated, the medical society withdrew its endorsement of the foundation in April 1972. The contractual relations and gentlemen's agreements of earlier years were breaking down. The early family planners had needed the endorsements of their colleagues in the medical society. But as the foundation changed its scope and mission, former officials admit, it neglected to include the medical society in its plans. Society members had not even been invited to the openings of the neighborhood clinics in New Orleans.

Double-Dipping?

In December 1972 the Louisiana State Medical Society sent a letter to Representative John Rarick (and copies to HEW officials in Dallas, other Louisiana officials, and health professionals throughout the state) presenting preliminary evidence for its belief that FHF took money from the Office of Economic Opportunity and the Department of Health, Education and Welfare for the same services. This was the first charge of double-dipping (*Times-Picayune,* December 28, 1972).

Representative Rarick asked for a federal HEW investigation of the foundation. The response from Family Health began a pattern of public counterattack that persisted through the following years. Instead of using one of the foundation's efficient but colorless public relations specialists as a mouthpiece, Beasley personally lashed out at the medical society.

He suggested that the actions of the society were jeopardizing the health care of thousands of poor people while trying to harm the organization, which he characterized as "the leading research and development center connected with family planning in the world." He brought what had been a covert philosophical disagreement between colleagues into the open. "There is a feeling among some medical society members . . . that I'm a phantom trying to get in the back door with socialized medicine. I'm for testing new methods for better delivering health services" (*Times-Picayune*, December 28, 1972). He interpreted questions raised about the fiscal practices of the foundation, particularly as they related to state and federal contracts, as attacks on his motives, health services to the poor, and the concept of family planning. As the feuding became public, observers predicted a classic confrontation between liberal and conservative, state and private care providers.

Social Impact or Chicanery?

In professional terms, the worst accusation that could be brought against a university-based research and development program is that it distorted or falsified its scientific results. State health personnel with the aid of officials in Louisiana's Division of Tabulation and Analysis were quietly conducting an investigation into the integrity of the research and statistics used by Family Health to claim success and promote its cause. The state health professionals smarted under the barrage of FHF criticisms, the open attacks on Charity Hospital, and the state legislature's limitations of their own budgets.

Accusations

First they disputed what FHF had listed as "a major accomplishment: the lowest cost per continuing patient per year of any United States program" (Family Health Research Group 1971:2). Not so, claimed the state officials (Louisiana, Health and Social and Rehabilitation Services 1973).[2] Although admitting that it is difficult to compare the cost of programs without specific information, they asserted that FHF could not possibly have had the lowest costs in the country. The state claimed that the private foundation was, if not the most expensive way, certainly more expensive than state delivery of the services. But the state had commissioned no objective or independent studies to back its contentions. No statistics existed that would support either side of the cost issue.

Next Louisiana health establishment professionals questioned the use or misuse of the state's vital statistics. Changing the rates for births, infant mortality, and illegitimacy was a major goal for the family planners.

Foundation reports seemed to make extravagant if not fraudulent claims of success in this realm. These summaries were often self-congratulatory while criticizing the services provided by the state of Louisiana (Family Health Research Group 1971, 1973). In response, members of the state health department published articles attempting to document, not the failure of the family planning program, but their claims to have altered the birth and death rates. In spring 1973, an article by James Gettys, Ben Freedman, and Ramson Vidrine (1973a) in the *Journal of the Louisiana Medical Society* praised the dedicated group of statisticians and social scientists working at FHF (many of whom were the authors' colleagues) but challenged the findings of the foundation's researchers.

In the article the analysts maintained that the family planning program had been in operation for too short a time and had served too limited a segment of the population to claim credit for trends that had already begun and were connected to far more subtle social influences than birth control availability. Women both inside and outside the program continued to have babies, but the trend toward smaller families was evident in Louisiana before Beasley's program and in other states without such programs. Even infant mortality had been dropping for decades. The only rate that showed embarrassing increases was that for illegitimate births to adolescent mothers, and no one wanted credit for that. After presenting elaborate tables and analyses, the authors pointed out: "Such figures are trivial in light of the fact that every parish in the state had a lower birth rate in 1965 than in 1964, and 60 of the 64 parishes had lower nonwhite birth rates in 1965—and all this occurred even before the Lincoln Parish demonstration" (Gettys et al. 1973a:80).

The most serious charge against the academic integrity of the program was based on a reanalysis of the major claims of success in Lincoln Parish (Gettys et al. 1973a; Freedman n.d.). Because sexuality outside of marriage is so resistant to social control, claims for altering rates of illegitimacy are rare. The report on the unusual, almost immediate impact of the program on illegitimacy was first presented to the American Public Health Association, was later published in a prestigious science journal *Social Biology*, and was widely cited by professionals as an example of what miracles a well-run program might produce. An article in *Science* (Harkavy et al. 1969) praised the dramatic results of the Lincoln Parish project.[3] The appearance of this laudatory article in such a responsible scientific journal prompted Ben Freedman, a state health department doctor with a long history in public health statistics and management, to recalculate the rates of illegitimacy, parish by parish, for the years in question.

Angered by what he saw as invalid data, he prepared a paper to demonstrate the dangers of "drawing conclusions from too great a limitation in number of events and in limiting the time duration of observations."[4] His analysis showed that greater reductions in birth and illegitimacy rates took place in a number of parishes without programs than in Lincoln Parish. The alleged decrease in Lincoln Parish was,

> without any qualifying reservations, not in accordance with the facts. Lincoln Parish experienced almost the same low illegitimate birth ratio in 1963 when it had no family planning program as it did in 1967 with the program. . . . However, take note that with the family planning program, the illegitimacy ratio in Lincoln Parish jumped up again in 1968 to practically the 1966 level. (Freedman n.d.:8)

Family Health's Response

Although all the critics acknowledged that the family planning effort in the state was expertly organized, they insisted that no serious claims of demographic impact could be made. Detractors of the program hinted obliquely at deliberate fraud, particularly in the Lincoln Parish materials, and willful distortion in other publications (Gettys et al. 1974). They suggested that using a five-year average for a single indicator within a parish would produce more realistic results. But the project as a demonstration and research model did not have five years to wait and hope for reductions in the gross rates. Nor could it convincingly link the decline to program performance. So the family planners stood accused of rushing into print and publishing misleading or self-serving interpretations of what might have only been random fluctuations within a larger pattern. A reply from Family Health consisted of technical clarifications of some data and sources, but it addressed none of the fundamental questions raised, particularly the validity of the Lincoln Parish data or the issue of whether FHF was piggybacking on the trend of falling birth rates in general (Serfling and Mather 1973).

Undaunted, the FHF Research Group released its last statistical report in early 1974. In this report, it included some new dimensions of analysis, but the conclusions remained the same: "In summary, the family planning activities of the Family Health Foundation in Louisiana have had a very significant impact on fertility in the state" (Family Health Foundation Research Group 1973:13). The reduction of nonwhite births was four times greater than in neighboring Mississippi, the group noted. Despite larger numbers of women entering the reproductive age span, total births had decreased.

Later in the spring, another article appeared in the state medical society journal. Placing special emphasis on new techniques of determining parity components and excess births, the critics engaged once again in the war of tables and formulas to conclude that

Family Health Foundation has stopped suggesting and implying; it has begun to boldly claim "significant" program impact on the vital forces of the state. In fact . . . no scientific or even pseudoscientific analysis of the program's impact has ever been published or made available by FHF to any state agency. If no valid analysis of impact/nonimpact has ever been performed, it seems fair to ask why, since the FHF's Research Group is more than capable of performing such an analysis. If such an analysis has been performed and withheld from "outsiders," there is an even stronger reason for posing questions. (Gettys et al. 1974:87)

But no acknowledgment of the challenge nor answers to these questions were ever proffered. By spring 1974 the foundation was in legal disarray and its statisticians, fearing possible indictments, had no reply.

The question of credibility within the national scientific community would ultimately have become serious. Different interpretations of statistics were only a symbol of the deep divisions between the foundation and the state bureaucracies. What the foundation called "a marked program impact" had been opened to interpretation. At the national level, no officials had questioned the statistical basis for the foundation's claims. The federal agencies appeared to believe that they had funded only successes. At the local level, despite the intensity of these battles within the medical establishment, the press did not report on these academic controversies.

"Our Own Little Watergate"

Members of the medical society also criticized a Family Health Foundation manuever to use the outreach workers to bring in more money. An internal FHF memorandum dated March 29, 1973, instructed nursing, clerical, and outreach personnel to begin an all-out campaign to visit the homes of as many welfare clients as possible during the following three months. Calls on nonwelfare clients were suspended, and nighttime or weekend visits were increased. As the memo acknowledged, "This renewed effort is necessary so that we will be in a position to negotiate a more satisfactory contract with DPW [Department of Public Welfare] than we have had in the past." In other words, the outreach program was temporarily modified to reach women who might not need family planning services but for whom the state would have to pay. For the period of the DPW push, the state had to pay under its contract, but clinic visits did not increase correspondingly.[5] "We would speculate that the April–June outreach campaign was mounted to . . . capture as much welfare money as possible before the end of the fiscal year" (Louisiana, Health and Social and Rehabilitation Services

1973:8). Although this ploy was later reported in the audit and the report of the Medical Advisory Committee, the press did not pick up on this issue with any fervor. The fact that the foundation needed to mount such an effort is mute testimony to its cash problems during 1972.

Preliminary Investigations

In April 1973, the federal grand jury requested by the medical society convened to investigate charges that the Family Health Foundation spent money in violation of the guidelines. These allegations originated in the regional office of HEW in Dallas and centered, at the beginning, on the arrangements made for portable health clinics and airplanes. The inquiries widened as the revelations of an HEW audit were revealed.

In what became typical scenarios, there were leaks from the grand jury to the media, revelations from a "Deep Throat" within the foundation, and increasingly overt machinations by involved politicians. For the year following the opening of the grand jury inquiry, reporters had almost daily copy for one of the hottest political stories ever in Louisiana, with a cast of characters unsurpassed since Huey Long's time. Foundation officials, particularly the dramatic Joe Beasley, began a year of hearings, publicity, and testimony. The attorney general called this "the most extensive investigation in the history of the state" (*States-Item*, December 1, 1973).

Gradually the grand jury and U.S. Attorney General Gerald Gallinghouse grew more acerbic about the charges under investigation. By August, charges were filed in federal district court citing possible violations of federal laws relating to conspiracy to defraud, mail fraud, obstruction of justice, and false statements (*Times-Picayune*, August 3, 1973). As the inquiry widened, not only FHF officials but the governor's brother, the top administrators of the Tulane Medical School, executives from companies subcontracted to FHF, and the financial records of the Rockefeller Foundation were subpoenaed.[6]

The grand jury studied the relationship between Family Health and the governor's office and family. The press gleefully reported that Governor Edwin Edwards' brother Marion had been taken to Latin America by the foundation in November 1972. Ostensibly his presence was to reassure Latin American officials that the governor of Louisiana had faith in family planning and to encourage trade relations between these countries and Louisiana. In a taped interview, Marion Edwards clarified his position.

You can spend your lifetime checking me out if you want to, and in the end you will find out three things, like I told you all across the years:

> everything I have done for this State is for my brother; you gonna find I
> am not gonna do anything wrong in the way of taking funds or anything
> else; you gonna find out the third thing, that I am a very conscientious
> person, that I like to help all the people that I possibly can. And Joe Beasley
> is just a person I like. I think he has got a great plan and a great program
> and I think it is something that is gonna ultimately save this world from
> starvation. And maybe your grandchildren may come and put their arms
> around me when I am old and gray and say, thank you for helping us save
> our lives. (*Courier*, December 19, 1973)

He also told reporters that he only wanted to help his brother promote
the foundation because it was such an important program for the state.
When questioned about his daughter's employment and salary in the
foundation, he replied that she was hired on her own merit. All he had
done was to call the foundation to introduce her. "I told them very
carefully and distinctly not to hire her because she was my daughter"
(*Times-Picayune*, July 28, 1973). Later the *Times-Picayune* (October 16,
1974) reported that Marion Edwards had written a group insurance
policy for a thousand FHF employees in May 1973, and had received
a $12,000 commission. Improprieties in the use of the airplanes were
consistently denied, and the truth has proved elusive. None of this
testimony resulted in indictments; however, these allegations stuck in
the public mind more tenaciously than the complexities surrounding
government regulations that were actually the issue.

Governor Edwin Edwards staunchly backed the activities of the
foundation and insisted that his only interest was "philosophical"
(*Courier*, October 19, 1973). Governor Edwards had worked to appropriate
state matching funds because the foundation brought millions of additional dollars into the state. Meanwhile, the attorney general and the
grand jury were investigating practices reported in the press as payroll
padding, patronage, and political payoffs. Gallinghouse charged that
"certain persons" received foundation funds for legal or consulting work
for services they did not perform. It was several years before the
implications of this accusation became known. Beasley defended the
work of the consultants, repeating many times in these hectic months
that he had personally requested the HEW audit and believed that it
would show no mistakes in handling more than $50 million in a five-
year span (*Times-Picayune*, August 13, 1973).

In August 1973, even as the grand jury investigations into the alleged
misuse of funds were attracting widespread attention, Beasley was named
dean of the Tulane University School of Public Health and Tropical
Medicine. Supporters of his appointment pointed out that Beasley was
an administrator with an international reputation and a star performer

who attracted tantalizing sums of money. Medical schools need infusions; the appeal proved irresistible. He intended to keep his position as chairman of the board of the Family Health Foundation, seeing it as a "complementary role" to the deanship; he viewed the appointment as a vote of confidence despite the audit and the grand jury investigations (*Times-Picayune*, August 13, 1973). The appointment concentrated even more public attention on federal actions and the affairs of the foundation.

Through the long hot summer the multipronged federal investigation gathered steam. The Department of Health, Education and Welfare was auditing what the press began to call "the controversial foundation." A draft report secretly leaked to the press well in advance of the official release revealed details of some of the allegations for the first time. It was rumored that advance copies of the HEW audit were left in the backseat of a reporter's car.

Official HEW Auditors' Report

The official HEW report was released in October 1973. Its major criticisms of the foundation centered on the use of federal money contrary to the regulations and to the goals of family planning (U.S. Department of Health, Education and Welfare 1973:1–105). One of the main conclusions of the report was that the state had been extremely lax, even negligent, in its supervision of the contracts channeled to Family Health. In fact, the HEW auditors recommended that the state of Louisiana be required to pay back the money involved in the transactions. Based on this conclusion, HEW later sued the state for recovery of the federal share of the misspent funds. The state in turn sued FHF for the money. The actual dollar amounts ranged cavalierly from thousands to millions, depending on who was speaking or which stage of investigation, audit, suit, countersuit, or negotiation the various levels of government were conducting. From the publication of the audit report, suits, charges, and countercharges continued to multiply. Even careful observers needed a scorecard.

Before the federal auditors began work, the Family Health Foundation had commissioned an exhaustive internal audit from the prestigious firm of Peat, Marwick and Mitchell, which revealed some questionable areas and possible federal violations (*Times-Picayune*, January 3, 1974). The private audit criticized accounting procedures that speeded the cash flow but obscured an accurate diagnosis of the foundation's true financial position. This and a number of other audits had been commissioned by the foundation to help establish sounder financial management practices, particularly for the confusing federal regulations, and were separate from the HEW audit. Nevertheless, both the press and the public remained confused about the intent and number of audits.

Family Health had purchased thirty-seven mobile health clinics with federal money. The HEW auditors maintained that federal guidelines prohibited the purchase of equipment with funds designated for services. These expenditures, totaling some $1.5 million, were not submitted to the state for approval but were charged to the state's contract with Family Health. This scheme raised questions about whether the required competitive bidding for equipment purchases had been conducted. Officials at FHF later claimed that the negotiations for the clinics represented an ordinary business decision for a private corporation (Kelso 1974).

The foundation had leased three airplanes and had purchased two with federal money and one from private funds. Such capital expenditures for equipment are generally not within the scope of federal regulations. The foundation viewed itself as a private corporation, a business that contracted to the state and federal government for services and justified the planes as "more cost-efficient in terms of personnel time, over-night expenditures, meals and services than ground transportation and commercial transportation costs" (*Times-Picayune*, April 17, 1973). But the HEW auditors were concerned, as was the grand jury, because state politicians (elected, appointed, or related by blood) had taken trips locally and to Washington, Latin America, and other places on the FHF planes. The planes were informally referred to as "the family planning air force."

The audit went on to contend that the foundation had rented office space in Washington, D.C., as a base for lobbying in the thirty-eight agencies that supported it. The foundation had spent money for entertainment, foreign travel, liquor, flowers, and apartments (two in New Orleans, one in Washington), all of which had no relation to family planning services. The foundation had hosted in lavish style the Regional White House Conference on Children in December 1970 and a meeting of the President's Commission on Population Growth and the American Future in January 1971. Lunches, receptions, cocktail parties, television promotions, and photographs were billed to the HEW grants at a time when, the *Times-Picayune* pointed out, welfare checks to mothers in Louisiana were being reduced (October 8, 1973). The media presentations sometimes left the impression that the lavish life-style at the foundation was completely incompatible with offering health services to the poor. Foundation officials argued in return that such social activities were practical, customary ways of doing business. The audit had provoked a philosophical disagreement between the mores of populism and those of capitalism.

The audit also raised questions about the misuse (later called *laundering*) of private donations as matching funds to consolidate a federal grant. Money from private foundations such as Rockefeller, Ford, and Kellogg was subject only to the grantor's wishes, not to the government's rules. This money could be used for discretionary purposes (the auditors argued that they were indiscretionary). There was evidence that the Rockefeller Foundation money might have been designated as matching funds on the state contract to provide birth control services, even though it had already been used for other purposes (U.S. Department of Health, Education and Welfare 1973:106–110). If the private grant money had been allocated as matching money (the nine-to-one standard), then it could only go directly to birth control services, not to peripheral activities however justifiable.

The practices of the foundation in awarding substantial salary increases to employees within a short period after hiring, giving large salary advances, and providing consultant or legal fees to employees already on the payroll raised eyebrows at HEW. These were the major areas of the government's investigation (*Times-Picayune*, October 4, 5, and 8, 1973). The auditors contended that many of these costs were incurred outside the contract periods, were unrelated to family planning services for welfare recipients, or did not conform to existing regulations.

Results of HEW Audit

The HEW audit directed the state of Louisiana to renegotiate its $10 million contract with Family Health. Without the spectacular revelations of the audit report, the negotiations of this contract would have attracted little attention. Governor Edwards had appointed as director of the state's new health agency (LHSRSA) Dr. Charles Mary, Jr., a graduate of the Louisiana State University Medical School who was not tied to the Tulane establishment. Dr. Mary was a young, dynamic director of Charity Hospital in New Orleans who was credited with introducing innovations in the surgery and intensive care units. On occasion the press called him "the wonder boy of Louisiana medicine" (*Times-Picayune*, October 11, 1972). Although the governor was openly supporting Family Health, Dr. Mary elected not to continue the laissez-faire practices that had brought so much trouble. Instead, the state would—as it had neglected to do before—supervise its contracts with the Family Health Foundation, even if these actions brought latent conflicts into the open. Dr. Mary told reporters that ignoring the audit report from HEW "would have constituted a dereliction of my duties and place in jeopardy federal welfare and health funds coming to Louisiana" (*Times-Picayune*, October 8, 1973). But, he was careful to add, the renegotiation of the contract was not a comment on FHF's spending practices or an accusation of fraud against anyone. His assertions that he intended to abide by federal regulations regardless of the consequences led to speculation that he would lose his job (*Times-Picayune*, October 8, 1973).

Meanwhile, Governor Edwards disarmingly assured the press that there was basically no evidence of wrongdoing at the foundation. There was only, according to the governor, a "personality conflict" between Dr. Beasley and Dr. Mary (*Times-Picayune*, October 5, 1973). Mary denied this and hewed steadfastly to the position that HEW expected the state to induce order and proportion into the contract and to begin more efficient monitoring (*Times-Picayune*, October 11, 1973). Mary was pressured by Charles E. Roemer, commissioner of administration for Governor Edwards, to sign a questionable retroactive agreement with FHF to legitimize the purchase arrangement of the mobile clinics (*Times-Picayune*, October 7, 1973). But Mary requested the opinion of the state's attorney general, William Guste, who concluded that signing an addendum to an already expired contract might constitute a conspiracy to violate a national statute. An editorial in the *Times-Picayune* speculated that behind Commissioner of Administration Roemer was the governor (October 7, 1973).

The official release of the audit brought forth an impassioned defense. Despite what others saw as a virtual catalog of alleged improprieties, Beasley declared that he was "very proud" of the HEW report. No evidence of fraud or stealing was clear, he claimed (*Times-Picayune*, October 5, 1973). When he accused the U.S. attorney general of intimidation and tyranny, Gallinghouse responded with a careful lecture on the workings of the law. "It would not be proper for me to make any special comment about anything that Dr. Beasley or anyone else may say about subjects of an impending investigation, however untrue, ridiculous or reckless those charges may be" (*Times-Picayune*, December 6, 1973). In a series of vivid interviews, Beasley blasted his critics and defended both the integrity and the ideals of his program. Speaking to the Rotary Club, he called the basic premises of the audit unfounded because the trouble was only HEW's interpretation of its own guidelines when applied to the unusual situation of Family Health. The application of new rules was just "Monday morning quarterbacking," since the government had full access to and knowledge of the contract during its four years. In this respect, he went on, Family Health was being treated like a public agency instead of a private concern or an ordinary business. Furthermore, he continued, there had been no conniving or scheming. No evidence showed that anyone in the organization had personally gained from the alleged transactions (*Times-Picayune*, November 14, 1973).

THE WEEKLY NEWSPAPER OF ● NEW ORLEANS

courier the

Vol. X, No. 23 / 1232 Decatur Street / New Orleans, La. 70116   Oct. 12-18, 1973

The 'S&F 84'/New Orleans' Poets/Lost Warehouse

Dr. Joe Beasley's $62 Million Baby
Immaculate Deception At The Family Health Foundation

Figure 6.1 Example of media publicity (*Courier*, October 12–18, 1973). Photograph by Warren Gravois from the Louisiana Collection, Earl K. Long Library, University of New Orleans. Reprinted by permission.

Formation of the Medical Advisory Committee

The state was in a quandary about the future of family planning and sensitive to the media barrage. A blue ribbon Medical Advisory Committee was formed. Among its members were some of the doctors and public health personnel who were criticizing Family Health in the journal of the state medical society. Some of the committee members were among the most vociferous opponents of the program or, at least, of its founder. Now they were in a position to recommend that the state contract with FHF be canceled. In a report of their findings, they reiterated some of their earlier judgments: The program claimed but did not prove that it had lowered birth rates; it was too expensive; clinic services had declined each year; and fraudulent charges for treatment had been filed (Louisiana, Health and Social and Rehabilitation Services 1973). Many of the committee members who had worked for public health in Louisiana for many years appeared to feel deeply wronged by the rivalry between the public and private sectors.

Beasley responded that the Medical Advisory Committee report was "inaccurate and even defamatory." The doctors had their facts wrong, he said, and did not understand that family planning depended on outreach, education, and opportunity, not just a visit to a doctor's office for treatment. At one point he called the committee a "lynching party" and the report by the head of the state's statistical services "a Mickey Mouse presentation" and an "Alice in Wonderland effort" (*Times-Picayune*, December 4, 5, and 6, 1973). He likened his foes to Nazis (*States-Item*, December 13, 1973) and pleaded for help in saving the foundation, which was doing so much good for poor women (*States-Item*, December 6, 1973).

You'll Have to Wait in Line to Sue

In December 1973, as the implications of the audit and the infighting became apparent, members of New Orleans's Board of Health remembered that they had a year earlier warned city officials of possible trouble in the three Model Cities clinics operated by FHF. Now the city was releasing an audit that focused on illegitimate expenses, including luxurious office furniture, excessive salaries and expense accounts for management personnel, the use of ambulances for nonemergency trips, and a top-heavy ratio of one manager to every 2.7 employees. Furthermore, the city claimed that the New Orleans Health Corporation, which was established to monitor and supervise the activities of FHF in the Model Cities clinics, was itself under the control of the foundation (*Times-Picayune*, November 29, 1973). But the Board of Health's concern came too late and was overshadowed by more dramatic local events and the increasing disenchantment with Model Cities management generally on the part of HUD and a new administration in Washington. In that light, the issue of how well FHF ran the Model Cities clinics became irrelevant.

December was a month of suits, accusations, allegations, denials, and realignment of alliances. The state's attorney general filed suit against the Family Health Foundation to return $700,000 ostensibly spent on the mobile health clinics but still untraceable. No denials were emerging from the foundation (*Times-Picayune*, December 20, 1973). Beasley resigned as its executive director (but retained position of chairman of the board) in a move widely construed as an attempt to placate state officials who had been suggesting that an administrative overhaul might be necessary before the state would renegotiate the contract (*Times-Picayune*, December 12, 1973). He was still chairman of the board, a dean, and the holder of other national titles and consultancies.

By the Christmas holidays of 1973, anyone who wished to investigate or sue Family Health had to stand in line. Auditors for the state, city, HEW, Housing and Urban Development, the U.S. Agency for International Development, and the General Accounting Office were all looking into the activities of what the newspapers had switched from calling the "controversial Foundation" to the "beleaguered Foundation" (*Times-Picayune*, December 11, 1973). Several politicians, like Commissioner of Administration Charles Roemer, abandoned their earlier roles as supporters and publicly acknowledged that problems were more serious than they previously imagined.

Family Health's contract with the state was canceled and could be renegotiated month by month only under stringent state supervision. But the pressure to continue offering the family planning and associated health services to poor women was intense. Not only did the federal programs mandate the services to welfare clients, but the money still mattered to the state, despite its embarrassment over previous mismanagement and neglect. There were red faces at some federal agencies, too, as the full impact of the HEW audit and the grand jury hearings began to hit home.

Clinics in the Grass—The First Half of 1974

The first scandal of 1974 was the discovery of six unused mobile health clinics in a weed-covered lot behind a motel on a bleak stretch of local highway.[7] Family Health had commissioned the clinics on the grounds that they were needed to operate and expand its statewide family planning program. Federal family planning guidelines encouraged innovations in delivery services, and the fact of the mobile clinics was not disputed. Only the financing was questionable.

The billing, bidding, and installation of the thirty-seven mobile clinics had been a paper chase for the grand jury and the federal auditors. The year before, the foundation officials had ordered the construction of the clinics and charged them to the state contract. The state obligingly paid. But the contractors went broke after building twenty clinics, and only fourteen were installed. However, the state had paid almost $2 million in advance for the entire order: $42,000 for construction of each trailer plus $12,000 for installation costs (*Times-Picayune*, January 9 and 10, 1974; *States-Item*, January 9, 1974). The clinics seemed to have been ordered without competitive bidding. The foundation had apparently paid unreasonable (some said "padded") prices and did so without authorization. Since HEW had subsequently reimbursed the state, it now insisted that the clinic money plus all other unauthorized expenses be returned to the government (U.S. Department of Health, Education and Welfare 1973:7–36).

Beasley and the Governor Look for Ways Out

In response to the public furor, the employees and friends of FHF sponsored a television broadcast to tell their side and appeal for community support. Edited sections of their movie, *To Hunt with a Cat*, were shown, and questions from viewers and reporters were answered live. Joe Beasley spoke as usual about the unique success of the program and blamed the current troubles on rumors, innuendo, and the local media, which he believed to be on the side of Charles Mary and the state health department. He justified the entertainment money spent as the way to attract larger grants to keep the program alive. "If you're going to catch big fish—you have to use big worms" (*Times-Picayune*, February 11, 1974). He charged that *laundering* was a Mafia term favored by the press and urged the foundation's friends to contact the governor. The press speculated on how much the movie and television hour had cost and who had paid for it.

Supporters of the foundation distributed a cartoon showing a diminuitive Joe Beasley beset by power politics in the form of Charles Mary, the medical establishment, press, and federal prosecutors. This depiction contrasted sharply with newspaper coverage, which portrayed Beasley as the mastermind behind an "immaculate deception" involving more than $62 million of foundation assets (*Courier*, October 12, 1973).

Within the foundation, the strains were palpable. Those directly involved have said that they developed problems of insomnia, stress, and misuse of alcohol or drugs; women experienced breakthrough bleeding, and men had elevated blood pressure and worried about heart attacks. An atmosphere of paranoia, suspicion, confusion, and fear often prevailed. Services to patients continued, but the work of the outreach workers became more difficult. Supporters feared the deterioration of a program in which so many hopes and careers were vested.

For the first time in public, Beasley admitted that some fraud might have occurred but denied that it was substantial (*Times-Picayune*, February 11, 1974). In March, with faculty unrest becoming visible, he resigned as dean (*Times-Picayune*, March 22, 1974). At the same time, the foundation hired a San Francisco law firm to defend it against the increasing allegations. The lawyer for the defense compared Joe Beasley to Galileo. "Honest people doing an innovative job envoke envy as Galileo did when he went to the flat-world people and said the world is round" (*Times-Picayune*, March 15, 1974). The law firm prepared an elaborate explanation, almost none of which was used in the newspapers. As it would continue to do, the defense contended that only small amounts of money ($10,000 to $140,000) were misspent, not the $2.6 million claimed. Even these amounts depended on how the regulations were interpreted.

The governor went to Washington to discuss the findings of the HEW audit. The audit appeared to vindicate Dr. Mary who, throughout the public controversy and sometimes seemingly in opposition to Governor Edwards, had steadfastly insisted that the spending habits of the foundation should be more closely monitored by the state. The governor was starting to temper his support for the program and to discuss options. Returning from Washington, he was overheard to mutter, "Quite candidly, I don't find that most doctors are very good administrators" (*States-Item*, February 15, 1974).

Governor Edwards saw three alternatives. First, the state could persuade HEW to permit it to renew its contract with Family Health but to enforce closer scrutiny and clearer guidelines. Second, the state could contract with another private agency. Third, the state could add family planning to the existing public health organization. The third option, the governor declared, should be the last resort because the record showed that other states had simply not been as effective in providing birth control services as private endeavors had. But his trip to Washington showed Edwards that HEW was not going to provide the state with an easy way out of the morass. The federal government insisted that $6.2 million had been improperly used and that the state should refund around $2.6 million of that sum because it had failed to monitor the money properly. The possibility of repaying a sum that large, said the governor, "is so remote it is not being given consideration at this time" (*Times-Picayune*, February 16, 1974).

Requiem for the FHF

Following this fateful meeting, the federal government announced that $6 million in contracts with the foundation would not be renewed even with state guarantees of surveillance. Edwards declared that the decision that he had hoped could be averted was "the requiem for the foundation." He added that some extravagances, "neither illicit nor illegal," were responsible for its downfall. Once these expenditures came to light, those within the medical profession who opposed public health in general and the foundation in particular had grounds for criticism (*Times-Picayune*, March 17, 1974).

The double blows of mid-March—the HEW cutoff of funds and the governor's abandonment—drew sharp retorts from Joe Beasley. "I don't plan to be thrown to the wolves. When someone thinks you're down, they all come out of the woodwork, especially the cowards. This is the vulture syndrome." He included HEW in the "out-to-get-us syndrome." "HEW is trying to cover up its mistakes on the welfare side by coming at us on the health side. They're trying to sweep us under the rug to cover themselves" (*Times-Picayune*, March 10, 1974).

From March 20 to May 8, the federal grand jury returned three sets of indictments for a total of seventeen counts against the four top officials of the Family Health Foundation. The first set of indictments listed five counts of conspiracy to defraud the government by making false claims for federal money and lying to federal authorities to cover up the alleged transactions with the mobile health units, since foundation officials had received $4,400 in extra costs for each of twenty-seven units. This was the alleged padding.

The second set of indictments contained seven counts of fraud, again in an alleged scheme to launder federal welfare money and defraud the government of more than $2 million. In the third set of indictments, the grand jury charged five counts of cheating the government out of $4 million through an elaborate plan to use Tulane University to gain extra money on its state contracts (*Times-Picayune*, March 20, April 3, and May 8, 1974). The sums mentioned in the indictments were different in technical respects from the sums mentioned in the audit and in subsequent trials. Each of the four officials pleaded innocent. Two were to go to trial.

The FHF's Last Word

At the same time, the Family Health Foundation produced its own response to both the HEW audit and the accusations (Kelso 1974). The press, which had been savoring every detail of the grand jury investigations, the audit, and the political infighting, made no mention of the analyses that employees of the foundation had mustered in their own behalf. The response fell into two parts: an expression of solid pride in the achievements of the model health care program and a spirited demonstration that the use of federal funds did not violate statutes or regulations. Although the response addressed many of the technical allegations of the audit and would form the basis for defense at the trials to follow, few members of the press or the public understood the legalistic regulations in conflict.

Family Health had defined itself as a model for the solution of the "broader cyclic cluster of problems called the welfare-dependency cycle" by providing family planning services and related assistance to poor women. In short, it claimed, the program had been desperately needed and was delivered as promised within the prescribed rates and with unprecedented success. Or, as Joe Beasley was fond of saying, "We could eat anybody's lunch."

Furthermore, the response contended, the state of Louisiana had not been lax in executing its contracts with the foundation. The foundation maintained that the intent of the federal law was to promote greater participation from the private sector as well as to ensure quality family planning. In keeping with this philosophy HEW was supposed to monitor the state but not the subcontractor directly. The Family Health Foundation insisted that the issues separating it from HEW were not differences in accounting and fiscal management, as the HEW auditors claimed, but those involving the selection of applicable statutes and regulations. Auditors misunderstood what Congress intended and which regulatory devices should be applied for welfare programs under Title IV-A (Social Security Act 42 USC 600-610). The report accused the auditors of retroactively applying irrelevant regulations and of lacking the authority to recommend refunds (or even to audit) because HEW had not established guidelines for dealing directly with subcontractors.

Said the foundation, all its expenditures were reasonable and proper under the circumstances. The broad circumstances were the unique conditions of a private corporation offering comprehensive medical services under a liberal but vaguely worded congressional mandate. The narrow circumstances were the regulations (themselves in dispute) surrounding one category of services (Title IV-A).

> By far the safer course for the State would have been to take the federal money, fatten its bureaucracy, and settle for results which, if unimpressive . . . were incapable of being misunderstood by auditors trained in the mechanical costs rules applicable to public agencies, but unfamiliar with the demands of producing quality family planning services. But Congress was demanding—and the State of Louisiana was uniquely willing to undertake to provide—more than the dismal failures of the past. (Kelso 1974:41)

The government justified the Washington office and the airplanes as reasonable expenses for a private corporation and as economies not precluded by the guidelines. As for the mobile clinics, "there is no statutory or regulatory authority for concluding that the IV-A funds were not to be used for the purchase of mobile clinics or that the amounts spent for these clinics was unreasonable" (Kelso 1974:15). (The first part of the statement is true; the second part was at the heart of the court actions.) The response also defended the channels of matching money on narrowly technical grounds.

The Family Health Foundation tried to get in the last word:

In achieving so much so quickly, it is natural Family Health has created controversy and has been misunderstood or felt as a threat by some. Nor, human nature being what it is, can Family Health have failed to arouse the envy of some. Although working largely with public monies, it is a private endeavor. Working in the private sector of medical practice, it is non-profit and oriented to service to the poor. But the fact remains that it is not competing with anyone, that its overriding concern for quality services to the poor does not translate into an ambition to be in the general business of providing health care. Its mission is solely research and demonstration at the service of the State, Federal and foreign government objectives, thereby to aid in formulating generic *human development* strategies that will begin to resolve rather than institutionalize the chronic and critical problems of welfare dependency and poverty and establish a population growth in balance with the resources available for the development of human potential. (Kelso 1974:24)

From Private Kingdom to Public Responsibility

The release of the audit findings, the governor's inability to defuse federal ire, and the first of the grand jury indictments against the leaders of the foundation in March were described in an editorial as the turning point in a classic Louisiana political war.

> As Louisiana political wars go, the Great Family Planning War has been brilliantly fought, one of the best ever. At stake were millions of dollars, thousands of jobs and great gobs of human ego. It has been a hard fight for high stakes.
>
> Poised on one side with the pro-Beasleys, were Governor Edwin Edwards, Commissioner of Administration Charles Roemer, U.S. Senator Russell B. Long, the Tulane University establishment, a full payroll of legal talent, the powerful black political group known as SOUL and key members of the legislature.
>
> On the other side, the anti-Beasleys, were state health chief Dr. Charles Mary, Jr., U.S. Attorney General Gerald Gallinghouse and the apparatus of the Justice Department, state Attorney General William Guste, the Dallas office of the U.S. Department of Health, Education and Welfare, the Louisiana Medical Society and the state public health bureaucracy. It was a pretty evenly matched fight between two evenly matched armies. (Allan Katz, *States-Item*, March 23, 1974)

It was predicted that the winners would be magnanimous in victory and resurrect the besieged foundation under new leadership.

Editorial speculation about the future of the foundation, its assets, and its mission ran high. The continuing audit listed deficits of $238,000 for the last day of February, and funds earmarked for employees' accrued leave had not been found. With the prospect of acquiring funds to cover the deficits unlikely, bankruptcy action was one possibility (*States-Item*, March 23, 1974).

Employees of the foundation feared that more indictments were planned. Income was dwindling, and the sources had dried up. Some employees were released, and sixty clinics closed; thirty-two others were slated for closure. The state was paying auditors to double-check all expenditures daily. The question in everyone's mind was, what will happen to the Family Health Foundation? Was there a possibility for compromise? Who would deliver the health services? Does a state take over a private foundation? Was there another alternative in the private sector?

Receivership

Suddenly some of the questions were answered. On May 14, a U.S. district court judge signed an order throwing the Family Health Foundation into receivership—the first major health program in the United States to be so treated. Its assets were seized; the seven top officials were ousted; and a receiver was quickly selected. The swift move permitted the foundation to stay open for services but severed it from the legal controversies swirling around its top management. Clinics around the state that had closed because of financial exigency were reopened (*Times-Picayune*, May 15, 1974).

What had begun in the eye of a hurricane ended in a storm of another sort. Federal marshals entered the foundation's headquarters, sealed the doors and records, and turned out the employees. For the first time in a decade, appointments could not be honored. Some of the staff members who were in the headquarters when the marshals arrived described to me the feelings they had about the foundation. Some were critical of the high rollers who had abused the finances and brought the foundation to its knees. Others feared that racial prejudice had contributed to its downfall, since most of the patients and many of the staff members were black (*Times-Picayune*, May 10, 1974). For all the trauma, the staff members showed a "rock-ribbed determination to tough it out, in court if necessary," said a prominent figure who was critical of the leadership of the foundation but praised the spirit of the staff. Although the quality of health care had not been challenged, the care-givers felt that they and their patients were the real victims of the year-long battle.

The patients' emotions ranged from insecurity to bereavement. "Now they're gonna treat us just like Charity." "Where we gonna get dignity now!" The evening clinics were closed. The number of personal appointments decreased, as did the follow-up activities. The atmosphere gradually became more like that of a public health clinic.

Reconstruction

A new health chief replacing Dr. Mary had been appointed, and he set up a task force of nonfoundation professionals to cope with the decisions involved in the state takeover of family planning services. "Inextricably tied into our planning is the unknown factor of the fate of Family Health. . . . Since it is not possible to invent a new foundation to perform FHF functions, the alternative is for the state to develop family planning services . . . and to do this by July 1, 1974."[8] The new planners were still wary of allowing "somebody's empire that is all powerful" or "an organization that is difficult to control or insists on evaluating itself."[9]

The task force had to determine whether family planning was a social service or a medical service. On that philosophical debate hinged its new structure and assignment in the state. Health and medicine won. Only the functions narrowly perceived as contraceptive services were to be left. The elaborate structures in community relations, communications, education, and research either were too expensive, duplicated existing services, or offended conservative sentiments. The AID grants for Latin America were terminating. Only the Parent-Child Development Center survived, funded by the Office of Economic Opportunity as a research and development experiment; the University of New Orleans assumed the contract. The programs for teenagers had been only a token, but the problems caused by adolescent pregnancies were overwhelming, particularly since the state bureaucracies had never dealt with teenagers, sex, and birth control before.

Both the federal receiver and the ad hoc committee had to sort out the problems, beginning with personnel. As many former employees as possible were absorbed into the civil service. Some who had been hired on patronage were fired. Apparently FHF had spent the retirement funds, so the state had to assume responsibility for incorporating employees into the retirement system and making unemployment payments that were in arrears.[10] Tulane University had to deal with tenured faculty on "soft money" and other commitments made with FHF funds.

Organizational complications were extreme. The state had little experience in family planning or in single-purpose clinics, having tended toward consolidation as an efficiency measure. Now it had to integrate family planning, postpartum care, and other gynecological services into the Charity Hospitals and public health units just as they were coping with a major health care reorganization in the state. Another problem was simply geography. The state's "welfare regions," Charity regions, public health regions, and other catchment divisions had to be integrated with the foundation's parish units. All patients had to be rechecked for eligibility under the various grant categories. It is impossible to see how a woman could ever have negotiated the maze during this period.

The task force agreed that the program should remain visible and discrete but above all, as the task force put it, "be financially cost effective and politically feasible."[11] Administrative tasks such as evaluation, accounting, and personnel were moved into comparable units in the state bureaucracy. Evaluation, in particular, was an urgent priority. Had such an office existed to objectively evaluate FHF's activities, "there is a good possibility that the present FHF situation would not exist."[12]

Even with access to FHF's records, the state personnel found that accurately counting the patients was impossible.[13] "The computer program was not clean," reported a number of those who had seen it. Sometimes expectations at the foundation had become confused with reality. A common projection was that the program would have 140,000 active patients by the end of 1974, but sometimes that figure appeared in newspapers or other statements as the actual number of patients. Women were retained on the computer records past a sensible cut-off point. At various times in 1974 the foundation claimed over 100,000 birth control patients; later estimates fall within the range of 60,000 to 75,000.[14] As a result of these recalculations, there was a sharp drop in patients during the first year of state operation.

This summary obscures but does not ignore the complex negotiations, turf battles, and redistributions of power and assets that took place as the foundation was disbanded. Many of the professionals who shaped the transition have since acknowledged that the innovative ideas borrowed from the foundation permanently changed their ways of thinking about health care. Many new systems of data and records management were incorporated into the state health bureaucracy. The employees, particularly a large number of nurses who transferred to the state, have been credited with bringing humanizing values to their new positions.

During the summer after the foundation went into receivership, a director for the newly minted state family planning agency was hired. A state plan to transfer family planning to the Health and Human Resources Administration was submitted and approved. On September 1, the private program became another state agency. The transition was efficient but without flair.

The Promised Revelations

Following the various allegations from the first published suspicions through the collapse of the foundation and into the subsequent trials is difficult. Chronological reconstruction, much less absolute determination of truth, is impossible.

Mobile Funding for Mobile Clinics

The case of the mobile clinics is the first example. The particulars of the clinic funding emerged at the first trial in January 1975. The foundation's own auditors, Peat, Marwick and Mitchell, had questioned aspects of this complex transaction before HEW and the grand jury picked it up. But for reasons that made sense only later, the financing included irregular elements. The sum of $4,400 was added to the cost of each of twelve of the modular clinics by a company called Parkway, Inc., which theoretically built mobile homes. With the approximately $53,000 made available, Parkway officials agreed to purchase consulting work on day care centers. This money was funneled to the Scholarship, Education and Defense Fund for Racial Equality (SEDFRE) in New York City.

SEDFRE was one of those vague, liberal-sounding organizations working for community change and racial harmony. On its board of directors, along with Julian Bond and James Baldwin, was a black New Orleans attorney and political leader, Nils Douglas, at that time head of the grass-roots black political organization, SOUL. Douglas was retained on the Family Health Foundation payroll for $20,000 (*Courier*, October 19, 1974; Mackintosh 1975:56). The executive director of SEDFRE was a former New Orleanian who had gone to school with Don Hubbard, another black lawyer who had an executive position in the foundation.

Ostensibly, SEDFRE was to use the money from the clinics to commission an advocacy report on the need for day care centers for working mothers. But SEDFRE was only the conduit through which the excess money from the clinics was to be delivered to Sherman Copelin, the aggressive young black director of the Model Cities program, which sponsored the neighborhood clinics. Copelin also used his involvement with SOUL to cement the relationship between the foundation and City Hall. He and Don Hubbard (among others) were reputedly responsible for the genocide accusations that had bedeviled the birth control mission, and they were involved in the systems of patronage that had soured the federal investigators on the foundation (Mackintosh 1975:56). The added costs on the modular clinics were referred to later as "Copelin's front porches" (*Times-Picayune*, January 16, 1975).

According to subsequent reconstructions, Oscar Kramer (an employee of FHF, later indicted and imprisoned) picked up a check for $10,000 (Mackintosh 1975). Don Hubbard (an employee of FHF, never indicted) personally delivered it to SEDFRE in New York. SEDFRE officials wrote a check to Copelin Associates. Day care was not discussed again. Miraculously, the genocide issue abated. The mau-mau scenes were not repeated at Family Health or in the community.

Because federal welfare money could be used to buy or construct buildings, an alliance between the foundation and the Model Cities program was disastrously tempting. Sherman Copelin, as director of the Model Cities program, could offer FHF the badly needed clinic space and the opportunity to expand the model of generic health care. But the Model Cities program had its own difficulties. City Hall moved much more slowly in setting up the health clinics than Family Health did in its statewide expansion. The Republican leadership in Washington was not committed to the war on poverty. As Dr. Beasley testified at a trial, "We were under pressure to build and get together those neighborhood health clinics and get them operational in a certain span of time, or the city of New Orleans would have lost millions of dollars and the people would have lost a chance for better medical care in the neighborhoods" (*Times-Picayune,* November 2, 1975). So Copelin was able to aid the foundation, which was already under stress, while forwarding his own Model Cities program.

Copelin had told the Grand Jury that a Family Health consultant had approached him in the men's room of the Saxony Restaurant on Canal Street with a roll of money in a rubber band. After a cryptic exchange appropriate to Grade B movies, Copelin said that he understood that the money was sent by the foundation in general and its director in particular. He could not remember how many payments had been made, what the total amounts may have been, or the dates and locations of the delivery of other installments. He acknowledged under questioning that some of the payments continued beyond his tenure in the Model Cities program. He did not admit complicity in the genocide and racism pressures or in the resulting patronage (*Times-Picayune,* November 2 and December 1, 1975). In an interview, Beasley confirmed that he had authorized money to Copelin because of his fears that Copelin would quit his job with the Model Cities program and leave the clinics in jeopardy. But Beasley went on to say that he had wanted the payments made legally and was not aware of how they had been conducted until after the fact (*Times-Picayune,* November 2, 1975). At other times, Beasley testified about his role in the payments to Copelin saying that he wanted "to arrange to take some of the financial pressures off Copelin . . . arrange a loan . . . and do it legally" (*Times-Picayune,* January 18, 1975). But Beasley insisted that he was unaware of the deceptions relating to the mobile clinics kickbacks and Copelin; these led to the conspiracy to defraud charge.

In the most striking explanation of these events, Beasley explained that he wanted to pay Copelin for serving as a consultant to help allay the fears of black genocide that had been raised in connection with the birth control activities. This he had expected could be done legally (*New*

York Times, January 22, 1975). According to this account, the foundation had needed Copelin's backing to dispel "the idea that the family planning program was aimed at black genocide or that FHF wanted to wipe out black children before they were born" (*Times-Picayune*, January 18, 1975).

Matching or Mismatching Funds

Federal investigators were also concerned about irregularities in the foundation's procedures to raise state or private funds to match the federal money at a ratio of nine to one. In yet another paper chase, the investigators turned up a series of financial moves that were popularly referred to as the "laundering scheme." Federal investigators alleged that when the foundation could not find externally generated funds, money for matching was channeled illegally through Tulane and other corporations.

On April 26, 1973, the foundation sent $235,000 to Software, Inc., of Norman, Oklahoma, a consulting and computer data firm working for FHF and the Division of Administration in Louisiana (Mackintosh 1975:56). On the same day, Software sent $205,000 to the private Fannin Foundation in Texas, supposedly a subcontractor to Software for FHF computer management. But this company existed only on paper and had no assets. Again, on the very same day, a check for $200,000 was sent to Tulane University as a straightforward gift designated for the Louisiana Family Planning Program. University officials testified that they saw no reason to question this check because private universities often receive such gifts and Family Health had been the beneficiary of many grants.

The $200,000 then went to the state of Louisiana so FHF could qualify to receive $1.8 million in federal money for family planning services. Notice that $35,000 was lost in the transaction, but $2 million was gained. The HEW auditors asked where the original money had come from? Who had profited in the interim exchanges? Was this illegal laundering, and, if so, who was responsible?

In March 1974, two of the controversial companies linked to FHF were dissolved: Software, Inc., and another formed to do business with Innovative Data Systems, owned by Commissioner of Administration Roemer. He at first denied all knowledge of their financial operation or of putative links to the scandals, although he did admit that his minor children owned Innovative Data Systems (*States-Item*, March 23, 1974). The laundering scheme was the subject of the third major trial, at which much of this information emerged.

Buying Support

The HEW auditors, looking at the FHF payroll, had wondered from the first if the foundation was buying political support. Evidence of campaign contributions to the coffers of prominent Louisiana politicians began to mount. Since nonprofit corporations such as Family Health should not make such contributions, FHF paid several of its own lawyers overtime for putative legal services. After taxes, of course, the additional compensation was contributed to politicians. The audit revealed contributions to the campaigns of two governors, two state senators, and a State Supreme Court justice (*Times-Picayune*, March 11, 1976; *Courier*, October 12, 1973). Because the auditors had exhaustively questioned employees about these practices, gossip had leaked out well in advance of the audit report, and the recipients returned the illicit contributions.

Through time, the foundation had increased its bevy of highly paid legal talent to help with the complexity of federal regulations and later to defend it against the rumblings about the misuse of funds. The *Courier* (October 12, 1973) reported that Senator Joseph Tydings of Maryland, a population policy activist, was retained at $40,000 per year; Harry Dent, former counsel to President Nixon and assistant to Robert Haldeman of Watergate fame, received $20,000. In addition, local attorneys with ties to Washington or San Francisco law firms were hired to contact the federal agencies for a gentlemen's chat on the interpretation and enforcement of the admittedly confusing regulations (Chandler 1974b:70). These visits, however, bypassed the Dallas Region VI HEW Office with which Family Health and their lawyers were supposed to be dealing. Foundation employees have commented that the HEW office in Dallas was offended by this and abandoned its earlier support of FHF when other problems surfaced (Chandler 1974b:70).

These issues were the primary ones to emerge from all the earlier allegations. Two people went to trial: Joseph Beasley, the flamboyant founder, and Oscar E. Kramer, Jr., a former top executive at the foundation.

The Trials

In early 1975, the great family planning war culminated in a series of trials. The intense media publicity focused more than ever on the charismatic personality of Beasley and on the contrasts between a visionary program and the tedium of financial maneuvering.

Just before the first trial began, the New York foundation that helped defend the Berrigan brothers and Daniel Ellsberg threw its support behind Beasley. The Bill of Rights Foundation sent out a nationwide mailing asking for contributions to the National Beasley Defense Fund. Supporters contended that Beasley was being prosecuted by the federal government "apparently for political purposes, in violation of fundamental constitutional liberties" (*States-Item*, December 17, 1974), because his views on birth control and medical treatment for the poor angered private physicians and government officials. A strong article in support of Beasley in the *Washington Post* (Chandler 1974b) and the letter from the Bill of Rights Foundation drew fire from the Louisiana State Medical Society, which referred to its earlier endorsement of family planning and hotly denied that it had ever attacked Beasley for moving into socialized medicine (*Times-Picayune*, December 29, 1974). This accusation that socialized medicine was the fundamental issue was to be raised as a defense several times.

> It is ironic that the land of independence, free enterprise, and private initiative should in the last 20 years have poured literally billions of dollars into noncompetitive public programs fostering welfare dependency. It is all the more ironic that we did so precisely to stimulate those characteristics of independence, private initiative, and free enterprise among the disadvantaged which we eschewed in dealing with them. The philosophical issue of *public* or *private* provision of services is crucial here as it is the basis of the present legal disputes. (Kelso 1974:6)

Just as Margaret Sanger had hoped to be tried on a First Amendment charge, Joe Beasley wanted a trial on the constitutional issues of health care delivery services. But the legal questions did not permit such an approach.

The First Trial

The first trial was on the charge of conspiracy to defraud the federal government by filing false claims for the purchase of the mobile health clinics. The government argued that the money had been spent to bail the foundation out of a growing deficit. Some of it was channeled to Copelin as a bribe, and the rest went to "lavish living" not connected to birth control (*Times-Picayune*, January 20, 1975).

Neither defense nor prosecution questioned the manipulation of money in the clinics deal. The chief disagreements were how much the man at the helm knew about the illegal activities, when did he learn about them, and what was his involvement in either initiating them or covering them up. Also at issue was whether such practices could be construed as legitimate accounting procedures given federal regulations. Copelin was not called as a witness. He had already admitted receiving the money.

The government's case rested primarily on the testimony of Eugene Wallace, another top official of the foundation, who had received immunity from his indictments in return for testimony against his two former associates. Under the sponsorship of the Government Witness Program, Wallace and his family had moved out of New Orleans, changed their names, and established new identities. Wallace testified that Beasley "made all the top level management decisions" (*Times-Picayune*, January 17, 1975) and had certainly made the decision to funnel money to Copelin. Although others had devised and carried out the plans, Beasley knew that the relationship with Copelin constituted a misuse of family planning funds. Wallace did, however, admit that Beasley was away from foundation offices "half the time" and often had to make decisions without all available data. Moreover, FHF had "constant political problems" and faced frequent solicitations for patronage, money, airplane rides, and other favors. Wallace testified that he recommended fulfilling requests such as the payoff, even knowing that they were illegal, "because they seemed to be the thing to do at the time" (*Times-Picayune*, January 17, 1975).

Oscar Kramer, on trial for the same charges as Beasley, took the stand to insist that he had carried out his responsibility to run the program without interference from the director. He claimed that he had masterminded the arrangements through SEDFRE, although the prosecutor sharply retorted, "Did he (Beasley) think it was manna from heaven?" Kramer admitted that he and Beasley had used conduits to provide money "for whatever parasite was trying to put the bite on the foundation" (*Times-Picayune*, January 17, 1975). Kramer also admitted that he had proposed the idea for the day care study and that he had hoped SEDFRE would support the deception to satisfy the auditors. (SEDFRE did not.) He insisted that in his capacity as business manager he had approved the money for apartments, planes, and entertainment. After this testimony that he, not Beasley, had managed the payoffs, Kramer's case was severed from Beasley's. He was tried separately and convicted two months later.

The defense argued that the tremendous confusion over the regulations governing the use of federal welfare funds had never permitted the foundation to act within clearly defined rules. Despite the apparent tedium of testimony about regulations, this trial was high drama. The defendant's attorney was Jim Garrison, the controversial and swashbuckling former district attorney of Orleans Parish, who had achieved national notoriety for his unsuccessful prosecution of Clay Shaw, a prominent local businessman charged with conspiracy in the assassination of President Kennedy.

Beasley's first trial ended in a hung jury, and a mistrial was declared. Two months later, the case was again tried. A lawyer with the state health and welfare agency described the investigation as "one of the most extensive if not the most extensive audits ever conducted by the Department of Health, Education and Welfare" (*New York Times*, April 24, 1975). In the second trial Beasley impatiently snapped. "Listen, man, I was making $150,000 a year in private practice before I left it to save the world. I don't need to rip anybody off" (*States-Item, Times-Picayune*, March 17, 1975). The other bombshell in this trial was "star government witness Eugene Wallace's testimony that he feared for his life." He claimed that his former employer had threatened to kill him with a shotgun if he testified against him (*Times-Picayune*, March 18, 1975). In separate trials Beasley and Kramer were convicted on the same charges of conspiracy to defraud by manipulating the money for the mobile clinics.

The Case Winds Down

Although appeals and other court appearances continued, the major dramas were over. The last trial in March 1976—for three counts of conspiracy to defraud the government by filing deceptive claims for $200,000 in matching money—was anticlimactic. It was quickly evident in the trial that the necessity to defraud had stemmed (again) from the precarious financial position of the foundation in 1973 and from the multiplicity of the laws, guidelines, and regulations then in effect. Ironically, after all the trials a government report was released outlining just how clumsy and vague the rules were (U.S. Comptroller General 1975). Beasley testified that he tried to abide by the regulations, had ordered the staff to cooperate in a complete audit, and hired a large number of lawyers to advise him on the complex laws. "I know as much about law as most lawyers know about kidneys, but I had to operate in that maze" (*Times-Picayune*, March 5, 1975). Governor Edwards was called as a character witness but quipped that the only thing he had ever gotten from Family Planning was some birth control pills that he had not taken (*Times-Picayune*, March 10, 1975). It is widely believed in the community that Joe Beasley's testimony was calculated to protect Tulane University, whose top officials were allegedly involved in or knew about the laundering. Others testified that it was permissible to use funds from HUD or Model Cities to attract more federal money as a match. The jury believed this and found the defendent innocent.

Because they were granted immunity for helping to build a case against the foundation's top officers, Copelin and Hubbard faced no federal prosecution (although they were repeatedly referred to as "unindicted co-conspirators" in the press) (*Times-Picayune*, June 6, 1975, and November 2, 1977; *States-Item*, March 19, 1975). Later they were both indicted by the state on charges of theft, but a judge ruled that the doctrine of double jeopardy protected them (*States-Item*, June 5, 1975). In November 1975, the federal district court denied Beasley a new trial on the earlier convictions. At issue was Copelin-Hubbard testimony that might have cleared him of charges that he had direct knowledge of payoffs or authorized them (*Times-Picayune*, November 6 and 26, 1975).

Beasley pledged to keep on addressing the sociomedical problems in the United States and abroad and "to find a way to limit unwanted births and break the welfare cycle unwanted births sometimes breed. The real losers are the people who can no longer avail themselves of Family Health Foundation services" (*Times-Picayune*, March 13, 1975). At the sentencing for the conspiracy to defraud conviction, Beasley requested probation because his losses were already great. He cited the deanship at Tulane and the directorship of the Family Health Foundation, not to mention "the damage to my work and field . . . the destruction and scattering of a unique technical resource which I have built, the damage to my personal reputation in New Orleans by being depicted a materialistic crook aimed at personal gain and so-called lavish life-style and the loss of financial independence and personal freedom" (*Times-Picayune*, April 24, 1975). Resigned to these losses, he compared himself to Job.

The judge sentenced Beasley to two years and instructed him not to blame others or portray himself as a victim.

> You have cast a shadow over all programs of this nature, because actions like yours encourage the belief that worthwhile programs for the poor are merely blinds for the diversion of public funds to private benefit. . . . I am convinced that you are an able and indeed a brilliant person. You have been afforded the highest advantages our society can confer. . . . It is therefore all the more tragic that you corrupted yourself and those about you. (*Times-Picayune*, April 24, 1975)

The final framework into which these extraordinary events can be fitted is not that of social science but that of a Shakespearean tragedy. It was, in fact, one of the prosecutors who suggested that the Bard's view of human nature was most apt. He recalled that

> Shakespeare's tragic kings would often caution their aides not to do anything rash, thereby hoping they could immunize themselves against any acts that might be committed in their name: . . . "Look, we've got a problem that

threatens to wreck the empire. Take care of it for me but don't let's have any on the record discussions of the details because what you have to do will probably be illegal." (*States-Item*, December 17, 1977)

Then, as now, unsubstantiated rumors circulate that the foundation was involved in unsavory activities with the Mafia, arranged for sex for political favors, or committed other dark deeds that have not come to light. The existence of these rumors testifies to the importance of the preceding events in the community where ordinary people still talk about what really happened.

7

Epilogue and Epitaph

*I wouldn't take a million dollars for any of my six kids, and I wouldn't give
you six cents for another one. Thank the Lord, they're all healthy.*
                                                              —A former patient

*From its inception until it was placed in receivership in May 1974, the foundation
obtained at least $53.6 million in Federal funds under 10 assistance programs
administered by nine Federal agencies . . . and indirectly from Federal agencies
through grants and contracts with 12 public and private intermediary organizations.
About 76 percent of its total Federal funding was for family planning services
throughout Louisiana; the rest, for other health-related services.*
                                                    —U.S. Comptroller General, 1975

During the decade from its beginning in a rural parish to the final
days of seige, the family planning program (under various names)
garnered over $62 million. Beyond the approximately $53 million from
the government were the grants from private foundations such as Ford,
Rockefeller, and others. Apart from the Comptroller General's summary,
no final accounting has ever been rendered. The foundation's record of
attracting money has probably not been equaled in Louisiana and certainly
has not been surpassed. With an annual budget of about $18 million,
it was one of the largest corporations in the state.

At one time Family Health employed over 1,000 people; 81 percent
of these were women and 52 percent members of racial minorities,
largely from the disadvantaged neighborhoods the program served.
Members of these groups accounted for 78 percent of all management
and professional positions. Because of the partnership with Tulane
University, the foundation had utilized the services of about 180 technical
experts in more than thirty disciplines. It was proud of its record in
employing more former welfare recipients than did programs in any
other state. For ten years, the organization was the largest family planning

program funded by the U.S. Department of Health, Education and Welfare; other states emulated it.

Measuring the intangible achievements of a health care delivery service is difficult. Because of the conditions of its demise, no one tallied the total number of patients served through the history of the program. Guesses vary, but certainly the number is in the hundreds of thousands. The computer programs and individual records have been lost. The federal auditors isolated only a small fraction of the total money spent as questionable. They never challenged the quality or the quantity of health care.   ◡

Why Did Family Health Fail?

Many people have theories about the ultimate causes for the collapse of the foundation. Soft money is always vulnerable. Changes in federal administrative priorities or regulations can capriciously cripple a program. Since the patients paid nothing toward the cost of their care, Family Health had no steady source of income. Birth control services had a solid foundation, but the expansions into community medicine and international population control were in pursuit of a dream built on sand.

Politics or Gender?

Most knowledgeable observers see the foundation's alliance with the Model Cities program as the turning point in its fortunes. In the latter program idealism was tainted by compromises with the political establishment, by the lure of money. When I asked professionals who worked closely with the foundation why it had failed, they said that "there were politicians interested in getting in on the gravy train and they didn't mind prostituting the poor." Others said that "nobody in the political establishment gave a damn about family planning. They weren't getting pregnant, losing their jobs and going on welfare." The politicians had, after all, been glad to turn the whole matter over to a group of college professors when there was no money involved, only controversy. A former FHF researcher analyzed the cause of the collapse: When "the family planning dog began to wag the state health department's tail," and when the potential for patronage and payoffs become evident, the political forces moved in.

A story about the collapse of the foundation circulates very quietly among some sources deeply involved in the program and others with reasons for disenchantment. In the most often repeated version, a former Family Health administrator was approached at a dinner party by a prominent state politician who said, in effect, "It is terribly sad and unfortunate that your career and the careers of others have been hurt so badly. But the program had to be destroyed. Dr. Beasley was too political. Through the program, anyone could mobilize as many as 70,000 women. After all, they had staff members out knocking on people's doors. It was too powerful a built-in constituency."

If this scenario of political force were true, however, why wasn't the constituency of women and loyal families mobilized on behalf of the foundation? Because to have converted patients into political pawns would have violated the canons of medical confidentiality. What the politicians did not understand was that no matter how politicized certain aspects of the foundation had become, the central core of medical services—dignity and respect for the patients—had not been breached. Nor does it appear that plans for organizing patients for other than health care were ever on the agenda.

The genocide accusations posed a valid threat to the program only in that they frightened the administrators into desperate acts of bribery. Once again, the medical and contraceptive services of the program had the credibility and stature to have withstood a few black militants. But the genocide confrontations deeply divided females from males in the black community.

This same division by sex became striking within the foundation. The entire cast of characters in the "great family planning war," accusers and accused, were men. The nurses, staff workers, outreach workers, and patients were predominantly female. But women had no opportunity to become involved in the larger administrative decisions. This is not to say that had the sexual distribution of responsibility been more equitable, the traumas would have been avoided. The women employed by Family Health, who worked conscientiously in patient care, did not hold positions of temptation.

Vague Federal Controls?

Because a federal agency has the term *community* in its name does not necessarily mean that its personnel understand the realities of communities linked by multigenerational bonds, poverty, discrimination, and heritage. The early family planners had tapped into these real communities in a way the federal programs often failed to do. The people in Louisiana tend to distrust carpetbaggers or Washington bureaucrats who try to "tell us how to run things." They often presume that outsiders do not comprehend how Louisiana politics really operates. As a corollary, Louisianians do not always play by rules made up by outsiders. This cultural isolation may have played a part in the failure of the Model Cities program.

The Department of Health, Education and Welfare perhaps deserves some blame for the demise of the foundation. According to one theory HEW turned on its prize protegé to avoid a larger investigation into how it had spent over 1 billion dollars in welfare money (the Title IV-A funds) and why it failed to write detailed guidelines on the management of grants (Chandler 1974a). "They had big money, but no big rules for it," said one former Family Health employee. In a convoluted fashion the government did take part of the responsibility for what happened. Some of the major issues in the trials hinged on the patent inadequacy of federal regulations. Just after the last trial resulting from the 1973 indictments, the U.S. Comptroller General's Office reported to Congress on what went wrong at Family Health. It concluded that the haziness of administrative controls for federal assistance programs had permitted the fiscal pioneering that destroyed the FHF, and it belatedly recommended that the guidelines be redrafted (although they never were).

In effect, the foundation had taken advantage of vague federal guidelines and lax supervision and had obtained money without question until it was too late. The Comptroller General's report outlined weaknesses in the administrative requirements of the funding programs, the lack of pre-award evaluations of the foundation's ability to manage money, the absence of sensible monitoring, the conflicting regulations on such matters as matching funds and patient eligibility, and the diversity of requirements among funding sources. At the same time, the report noted that "the foundation received extensive favorable publicity and recognition by Federal officials, particularly for its innovative approaches and its reported achievements in the Family Planning program" (U.S. Comptroller General 1975:9). Even the bureaucrats had been beguiled by the drama of solving serious social problems.

Although questions were raised about the foundation's handling of money as early as 1970, no one at the local, state, or federal level had authority to reconcile the differences of interpretations about federal regulations or mandate controls that might have averted the collapse. In the seven years of foundation-federal friendship, the foundation was involved in eighty-nine funding agreements (eighteen grants, three direct contracts, and sixty-eight indirect third- or fourth-party contracts). Even the Comptroller General's Office was unable to trace some money accurately (a list of sources of federal money is given in Appendix A). Each funding action required a proposal, but the form and requirements varied widely. Time periods covered differed and often overlapped. Some programs provided cash advances; others reimbursed for expenses already incurred. Matching fund requirements, as we have seen, differed strikingly among different levels of government. Title IV-A funds were for welfare women, but low-income women (who were much more numerous) qualified under Titles V and X. "These diverse requirements complicated the foundation's fiscal management responsibilities and thereby contributed to the deficiencies which eventually caused the foundation to be put into receivership" (U.S. Comptroller General 1975:24). Once the money had been given out, everyone assumed someone else was monitoring its use.

A Conspiracy?

Conspiracy theories for the end of the foundation still abound in the community. What they have in common is a belief that some powerful men in Louisiana chose the Family Health Foundation as an arena in which to carry out larger power plots and vendettas. Some see the conflict as between conservative capitalist medicine and the liberal ideal of government-supported free health care for the poor. Certainly Joe Beasley did.

> The charges on which I go to jail were simply a convenient device by which a segment of organized medicine was able to destroy a program that provided free family planning and child nutrition information to the poor. Unfortunately, there are some doctors—dinosaurs slowly drifting into their own Ice Age— who regard any government program as competition that might be doing them out of a few dollars regardless of the social needs or realities. (*States-Item*, December 9, 1977)

Another speculation is that segregationists were offended by the concentration of effort and money on a largely black population and by the lack of punitive restraints for reproductively active women on welfare (Chandler 1974a). The press is still believed to have overemphasized the lavish-life-style issue and to have ignored the fact that a private corporation with a contract to deliver specified services has business considerations that differ from those of a public antipoverty agency (Chandler 1974a:71). Proponents of the conspiracy theories point to the crusading zeal, unusual in Louisiana, with which the federal and state agencies pushed to end the foundation and to prosecute its principals.

Robin Hood?

One factor stands out in popular consciousness. The foundation as a corporation had a life and character of its own but was all too frequently identified with only one person, Joe Beasley. Charismatic power and bureaucratic responsibility mixed poorly. No one has seriously suggested that Beasley took money for himself, but clearly he sought fame and a place in history.

Beasley was shown to be a poor judge of character when hiring associates. His selection of individuals who had opposed him or the goals of the program (as in the genocide case) or who were political appointees created a staff with weak loyalties, who leaked information and in other ways damaged the program (Mackintosh 1975:58). Vision, ideals, and charisma could not replace sound administration.

The role that Beasley's personality traits played in the collapse of the foundation is a favorite topic of speculation. It is said that he did not understand how to play Louisiana politics, variously described as Byzantine, medieval, or feudal: He was an outsider who lacked the school and family ties that bind politicians together. Others feel strongly that he was betrayed and martyred in a cruel system. "He wanted to help people, so they axed him." "He sought to solve the world's population problem. They call him an enemy of the people" (Chandler 1974a:1). Many poor people in New Orleans remember him as a folk hero in the Robin Hood mold: They believe that he took money from the rich in a good cause.

Why Did the Foundation Succeed?

Even the most vociferous critics of Family Health do not question its fundamental claims of achievement. The program was racially integrated. Dignity and respect for women were more than a motto. Not one single charge of patient maltreatment was leveled at the program. Given the revelations of the feminist movement about "medical male-practice," involuntary sterilizations performed on poor women in other states, and related sexist abuses, this fact is remarkable. There was no coercion. The medical services offered by the Louisiana Family Planning still serve as a model in the United States (for a list see Appendix B). Many key administrators in family planning or maternal-child health care systems around the world were trained in Louisiana.

Quality and Compassion

Beasley and his team made family planning a household word, created the expectations of humane health care, and met the demand. As one doctor said, "When the dust settled, the discussions were on a higher plane." Observed a black community leader, "Family Health did more to change public medical services than any group in the state ever had. It set a model for how services should and could be. People got used to quality services and began to demand them from Charity and welfare." Another doctor summarized, "Private doctors were affected too. The experience changed a lot of sloppy attitudes about sexism and racism and drove some of the more virulent attitudes underground." Former patients were more assertive: "I'm gonna make them treat me better." "Health is my right, I don't just have to take anything." Adds another woman, "Family Planning was a helping hand to women. It set a lot of women on their feet. If it weren't for them, we'd still be caught." Although the educational mission of the program was primarily directed to poor families, possibly the greater impact was on the culture and attitudes within the wider community. But these intangibles are impossible to measure, much less to prove.

The strategy of identifying high-risk women in their childbearing years and concentrating medical resources on them was an important case of primary-care epidemiology. The family planning program tried to break the complex causal chain of illness and death by new health care delivery. Some Louisiana doctors have compared this approach to the successful rubella campaign in which a massive public health crusade of vaccination and education alerted doctors, women, and the public to the dangers for children whose mothers contracted this mild disease in the first three months of pregnancy. Many of the birth defects, deaths, and retardation resulting from rubella have been prevented. Family planning worked toward the same goals.

Mothers and Mortality

What about the program's objectives of lowering birth rates and rates for maternal and infant mortality? An independent study of these statistics for the years 1970 to 1974—when the program's activities could be expected to show an impact—revealed that the birth rate in Louisiana decreased by 11.5 percent and infant mortality by 25.6 percent. Part of the decrease in infant deaths resulted simply from the decline in birth rates nationwide. But the gap between Louisiana's and national figures was narrowing substantially, despite the large nonwhite population in the state. "This is a significant and praise-worthy reduction in number of infants who die. Louisiana infant mortality in 1974 compares favorably with the total US infant mortality of 16.7 in 1974" (Dickey 1976:2). Louisiana's rate was 18.8 per 1,000 births, still higher than the national average but greatly improved over that for earlier decades (see Figures 7.1 and 7.2). The decline in infant deaths was slightly higher for black babies than for white babies—a favorable sign.

The biggest change occurred in deaths for child-bearing women. Decreases in maternal mortality were impressive for both blacks and whites. Even adjusting for the lower birth rate, the reduction was 51.5 percent. The only unpromising part of these figures is that black maternal death rates remained three and one-half times as high as those for white maternal mortality.

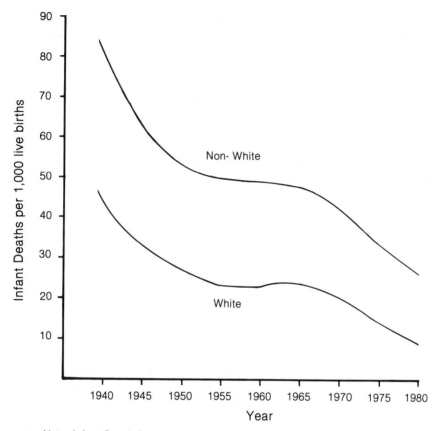

Note: Infant Death Rate = Deaths under one year of age per 1,000 live births

Figure 7.1 Infant deaths in Louisiana, 1940–1980, by race (Source: Louisiana Vital Statistics Report, Department of Health and Human Resources)

This very dramatic decrease in the incidence of maternal deaths suggests that obstetrical care has been improving at least as much as pediatric care during this five year period. *A major cause for this improvement . . . has been the availability of family planning services rather than an improvement in prenatal or delivery care.* (Dickey 1976:3; emphasis added)

A Recognized Cause

Perhaps the ultimate measure of the program's success is seen between the lines of official actions and statements. Not one single politician or health official, no matter how angry or embarrassed, suggested that saving family planning services was not a justifiable goal. Their only question was how. Although they did not see family planning as the

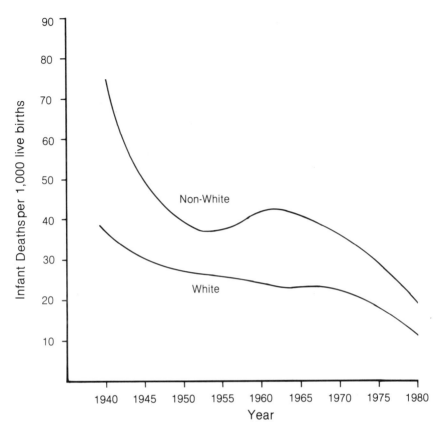

Note: Infant Death Rate = Deaths under one year of age per 1,000 live births

Figure 7.2 Infant deaths in Orleans Parish, 1940–1980, by race (Source: Louisiana Vital Statistics Report, Department of Health and Human Resources)

keystone of family health and social justice, only a decade earlier their counterparts had not viewed birth control programs as a legitimate concern of public health. Somewhere in that ten years the efforts to educate the community had taken root and blossomed.

Although this aspect has never been systematically analyzed, it has been said that the foundation was a significant factor in job training and career development. Minorities and women were given chances for advancement, retraining, and middle-class employment. Many have cited the education and financial assistance provided by the foundation as determining influences in their lives, and they now miss the excitement of the program. Dr. Arthur Fort, brought in from the outside to help save the foundation, says, "They were the most creative people I've ever met." Another administrator concludes, "We did a lot of good no matter what happened. We had a wonderful fantastic time."

Aftermath

By the end of 1977, Dr. Joseph Beasley had lost his last court appeal. In December, he reported to federal prison at Eglin Air Force Base in Florida where some of the Watergate principals had been imprisoned. There he served over seventeen months of the two-year sentence; the rest was spent on close probation. During the three years between the collapse of the foundation and the beginning of the prison term, he had supported himself and his expensive legal battles with a private medical practice in a historic old neighborhood in New Orleans. Many former patients from the foundation came to his office. While he was in prison, the Louisiana State Board of Medical Examiners revoked his license to practice in the state.

The Powerful Men

Today, Beasley is the Bard Center Fellow in Health and Nutrition at Bard College in New York. A grant from the Ford Foundation has permitted him to write about the impact of nutrition on health in the United States. Through the Bard Center, the Kellogg Foundation has agreed to fund an additional large-scale research project to demonstrate the effects of good prenatal nutrition on normal births and healthy babies. As director of the Department of Metabolic Medicine and Nutrition at Brunswick Hospital Center in New York, he practices clinical medicine and works on health care delivery systems to correct what he calls the fundamental problem facing civilization today.

A major proportion of the brain potential of hundreds of millions of the world's children is being lost through inadequate intrauterine and early childhood nutrition. The technology is now available to remedy this most basic of all needs and to preserve and release the enormous human creativity involved so that intact human beings around the world can successfully deal with the problems and opportunities facing them.[1]

He admits ruefully that it may be too late to save the world, that humanitarian concerns for sick and dying children are only a joke to cynics and politicians. Nonetheless, he speaks forcefully about building new medical models and utilizing new technologies to address the problems of international malnutrition.

Nationally and internationally, his reputation suffered less than it did in Louisiana. Many who worked with Beasley in family planning and population control regard him as a crusader beset by red tape and venality and victimized by black activists, power politics, and petty bureaucrats (Chandler 1974a). Now he has distanced himself from the earlier turmoil, "I am at peace with myself" (*Times-Picayune*, January 1, 1978). He refers to his time in prison as a detour in his career that made him a better person and adds that instead of bitterness he feels only pride in the achievements of the program.[2]

Sherman Copelin, the black director of the Model Cities program, testified to the grand jury about taking bribes from the Family Health Foundation officials, but he did not participate in their trials. Later he was implicated in another scandal involving the terms of the contract between Superdome Services, his minority-owned janitorial company, and the state for services to the new Superdome in New Orleans. His lucrative relationship with politicians revived the gossip surrounding the family planning program. In 1981, Copelin announced his candidacy for city council. He lost. One black leader said, "He won't be forgiven for hurting what helped poor women and children. A big hunk of the black community won't forget." Or as a journalist observed, "Along with the money exchange, the most disturbing thing about the testimony was the suggestion that Copelin was prepared to submarine the birth control program so important to poor families if he did not get the pay-off" (*Times-Picayune*, December 13, 1981). He has since lost another election for the highly politicized position of district tax assessor. The spectre of his involvement with Family Health continues to haunt Copelin in the community.

Edwin Edwards was elected by a landslide majority for a third term as governor. His role in the Family Health Foundation problems has been forgotten in the wake of other events. In 1985 he went to trial in federal court on charges of racketeering in a complex case involving other aspects of the health care delivery system in the state.

The Program

Today, the family planning program in Louisiana is only one part of a large state bureaucracy and must compete with other health agencies for limited funds. The social pathologies that family planners hoped to address are still alive. A small dedicated staff works hard for the program, but the crusading zeal is gone. The outreach worker system is too costly to maintain, and its effectiveness is diminishing.

With the loss of the foundation, no concerted drive is being made to reach women in need of medical services or to provide them with sex education, reproductive counseling, and related health care. The family planners assume that patients know enough to take responsibility for themselves and that older women who have reached their desired family size understand their choices for fertility management. The waiting rooms do not sparkle; the lines are sometimes too long. Often the educational effort is more perfunctory than liberating.

The patients too have changed. Because the eligibility rules have been tightened, the patient population has become largely welfare recipients. Now the central focus is teenagers; delivering contraceptive services to them before that critical first pregnancy is difficult. The lack of outreach has contributed, many believe, to soaring birthrates among teenagers. The foundation was just beginning to concentrate on this special high-risk group when it was closed; rates of adolescent pregnancy have increased 50 percent since that time.

In 1974, abortions became legal in Louisiana, although not without heated legal battles and sidewalk dramas. The Family Health Foundation had planned to take a public stand favoring legalized abortion because of its disapproval of illegal abortion. Although this approach would have brought the powers of Catholic and fundamentalist outrage down on it, foundation staff members believed that community sentiment was strong enough to have won this last battle. In large measure, their contribution was indirect. Opening the doors to birth control had helped open the doors to abortion.

In 1983, Planned Parenthood opened in Louisiana, one of the last U.S. states to have a chapter. Planned Parenthood had been excluded from Louisiana, first by Beasley's deal with the Catholic Church and then by the controversies and the aftermath of the collapse of the foundation. The organization is proceeding with caution. It has applied for no state or federal money, which in any case is increasingly scarce. It will use a sliding fee scale and raise money from private sources. The new clinic will offer contraceptive assistance to women of all social classes. Sex education, not systematically available through private physicians or the schools, is a major focus. The clinics will provide a welcoming atmosphere particularly for adolescents and women who are first-time users. Planned Parenthood will do only what it did in the half century after Margaret Sanger challenged the laws: run good birth control clinics. Expanded maternal and child health care will be the indirect result of family planning. Louisiana will not lead the world in population control, but the state's medical model reflects the principles first developed in Lincoln Parish.

Women, Poverty, and Reproductive Rights

Only in Louisiana under the umbrella of private corporations had the daring for family planning reached the magnitude originally envisioned by Congress. Investigations of programs in other states revealed that they had similar problems stemming from vague regulations and inadequate supervision (U.S. General Accounting Office 1975). All the programs had money problems, particularly in finding matching funds even after the requirement was reduced from 25 to 10 percent.

The success of Louisiana's outreach worker system contrasted sharply with other programs that expected welfare caseworkers to spread the word (U.S. General Accounting Office 1975). In states without outreach the majority of women learned about the family planning program from a friend, relative, or another patient and not through the welfare organizations. Turnover among caseworkers was very high, their loads were heavy, and often the paperwork precluded the rapport and counseling that birth control requires. Many caseworkers had received no training in dispensing this sensitive information, were discouraged or prohibited by their supervisors from discussing it with welfare women, felt embarrassed, or were hampered by the lack of literature to hand out. This poor delivery service resulted in an enormous waste of money; clinics could not operate at full efficiency if women were not referred. Furthermore, the stereotypes of welfare women as "baby machines" were reinforced.

The contrasts between the Louisiana family planning program and those of other states were spectacular. Programs in most states had no follow-up procedures for missed appointments, no mechanism for reinstating patients who had left, and no means of identifying the reasons why. Patient dropout rates were high, and broken appointments ranged from 30 to 70 percent of those scheduled (a much higher rate than in Louisiana). None of the states effectively used third-party payment systems such as Medicaid, and all had strikingly inadequate systems for accounting, benefit structures, eligibility screening, and personnel training. Costs per patient ranged from $16 to $219 (U.S. General Accounting Office 1975:ii).

Although the original inspiration for the development of family planning services had come from the federal government, the responsibility was shifting to the states by the mid-1970s. States either contracted with private agencies like Planned Parenthood or developed their own initiatives (Jaffe et al. 1973). In contrast to the glory years, the money appropriated dwindled as the patient population grew larger. But family planning was no longer a high priority: The National Center for Family Planning Services in HEW was reorganized, and both the number of staff positions across the country and the visibility of family planning services were reduced. The number of grants to sustain ongoing programs or for research on population control, contraceptive technology, and reproductive management had also declined by 1974. The national program had peaked by 1974 (Dryfoos 1976:89).

At its height, family planning had a national policy, massive funding, and, briefly, its own specialized bureaucracy. Age-old contraceptive policies and class biases had been replaced by new and enduring standards for the nation. Acceptance of family planning had outpaced even the most optimistic estimates, growing at an average annual rate of 32 percent for the first five years. As Frederick Jaffe, president of Planned Parenthood, argued, this experience confirmed the hypothesis that when cost and other barriers are removed from access to a valuable medical service, social class differences disappear (1973). The family planning movement brought a new accountability to health care systems, gave space for assertiveness for millions of U.S. women, and offered more rational alternatives in making health systems responsive to social goals.

The national family planning movement is no more. Neither the vision nor the funding has been sustained. No new contraceptive technologies have been marketed for a mass audience since the pill and the IUD. Money and initiatives for research for a better mousetrap are lower with each federal budget. In fact, more money is now spent for research and programs in infertility than the control of fertility. Sterilization has become the favorite means of birth control for both females and males. Within the health care delivery systems in this country, birth control services are not seen as the cornerstone of maternal and infant health. Such services are walled off although available to those who seek them.

Abortion Controversy

Two issues that were marginal to the drives of the 1960s have grown to dramatic proportions and now occupy center stage. The first is the abortion controversy, and the second is the increase in adolescent pregnancies. Both are, as was the family planning movement, inextricably tied to society's view of the proper status of women, the cultural controls on sexuality, and the role of family structure.

In the arguments, organizations, picketings, and bombings that surround the abortion debates, many seem to lose sight of the middle ground—the prevention of unwanted pregnancies. Yet with birth control technology still so awkward and the social expectations of sexual activity so pervasive in the media, unplanned pregnancies are frequent. Abortion availability, new technologies, and a delivery system have expanded dramatically with the Supreme Court decision legalizing it. An examination of the agenda of the antiabortion foes will reveal some of the same confusions about birth control and abortion as women voiced when describing folk remedies (Willson 1985). The IUD is damned as an abortifacient, not applauded as a means of birth control under medical supervision. Sometimes birth control clinics that offer no abortion services have come under fire (Owens 1985).

At the very heart of the abortion controversy are the same questions about women that Margaret Sanger faced and that the early family planners addressed. Who controls the bodies of women: husbands, the church, the government, the medical establishment, economic forces, or ethical systems in flux and in conflict? If women are free to choose birth control, what will happen to the sanctity of the family, asked the opponents of Margaret Sanger. In the current debate, the antiabortionists assert the primacy of the fetus over its mother and her body and have been criticized for ignoring the need for social support systems for the mother and the child after birth.

Supreme Court decisions have legalized the sale and importation of birth control devices and the rights of couples and women to seek contraceptive services from doctors. Other court decisions have freed public institutions to serve poor women with family planning services. Indeed the reproductive rights of women are no longer questioned. Even the Catholic Church, so long an ardent foe of birth control, came to the public position that it could not mandate decisions for the entire nation, only for its believers.

Adolescent Pregnancies

Today's most immediate problem is adolescent pregnancies, with their severe health and social consequences. I am impressed by the number of professionals who insist that the root of the problem rests with males, not with females, but they admit that they have no agenda for reaching males. Although teenagers are avid viewers of television and consumers of products, no media advertising campaigns have been waged to encourage the use of condoms or other minimal birth control practices. More energetic campaigns such as those used in European countries have not been undertaken by policymakers.

A special subset of the problem is black teenagers, both poor and pregnant. In growing numbers, black leaders have articulated the issue. "It is the single most important problem confronting the black community today," says Eleanor Holmes Norton, the former director of the Equal Employment Commission. Black columnist William Raspberry has called it "babies making babies." In the past, the social illness of segregation and racial prejudice has been blamed for the problems of blacks in the United States. Now the statistics are seen in new light. In the early 1980s, more than 50 percent of all black births were illegitimate, and in some large city ghettos, the figure may approach 90 percent. The difference between the mobile middle class—with small family size, delayed marriage, college educations, and employment—and the "underclass" is enormous. Study after study has found correlations between single-parent families and child abuse, truancy, low school achievement, suspensions, drop-out rates, unemployment, and juvenile delinquency (*Time*, December 9, 1985).

Teenage pregnancies, whether among blacks, whites, or Hispanics, still include today the same dangers the family planners were cataloging. There are enormous medical risks for both mother and child, major incidences of sexually transmitted diseases, and high costs for government social services. More than half of the $10 billion paid nationally to families with dependent children went to women who had begun the family cycle with an adolescent pregnancy (*New York Times*, October 23, 1983).

The original family planning movement was directed at (presumably married) women who wished to limit or space their children and needed the corollary medical services. The extensive programs provided the basic information and counseling. Teenagers were almost an afterthought, and the current epidemic of early teen pregnancies was a statistically minor trend at the time. But teenagers have come to represent a major problem that is, according to *Time* magazine, "corroding America's social fabric."

> The subject of teenage pregnancy seems to raise almost every politically explosive social issue facing the American public: the battle over abortion rights; contraceptives and the ticklish question of whether adolescents should have easy access to them; the perennially touchy subject of sex education in public schools; controversies about welfare programs; and the precarious state of the black family in America. Indeed, even the basic issue of adolescent sexuality is a subject that makes many Americans squirm. (*Time*, December 9, 1985)

It might seem self-evident that sex education is an answer. But few issues in the United States arouse such public and private intensity yet have resulted in so little action. In Louisiana, for example, only in 1979 did the legislature permit schools to teach sex education in grades seven through twelve. Parents have the option of keeping their children out of the classes. In any case, few schools can offer much instruction because of a shortage of teachers for the subject. For some children, beginning instruction in sexual values in the seventh grade is too late; a school for pregnant teenagers in New Orleans served many fifth-graders (the school has since been closed and no alternative offered).

Some of the same churches that sponsored the family planners in the 1960s have started classes to help bridge the gap.

Although teaching teenagers family planning and sexual responsibility is one aspect of the solution, it is the part under strong attack from the Reagan administration. The current Congress as well as the administration has made moves against Planned Parenthood, written bills to force parental consent for teenagers seeking contraceptive information and services, and issued statements equating sex education with promiscuity (Wilson 1985).

Federal Policy and Female Poverty

The national debate in the halls of Congress during the Reagan years has taken strange turns. The decades of family planning services both at home and abroad have come under continual fire from the so-called pro-life forces. Many family planning supporters who have voted for the U.S. funding for AID and UNFPA have been stridently accused of being antilife and proabortion (Willson 1985). It is often difficult to follow the complexities of the House and Senate maneuvering through postponements, amendments, filibusters, and reauthorizations. Provision of Title X funds for the Family Planning Assistance Program—the largest and most important category of federal aid to family planning—has been under congressional attack since 1980. There have been efforts to reintroduce and even mandate "natural" family planning as the only birth control method. Counseling and services to teenagers have also been under attack.

Today in the United States, poverty wears a feminine face. The number of female-headed households is growing faster than any other type of U.S. family and for black families stands at over 50 percent. "Two out of three adults in poverty are women," reads a recent poster. "One out of every five children live below the poverty line and the rates are increasing," says a television newscaster.

What has come to be called the feminization of poverty has complex causes, many related to patterns of job discrimination and underemployment (*Signs* 1984). But, apart from the economic analyses of recent years, one fact stands out: There is a cyclical structure that begins with the birth of a child. From that point, women are enfolded in patterns that they did not create. What kind of job can women with children get? What kind of education can they get? Can they find day care, support systems, child support judgments from the courts, medical help? The vicious circle of poverty, which the family planners addressed, is entered at child birth. Women are far more likely to live in poverty if they are raising children alone.

Under the Reagan administration, officials have not publicly acknowledged a role for the U.S. government in fertility management. This approach contrasts dramatically with the sight of President Nixon on national television proclaiming that the touchstone of U.S. family planning policy is the right of women to have access to the methods for choosing the number of their children.

The Politics of Infant Mortality

This book began with a description of Louisiana as an underdeveloped country, characterized by the high rates of illegitimacy and infant deaths and their sad relationship to class and color. The story should end, twenty years later, with a report on the status of these problems.

The Picture in 1980

Even though the record on infant mortality had improved by 1980, it remained poor relative to that for the rest of the country. In the greater New Orleans area, the infant mortality rate was higher than that in the rest of Louisiana, and the racial differences were striking (see Figures 7.1 and 7.2). White infant mortality was 12.1 per 1,000, lower than the national average, but the black rate was more than twice as high, 25.8 per 1,000. Although the fertility rates of older women had been declining, national trends showed rising fertility rates among teenagers, particularly among those between 10 and 14 years of age. Again, black women represented a disproportionate share.[3]

In 1980, the infant mortality rate for Orleans Parish was 20.3 (per 1,000 births) compared to the rate for the rest of the country of 12.5. The gap between these two rates has been widening. The rate for the state of Louisiana is second from the bottom; only that for neighboring Mississippi is lower. Today, the reason for this rate is quite specifically pregnancies among adolescent girls. In New Orleans, one out of eight females between the ages of 15 to 19 is pregnant; the majority of illegitimate births are to black adolescents; and 40 percent of the births in the parish are illegitimate. In Louisiana, one out of every five babies is born to a teenage mother (*Times-Picayune/States-Item*, January 17 and 22, 1986). These young mothers are more than twice as likely as an older woman to give birth to a dead, damaged, or premature infant (*New York Times*, October 23, 1983). Now, as in the past, these girls do not seek or know how to find prenatal care. Pregnancy is the single most frequent reason for dropping out of school. According to police reports, child abuse cases are increasing, and teenage mothers are responsible for about 30 percent of the total.

Health planners estimated that the incidence of babies with low birth weights in Orleans Parish is twice the national average. About half of new mothers had less than three prenatal checkups. Even though Charity in New Orleans is famous for its premature nurseries and other hospitals are also adding neonatal intensive care units, the situations leading to high-risk pregnancies should be prevented before a premature, high-risk baby arrives. This statement sounds strikingly familiar: Nearly twenty-five years ago statistics like these were the battle cry for family planning.

A Federal Agency

Coincidentally, just as the Family Health Foundation was collapsing in 1974, the federal government created regional agencies to investigate the rising costs of health care and coordinate the development of new hospitals or medical programs. One staff member of the New Orleans Area/Bayou-River Health Systems Agency, Inc., said, "Every new hospital bed is a bar of gold for somebody, but who looks after the powerless?" The new agency wrote a comprehensive health systems plan that identified major concerns in community health: preventable diseases, venereal disease, high blood pressure, accidental deaths, alcohol, diabetes, environmental quality, and dignity for the elderly. But its highest priority— the touchstone by which all area health programs were to be judged— was a reduction in infant mortality by at least 25 percent (New Orleans Area/Bayou-River Health Systems Agency 1980:4). In 1982, the New Orleans area health agency was dissolved despite its federal funding and its noncontroversial reputation. New hospitals built for profit or other private medical programs were no longer required to commit themselves to community health care goals such as reduction in infant mortality.

Specialists in health planning ask why does an area with two medical schools, an immense public hospital, a favorable doctor-patient ratio, many specialists, and services such as counseling for sickle cell anemia and other genetic disorders continue to suffer from a high infant mortality rate? The answer must lie in the historic and cultural configurations of health care services, the federal barriers to the medically indigent, poor coordination, or maldistribution of existing services. For example, the current state-run family planning program has few ties to prenatal services and the state Maternal-Child Health Program. Charity Hospital and its satellite clinics offer prenatal care but little in the way of education. Other hospitals offer more pregnancy education but leave prenatal care to private doctors who may not see women early in pregnancy. Because information about the availability and qualifications for these services is not widely available, the programs often do not reach the audience for which they were designed.

A Local Initiative

In 1983, Mayor Ernest "Dutch" Morial, the first black mayor of New Orleans, proclaimed the Year of the Healthy Birth. Several hundred community leaders, politicians, health professionals, and educators met to discuss the city's abnormally high rates of infant mortality, teenage pregnancies, and child abuse. The participants hoped, as many had before them, that education (disseminated by mass media, school programs, radio spots, and retraining seminars for nurses) would help to change the patterns of poor nutrition and inadequate prenatal care. A project called Improved Pregnancy Outcome was started by the state's Maternal-Child Health Program and the mayor's group. It, too, started in northern Louisiana as a pilot project "to work up some experience before we came to New Orleans" (*Times-Picayune*, May 23, 1983).

The intent of these meetings—led by the mayor and his wife, Sybil Morial—was to acquaint the community, as well as expectant mothers, with the factors that lead to healthy babies. The participants recognized that medical problems have a social and cultural basis. The new community coalition announced its motto: "to put pregnancy on a pedestal." It focused on the fact of pregnancies but not on the immense constellation of pressures—economic, social, or emotional—that produce unwanted babies. It did not address sex education, birth control availability for adolescents, or the extraordinary social costs for these girls. Everyone tread carefully around the racial differences in the statistics. No one commented on the fragmentation of health care for the poor nor was mention made of male responsibility, particularly that of black males (*Times-Picayune*, May 23, 1983; *New York Times*, November 13, 1983). Paralleling the piecemeal programs for adolescent mothers and their offspring in the rest of the country, funding for this program is short-lived and will not be renewed.

With no sense of irony, the *New York Times* (November 13, 1983) published an editorial praising New Orleans for developing a creative health care delivery system.

> The only thing wrong with what's going on in New Orleans, where Mayor Ernest Morial has rallied community leaders to focus on the increasing numbers of teen-agers having babies, is that it isn't going on everywhere. ... The New Orleans meeting deserves emulation in every city where teenage pregnancy is a problem. This local initiative stands out because concern at the national level seems so minimal.

Notes

Chapter 1. More Folklore than Folk Care

1. This story was first published by David Chandler (1974b). The speaker, Jacqueline Harvey, was kind enough to repeat it on December 3, 1981. She is articulate, even poetic, and her tale is typical of other personal stories I have collected. Reprinted by permission.

2. Louisiana Health and Social and Rehabilitation Services Administration, Division of Health Maintenance and Ambulatory Patient Services, *Statistical Report of the Bureau of Vital Statistics*, prepared by the Division of Tabulation and Analysis, 1960–1970.

3. Longer accounts of the impact of the birth control movements in the United States and Great Britain can be found in many sources. Excellent historical analyses include those by James Reed (1978) and David Kennedy (1970). For a well-documented feminist history, see Linda Gordon (1976). A good general history that emphasizes the British experience is Peter Fryer (1965).

4. For personalized accounts of the birth control movement, see Margaret Sanger's autobiographical works (1931, 1938). She also edited a fascinating selection of women's letters about their reproductive histories and dilemmas (1928).

5. For more recent assessments, see Hyatt Medical Management Services (1980); or a publication of the Louisiana Department of Health and Human Resources (1980). These statistical reports, however, were prepared for planning purposes and contain no ethnographic information.

6. For further sources on illness and health care delivery services in the South, see John Ettling (1981) or Elizabeth Etheridge (1972). Both books emphasize the role of cultural factors such as diet and sanitation as well as interventionist strategies for curing social problems. Articles on other programs may be found in a special issue on disease and the social environment in *Southern Exposure* 1978.

7. The folklore material reported in this chapter is from interviews with women in St. James Parish in 1968 and in New Orleans since then. I have talked with a number of people with similar firsthand experiences—nurses, doctors, women who have tried at least some of the techniques mentioned, and some who performed or assisted in illegal abortions. The same stories occurred repeatedly but independent of each other. I also wish to acknowledge student

papers, published and unpublished, which are catalogued in the University of New Orleans Folklore Archives (New Orleans, Louisiana). I wish to credit unpublished papers by Christine Pleasanton, "Folklore on abortion and contraception"; Gwen Mueller, "Beliefs and superstitions surrounding pregnancy"; and Stephen Nodruft, "The medical student and physician: Past and present." Published papers from these collections include Trahant (1981) and Grayson (1981).

8. This information about illegal abortions is not published in any systematic form nor is it likely to be. Through the years and particularly since the beginnings of the women's movement, I have heard these stories from my friends and students in Louisiana. Doctors or medical professionals have confirmed these accounts. I have also had the opportunity to interview a former abortionist who made some of the same observations. I would like to thank all those who shared their experience or knowledge with me. They would not want to find themselves listed.

Chapter 2. Margaret Sanger Comes to Louisiana

1. The growth of this early idealism and the proposals for medical solutions can be traced in Platou et al. (1964), an article on battered children in New Orleans. An unpublished research manual (Lennox et al. 1964) shows the early concerns with infant and maternal mortality. Beasley's unpublished Masters of Public Health thesis from Tulane (1964) puts forth a hypothetical and naive design for initiating a family planning program in New Orleans.

2. This list has been adapted from numerous publications, reports, speeches, and interviews. For further details, see Beasley (1969a, 1969b, 1972), Coyle (1968), and McCalister et al. (1973).

3. This list included the governor, state attorney general, representatives of Louisiana's State Board of Health, Department of Hospitals, Department of Welfare, Medical Society, the Tri-Parish Medical Society, the regional Charity Hospitals, local police juries (elected county officials), the public health unit staff, welfare agency staffs, plus appropriate medical, religious, civic, and educational groups.

4. Catholic intransigence was waning. For a spirited analysis of why Catholics should change their minds and policies, see John Rock (1963). Everything you ever wanted to know about birth control from a Catholic point of view (and a convincing one) is to be found in John T. Noonan (1965).

5. Confidential internal memorandum by Joseph Beasley, March 11, 1966, p. 2.

6. For an excellent insight into the U.S. government's role in research and marketing of contraceptives, see Carl Djerassi (1979). Djerassi, the "inventor" of one of the steroids used in the anovulant (drug that suppresses ovulation), is disenchanted with prospects for a technological breakthrough in birth control technology. Another criticism of the state of the art in fertility management is the result of a conference in 1979 on Ethical Issues in Human Reproduction

Technology: Analysis by Women. The resultant book (Holmes et al. 1980) provides an excellent description of the many facets of feminism and birth control.

7. A complete depiction of federal activity at this time may be found in the inaugural volume of *Family Planning Perspectives*, vol. 1, no. 1, 1969, that first reported on the Louisiana program. In this issue see also articles by Jeannie Rosoff and Frederick Jaffe. The statistical assessments of need used during this period derive from Office of Economic Opportunity data (1968 and subsequent updates) and Planned Parenthood–World Population's call to action, *Five Million Women—Who's Who among Americans in Need of Subsidized Family Planning Services* (Varky et al. 1967). A short but independent analysis was prepared by the American Enterprise Institute for Public Policy Research (1970).

Chapter 3. Building the Model

1. Grant applications, reports to funding sources, and summary articles about the program (Beasley 1969b:8–9) contain complete lists and charts of the interlocking and cooperating institutions with descriptions of how they officially related to the operations of Louisiana Family Planning, Inc.

2. From February to July 1965, home visits with interviews were conducted for 1,124 households in a proportionate sample drawn from the census tracts in the New Orleans standard metropolitan area (households were also assigned to one of eight socioeconomic groups). These types of surveys have been widely used in underdeveloped countries to determine knowledge, attitudes, and practices (KAP) about the introduction of birth control programs. Copies of all forms, schedules, step-by-step interviews, and coding instructions are to be found in Carl L. Harter et al. (1965). Sampling procedures and a sociological rationale for the approach can be found in Harter's dissertation (1966) or Harter (1968b). The Children's Bureau grant PH-40 supported these surveys and many others.

3. Although the New Orleans Family Survey interviewed both females and males, blacks and whites, the majority of the data that entered the technical literature concerned black females. Census figures and poverty information, coupled with black infant mortality, illegitimacy, or female-headed households, warranted a closer look at the attitudes of this subpopulation. It was estimated that any health agency would serve more blacks than whites in New Orleans.

4. The sample of 106 was drawn from a list of all medically indigent women, black or white, who delivered at Charity Hospital or at home during the prior year but whose babies were stillborn or died within the first year of life. For a full report, see Beasley, Harter, and McCalister (1966). This specialized study focused on the problems of infant mortality as did others that followed.

5. There is voluminous literature in anthropology, sociology, and history about the nature of black family structure. A statistical presentation on the theories and controversies current at that time can be found in Daniel P. Moynihan et al. (1965). The Moynihan report was itself the focus of much controversy. For that analysis, see Lee Rainwater and William Yancey (1967). Many of the report's arguments centered on the putative matriarchy among

blacks. For an excellent analysis of this concept, more properly called matrifocality, see Carol Stack (1974).

6. For insights and excellent statistical analysis from the Family Survey data, I am indebted to an unpublished manuscript, "Family Structure in New Orleans through Two Generations," by Ann Fischer and Virginia Ktsanes, loaned to me by the latter. The most extensive and accessible article taken from these surveys is Fischer et al. (1968).

7. A more extensive description of the impact and development of the indigenous health auxiliaries system can be found in V. Djukanovic and E. Mach (1975), or N.R.E. Fendall (1972). Paramedical or auxiliary workers have long been a necessity in Third World countries. There, a ratio of one doctor to 200,000 patients may be commonplace, and alternatives to the hierarchical style of Western medicine have to be found. Since the few westernstyle medical practitioners are overburdened and poorly distributed, elaborate systems of traditional care fill the gap (midwives, herbalists, diviners, shamans, and bone-setters). In the 1960s many nations made policy decisions to train nonprofessionals to provide selected aspects of health care. For example, midwives were trained not only to deliver babies but to recruit for family planning, distribute birth control pills, or even insert IUDs (McClain 1981). The concept of applying ideas from the Third World has met with resistance in the United States, where licensing and certification are strict.

8. Thousands of women were registered with the program. Since thorough records were kept, it is possible to construct a picture of a "typical" woman in the program. The files show that she

- was black (94 percent)
- was 24 years old or younger (56 percent)
- already had three children or fewer (65 percent)
- had not completed high school (69 percent)
- had her first pregnancy before the age of 18 (50 percent)
- had used either no previous contraception at all or methods not considered effective
- entered the program because of postpartum referral (61 percent)
- adopted some form of contraception, probably the pill, after entering the program (96 percent)
- was married or had been married and separated (69 percent)
- admitted that she "took a chance and got caught" on her last pregnancy (81 percent)
- was poor but did not receive welfare assistance (80 percent)
- spent between two and three hours with the staff of the clinic on her first visit but only 10 percent of that time with a doctor (100 percent).

These statistics are adapted from charts in Beasley and Frankowski (1970) and Beasley et al. (1971).

9. Minutes of the staff meeting, Louisiana Family Planning, Inc., December 11, 1967, p. 2.

10. At an American Public Health Association meeting, a panel that included Beasley and Christopher Tietze urged the profession to back reforms in abortion laws (*Medical Tribune,* November 21, 1966). At a meeting with Planned Parenthood–World Population, Beasley, along with Margaret Mead, advocated abortion availability as a part of humane family planning (*New York Times,* November 24, 1968).

11. Minutes of the staff meeting, Louisiana Family Planning, Inc., April 5, 1968, p. 3.

Chapter 4. From the Possible to the Impossible

1. No record or history of the program's development was maintained. For the period of mid-1967 to the end of 1970 (the rise of the Orleans Parish Demonstration Project and Louisiana Family Planning, Inc.), the best source of information is a dissertation by John Wells (1972). Emphasizing managerial techniques, he drew heavily from accounting records, patient data, narrative reports, training records, and general correspondence, all now unavailable. Published accounts such as Beasley and Wells (1971) are drawn from the same sources.

2. To receive federal funds that require matching the grantee agrees with the grantor to assume some fixed proportion of the total grant as a condition of receiving it. Sometimes this is revenue from another source. Sometimes it is in-kind contributions such as services or facilities from other agencies.

3. The first major set of hearings was *The Growth of the United States' Population* (U.S. Congress, Senate, Committee on Labor and Public Welfare 1966). See also U.S. Congress, Senate, Committee on Foreign Aid Expenditures 1965; 1966; 1967). For a contrast to the governmental hearings, there are many popular and widely read accounts of the population crisis. See Garrett Hardin (1969), the Club of Rome's *Limits to Growth* (1972), or Paul Ehrlich (1968).

4. The program was drawing attention in the popular as well as the scientific press for its social and medical breakthroughs. See Farnsworth Fowle (1968), Arthur Gordon (1970), Joseph Lelyveld (1970), the *New York Times Magazine* (July 19, 1970), and *U.S. News and World Report* (1969 and 1973). Local articles were uniformly enthusiastic about the program (*Times Picayune,* September 26, 1971). In particular, see a series of articles that coincided with the opening of the clinics in Orleans Parish (Kahn 1967). Within some demographic circles, complimentary analyses were appearing (Westoff and Westoff 1971:315–318).

5. Beginning in 1967, Title X of the Foreign Assistance Act authorized grants, contracts, and loans for programs relating to population growth in friendly foreign countries. Nonprofit organizations both in the United States and in foreign countries were included in the list of eligible recipients. The programs relating to population growth included—but were not limited to—demographic statistics, research, training, construction and staffing of clinics, manufacture of medical supplies, dissemination of information, and provision of medical assistance and supplies. The Agency for International Development was responsible for administering Title X funds. During fiscal years 1971 to 1973, $344.7 million

in Title X funds were obligated for population growth projects. Of this total, the Family Health Foundation was granted over $3 million (U.S. Comptroller General 1975:50).

6. At the request of numerous congressional committees, as well as members of the White House Staff, the officials of the Louisiana Family Planning, Inc., also under the name of the Family Health Foundation, furnished data, technical advice, and testimony for deliberations on these major pieces of legislation: (1) The 1967 amendments to the *Maternal and Child Health Act* (Title V), providing increased HEW funds for family planning services; (2) Title X of the *Public Health Service Act*, known as the Population Act of 1970, establishing and funding the HEW's National Center for Family Planning Services; (3) The Title IV-A major amendments of 1969 to the *Social Security Act*, including family planning among accepted services to receive matching funds from HEW; (4) H.R. I of October 1972, providing a nine-to-one match of HEW to state funds and making family planning services a mandatory part of statewide health services. A complete list of congressional hearings is included in the bibliography.

7. Tulane University marketed Beasley as thoroughly as the family planning program marketed contraceptives. A handwritten note on a file copy of his M.P.H. thesis says,

This is good for *Tulanian* piece. Do from this angle:

He looks like a young corporation executive and he sprinkles his speech with phrases like "management systems," "application of technology." He drives himself so hard and tirelessly he probably would occupy a spot on an insurance actuarial table with some top flight corporative executives. But despite his corporation aura and his preoccupation with hardware and systems of modern management, Dr. Beasley is concerned not with profit but with people, particularly children. (Howard-Tilton Special Collections, Tulane University)

Chapter 5. The Peak Is Reached

1. In summer 1973, the Family Health Foundation gave its last major testimony in Washington. An extensive document submitted to a House subcommittee on appropriations (1973) includes a thorough but grandiose summary of the entire program and its plans for future expansion.

2. By 1972, at least fifteen theses or dissertations leading to graduate degrees at Tulane or other universities had been funded entirely or in part by Family Health Foundation. All credited the assistance of the foundation in providing them extensive access to program data. Several dissertations were instrumental in the creation of the program (Harter 1966; Moore 1968; Wells 1972). Others were plans for introducing family planning based on the Louisiana model into other countries (Lantum 1970, for the Cameroons; Onel 1972, for Turkey; Scofield 1970, for Brazil). Elizabeth Bennett (1972), Rose A. Britanak (1972), and Benjamin Barrentine, Jr. (1960), studied nurses and outreach workers as they took on increased clinical responsibilities and developed new job descriptions and educational requirements. Others concentrated on the structure and attitudes within

families that influenced decisions to use contraception (Parrish 1969; Maultsby 1971). Some were technical applications. Heartwell (1972) applied queuing theory to investigate how people wait, how long each function of clinic operation takes, and how to expedite the process. Family planning was also analyzed as a business, economic processes, or a management problem (Wells 1972; Dunbar 1973; Cook 1971). Elaborate models and mathematical descriptions for the adoption and use of oral contraceptives (Hawkins 1969) and a macrosimulation model for human fertility (Mather 1975) were developed. The study of asymptomatic gonorrhea (Ahmad 1970) broadened the scope of clinic services. From these efforts and the other studies funded from the same agency, many papers were read at meetings and published in professional journals.

3. Colposcopy is a safe and painless diagnostic technique for looking at the tissue surface cells of the mouth of the uterus or cervix with a microscope.

4. Several local studies were in progress at this time (Fischer and Ktsanes 1971). With the expanded federal liberalization of guidelines and funding, some small-scale programs to test delivery of services to adolescents were under way through Family Planning. Because good records were kept, systematic sampling and follow-up investigations were possible even after the 1974 administrative changes.

5. Negotiations originally involved Louisiana Family Planning, Inc., and the Community Action Program (CAP). By 1971, some of the birth control agency activities were funded through OEO as the health component of the Model Cities program. To implement its comprehensive demonstration program, which included over forty projects, New Orleans garnered Model Cities grants totaling $28.8 million from September 1970 through February 1975. Of this total, the foundation received $6.6 million directly for the neighborhood clinics. After fiscal 1974 the Model Cities program, along with several other HUD programs, was consolidated under HUD's Community Development Block Grant Program (U.S. Comptroller General 1975:49).

6. For an anthropological-linguistic account of black child rearing and language learning in Louisiana at this time, as well as an inadvertent criticism of interventionist strategies, see Ward (1971).

7. Objective accounts of these events are nonexistent. Many people whom I have interviewed were witnesses and/or participants. Chapter 6 outlines the grand jury and trial proceedings, in which further testimony confirms some of the major allegations about payoffs, patronage, and the genocide threats. Douglas R. Mackintosh's account (1975) is the best reconstruction available, since he conducted interviews immediately after these revelations became public. Even so, his article lacks both the tempering of time and an analysis of motivation. David Chandler (1974a, 1974b), a journalist and apologist for the program, omits all discussion of the effect of the genocide controversy on the eventual collapse of the foundation. Beasley's lectures at Harvard University (1973) contain his personal views on the politics of ethnicity and birth control. His personal communications with me in 1983 contributed to this account. I heard about these meetings from a number of people who were there, and I attended a meeting in 1972 that was similarly disrupted by black militants who stood in the back of the room and shouted threatening slogans about genocide.

8. The term *mau-mau* was invented by Tom Wolfe, *Radical Chic and Mau-Mauing the Flak Catchers*. Although he did not know of the events in New Orleans, he described scenes in offices of the war-on-poverty programs that were paralleled locally. His vivid analysis of the interethnic relationships within the war-on-poverty bureaucracies remains a classic.

9. For a record of these debates and findings on involuntary sterilization or other abuses linked to family planning, see U.S. Congress, Senate, Committee on Labor and Public Welfare, *Quality of Health Care—Human Experimentation* (1973:1446ff).

Chapter 6. The Great Family Planning War

1. Letter from Dr. Ben Freedman to State Attorney General William Guste, December 27, 1973.

2. Although claims of lower costs had been made in print by the Family Health Foundation from time to time, the specific report that raised the hackles of the Division of Tabulation and Analysis of the Louisiana Health and Social and Rehabilitation Services Administration (LHSRSA) was the "Statistical Analysis of the Louisiana Family Planning Program, 1967–1971," an unpublished report submitted to the state by the Family Health Research Group; the quotation is from p. 2.

3. This article was previously cited as the rebuttal to Blake (1969) in which the worth of the kind of family planning programs outlined for the poor was questioned. In the rebuttal article, the authors ardently supported the concept of government-supported family planning and cite Louisiana as an example of how well it can work. The senior author, Oscar Harkavy, was an official of the Ford Foundation; Frederick Jaffe, an officer of Planned Parenthood–World Population, had frequently testified along with Beasley before congressional committees on family planning.

4. This unpublished paper (Ben Freedman, n.d., p. 1) actually began as a letter to the editor of *Science*. Copies were sent to the authors of the article and to Kingsley Davis, a prominent demographer who had helped with the Blake article and who had expressed reservations about the Louisiana program. The editor of *Science* declined to publish the rebuttal on the grounds that the Louisiana illegitimacy data were only a small part of the whole article and that any disclaimers should be made within the pages of the journal that actually accepted the original article. In a letter (September 16, 1970), the assistant editor of *Science* closed the journal's case: "The title implies that Beasley is biased, the text that he was in a rush to get into print. Such may be the case, but one cannot say it in *Science*."

5. These allegations, as well as others to be discussed, were later included in the audit conducted by the Department of Health, Education and Welfare in 1973. State investigators, particularly those working under the Medical Advisory Committee, also later submitted reports on these matters (December 5, 1973). These mimeographed reports were designed for internal use only.

6. A New York spokesperson for the Rockefeller Foundation announced that he could not remember ever having been involved in criminal charges before and that the foundation would cooperate because both officials and the public had the right to know (*Times-Picayune*, October 18, 1973).

7. The missing family planning clinics paralleled an earlier scandal in that parish in which drainage pumps, the cornerstone of a modern drainage system, sat uninstalled in the weeds. The parish still floods regularly.

8. Minutes of the Family Planning Committee, New Orleans, May 2, 1974, p. 1. This was not an ad hoc or advisory committee. The minutes were loaned to me by Dr. Ben Freedman.

9. Minutes of the Family Planning Committee, May 23, 1974, p. 2.

10. Minutes of the Family Planning Committee, May 10, 1974, p. 2, and June 6, 1974, p. 3.

11. Minutes of the Family Planning Committee, June 6, 1974, p. 3. This quotation was from the final meeting of the task force. Instead of minutes it wrote a summary of activities.

12. Minutes of the Family Planning Committee, June 6, 1974, p. 4.

13. Minutes of the Family Planning Committee, May 23, 1974, p. 1.

14. The committee agreed that it needed accurate estimates of the patient population to be served, and the foundation had not provided it with any of the essential patient data requested. Thus when it conducted its own investigation, "the Task Force found that only 60% of the clients being served by the Family Health Foundation were classified as Title IV-A eligibles and potential. FHF had not known about new income thresholds approved by Family Services for welfare eligibility." Minutes of the Family Planning Committee, June 6, 1974, p. 3.

Chapter 7. Epilogue and Epitaph

1. From a letter of transmittal by Dr. Joseph D. Beasley and officials of the Bard College Center, in a contract grant report to the Ford Foundation, *The Impact of Nutrition on the Health of Americans: A Report to the Ford Foundation,* July 1981 (unpublished report).

2. Personal communication, Dr. Joseph D. Beasley, July 20, 1983.

3. For similar analyses of these statistics and the implications for health policies in the state, see "Goals to Grow, Framework for the Future: A Citizens Task Force Report on Welfare and Poverty," 1975; New Orleans Area/Bayou-River Health Systems Agency, Inc., 1980; or *Children of the Bayou State,* the Bureau of Child Development, 1979.

References

Washington Post, Washington, D.C.
New York Times, New York City
Times-Picayune, New Orleans
States-Item, New Orleans
Vieux Carre Courier, New Orleans
Louisiana Weekly, New Orleans

Ahmad, Mohammed Mitwalli. 1970. The study of the occurrence of gonorrhea in post-partum women. D.P.H. dissertation: Tulane University, New Orleans.

Alan Guttmacher Institute. 1977. *Abortion: Need, Services and Policies: Louisiana.* New York: 515 Madison Avenue.

American Enterprise Institute for Public Policy Research. 1970. *The New Family Planning Program.* Special Analysis no. 27:1–16.

American Medical News. 1974. Birth control "empire" periled by fraud probe. February 18:1ff.

Andrews, Susan R., Janet Blumenthal, Dale Johnson, Alfred Kahn, Carol Ferguson, Thomas Lasater, Paul Malone, and Doris Wallace. 1982. The skills of mothering: A study of Parent-Child Development Centers. *Monographs of the Society for Research in Child Development.* Series no. 148, vol. 47, no. 6. Chicago: University of Chicago Press.

Applied Health Sciences Department. 1972. *Fertility, Family Structure and Family Planning: Narrative Report. Summary of programmatic research, PH-40.* New Orleans: Tulane University.

Arrowsmith, Janet. 1979. Charity Hospital: A brief history. Unpublished manuscript on file, Tulane University Medical School Library, pp. 1–33.

Barrentine, Benjamin F., Jr. 1969. Indigenosity: Its substantive meaning as relates to the utilization of non-professional personnel in family planning clinics serving low income neighborhoods. M.S. thesis: Mississippi State University, State College: Mississippi.

Beasley, Joseph D. 1964. The design of preliminary studies necessary for the initiation of a family planning program for Orleans Parish, Louisiana. M.P.H. thesis: Tulane University, New Orleans.

———. 1967a. Benefits of family planning to family health. Teaching Family Planning in Medical Schools, *Proceedings of the 4th Annual Macy Conference.* Ann Arbor: University of Michigan. Josiah Macy Jr. Foundation. Reprinted in McCalister, Thiessen, and McDermott, *Readings in Family Planning,* pp. 51–60.

———. 1967b. The United States: The Orleans Parish Family Planning Demonstration Program (New Orleans, Louisiana). *Studies in Family Planning* 11(25):5–9.

———. 1969a. The community aspects of family planning: A medical educator's point of view. *Journal of Medical Education* 44(2):98–103.

———. 1969b. View from Louisiana. *Family Planning Perspectives* 1(1):2–15. Reprinted in *The Survival Equation: Man, Resources and his Environment,* edited by Roger Revelle, A. Khosla, and M. Vinovskis. Boston: Houghton-Mifflin.

———. 1972. Overcoming resistance to family planning. *Journal of Medical Gynecology and Sociology* 6(6):19–28.

———. 1973. Lectures on public policy at Harvard University. Unpublished manuscript on file, Littauer Library, Harvard University, Cambridge, Massachusetts.

Beasley, Joseph D., Elizabeth Bennett, Ralph Frankowski, and C. Morton Hawkins. 1968. *Louisiana Family Planning Program and Procedures Manual.* New Orleans: Louisiana Family Planning Program, Inc.

Beasley, Joseph D., Thomas Durel, and May Wells Jones. 1973. Community health programming: Medical media for the people. *Biomedical Communications* 1(2):18–39. Reprinted in *Nursing Digest,* September 1973, pp. 28–32.

Beasley, Joseph D., and Ralph F. Frankowski. 1970. Utilization of a family planning program by the poor population of a metropolitan area. *Milbank Memorial Fund Quarterly* 48:241–281.

Beasley, Joseph D., Ralph F. Frankowski, and C. Morton Hawkins. 1969. The Orleans Parish Family Planning Demonstration Program: A description of the first year. *Milbank Memorial Fund Quarterly* 47:225–253.

———. 1971. Evaluation of national health programs: Louisiana family planning. *American Journal of Public Health* 61:1812–1825.

Beasley, Joseph D., and Carl L. Harter. 1967. Introducing family planning clinics to Louisiana. *Children* 14(5):188–192.

Beasley, Joseph D., Carl L. Harter, and Ann Fischer. 1966. Attitudes and knowledge relevant to family planning among New Orleans Negro women. *American Journal of Public Health* 56(11):1847–1857.

Beasley, Joseph D., Carl L. Harter, and Donald V. McCalister. 1966. Aspects of family planning among low-income, "high risk" mothers. *Advances in Planned Parenthood,* vol. 2. International Congress Series, no. 138, pp. 197–204. New York: Excerpta Medica Foundation.

Beasley, Joseph D., and Vestal W. Parrish, Jr. 1967. A progress report on a Southern rural family planning research program conducted in Lincoln Parish, Louisiana. Advances in Planned Parenthood, *Proceedings of the Excerpta Medica Foundation,* vol. 3, pp. 29–36. New York.

———. 1969. Family planning and the reduction of fertility and illegitimacy: A preliminary report on a rural Southern program. *Social Biology* 16(3):167–178.

Beasley, Joseph D., and John P. Wells. 1971. Louisiana: Developing and managing a statewide family planning program. *Family Planning Perspectives* 3(4):68–79.

Bechtel Corporation. 1971. Masterplan for Satellite Clinics for New Orleans. New Orleans: New Orleans Area Health Planning Council (prepared for Louisiana Family Health, Inc.).

Bennett, Elizabeth A. 1972. The Determination of Perceived Educational Needs of Nurses Employed in Maternal Health and Family Planning Services. Ed.D. dissertation: University of Southern Mississippi, Hattiesburg.

Black, Timothy. 1972. Ten institutional obstacles to advances in family planning. *New Concepts in Contraception,* edited by Malcolm Potts and Clive Wood, pp. 43–55. Baltimore: University Park Press.

Blake, Judith. 1969. Population policy for Americans: Is the government being misled? *Science* 164:522–529.

Blumenthal, J. B., Susan R. Andrews, and Gerald Wiener. 1976. Five-year summary of the New Orleans Parent-Child Development Center, grant no. DHEW-90-C-381. Washington, D.C.: Office of Child Development (ERIC Document Reproduction Service no. ED 211-237).

Bobo, James R. 1975. *The New Orleans Economy: Pro Bono Publico?* New Orleans: Division of Business and Economic Research, College of Business Administration, University of New Orleans.

Bogue, Donald J. 1970. *Family Planning Improvement through Evaluation.* Chicago: Community and Family Studies Center, University of Chicago.

Brandon, Elizabeth. 1976. Folk medicine in French Louisiana. In *American Folk Medicine,* edited by Wayland D. Hand, pp. 215–234. Berkeley: University of California Press.

Britanak, Rose A. 1972. A study of the dynamic role of registered nurses in a family planning clinic. D.P.H. dissertation: Tulane University, New Orleans.

Chandler, David. 1974a. He sought to solve the world's population problem. They call him an enemy of the people. *Southern Voices* 1(4):66–71.

——. 1974b. The people vs. Family Health. *Washington Post,* October 20, Section C-3.

Club of Rome. 1972. *Limits to Growth.* New York: Universe Books.

Commoner, Barry. 1971. *The Closing Circle: Man, Nature, and Technology.* New York: Knopf.

Cook, William D. 1971. The demand for contraceptive information, goods and services: An analysis of the Orleans Parish Family Planning Program. Ph.D. dissertation: University of Chicago.

Correa, Hector, and Joseph D. Beasley. 1971. Mathematical model for decision making in population and family planning. *American Journal of Public Health* 1:138–151.

——. 1974. A model for personnel planning and administration in a family planning program. *Public Health Briefs* 64(11):1095–1096.

Correa, Hector, Vestal W. Parrish, and Joseph D. Beasley. 1972. A three-year longitudinal evaluation of the costs of a family planning program. *American Journal of Public Health* 62(12):1647–1657.

Coyle, Joseph T. 1968. Family planning and the worth of a child. *Tulanian,* May, pp. 10–19. New Orleans: Tulane University.

Davis, Karen, and Cathy Schoen. 1978. *Health and the War on Poverty: A Ten-Year Appraisal.* Washington, D.C.: Brookings Institution.

Davis, Kingsley. 1967. Population policy: Will current programs succeed? *Science* 158:730–739.

Dent, Tom. 1979. New Orleans versus Atlanta. *Southern Exposure* 7(1):64–68.

Dickey, Richard P. 1976. Lowering infant mortality—the obstetrical problems. Paper presented to the Louisiana State Medical Society Educational and Research Foundation Committee on Pediatric and Adolescent Health, Shreveport. Mimeo.

Dienes, C. Thomas. 1972. *Law, Politics and Birth Control.* Urbana: University of Illinois Press.

Djerassi, Carl. 1979. *The Politics of Contraception.* New York: Norton.

Djukanovic, V., and E. Mach, eds. 1975. *Alternative Approaches to Meeting Basic Health Needs in Developing Countries: A Joint UNICEF-WHO Study.* Geneva: World Health Organization.

Dott, Andrew B., and Arthur T. Fort. 1975a. The effect of maternal demographic factors on infant mortality rates. Summary of the Findings of the Louisiana Infant Mortality Study, Part I. *American Journal of Obstetrics and Gynecology* 123:847–853.

——— . 1975b. The effect of availability and utilization of prenatal care and hospital services on infant mortality rates. Summary of the Findings of the Louisiana Infant Mortality Study, Part II. *American Journal of Obstetrics and Gynecology* 123:854–860.

——— . 1976. Medical and social factors affecting early teenage pregnancy: A literature review and summary of findings of the Louisiana Infant Mortality Study. *American Journal of Obstetrics and Gynecology* 125(4):532–536.

Dryfoos, Joy G. 1976. The United States National Family Planning Program, 1968–1974. *Studies in Family Planning* 7(3):80–92.

Dunbar, Sam B. 1973. A general conceptual model of consumer behavior for family planning clients in Orleans Parish. M.S. thesis: Louisiana State University, Baton Rouge.

El-Ansary, Adel I., and Oscar E. Kramer, Jr. 1973. Social marketing: The family planning experience. *Journal of Marketing* 37:1–7.

Ehrlich, Paul. 1968. *The Population Bomb.* New York: Ballantine.

Etheridge, Elizabeth. 1972. *The Butterfly Caste: A Social History of Pellegra in the South.* Westport, Conn.: Greenwood.

Ettling, John. 1981. *The Germ of Laziness: Rockefeller Philanthropy and Public Health in the New South.* Cambridge, Mass.: Harvard University Press.

Family Health Foundation. 1973. *A Funding Request Submitted to the Department of Health, Education and Welfare, the Louisiana Family Planning Program.* New Orleans, Louisiana, September 10, 1973.

——— . 1974a. Quarterly Report. New Orleans: Louisiana Family Planning Program. Mimeo.

——— . 1974b. Written works of the faculty and staff (published and unpublished) of the Family Health Foundation; prepared by the Education Materials Center,

Tulane University. On file, Tulane University Medical School Library, New Orleans.

Family Health Research Group. 1971. Statistical Analysis of the Louisiana Family Planning Program, 1967–1971. Pub. no. 1, December 2, New Orleans. Mimeo.

————. 1973. Recent trends in Louisiana fertility. Second revision, January 5, New Orleans. Mimeo.

Fendall, N.R.E. 1972. *Auxiliaries in Health Care: Programs in Developing Countries.* Baltimore: Johns Hopkins University Press.

Fischer, Ann, Joseph D. Beasley, and Carl L. Harter. 1968. The occurrence of the extended family at the origin of the family of procreation: A developmental approach to Negro family structure. *Journal of Marriage and the Family* 30:290–300.

Fischer, Ann, and Virginia Ktsanes. 1971. Pregnant teenagers: A study of some who marry and some who do not. New Orleans: Louisiana Family Planning Program. Unpublished paper.

————. n.d. Family structure through two generations. Unpublished paper.

Fowle, Farnsworth. 1968. Human science of family planning. *Rockefeller Fund Quarterly,* no. 2.

Freedman, Ben. n.d. Statistics are neutral, but people . . . ? Report to Louisiana State Health and Social and Rehabilitation Services Administration. Mimeo.

Freedman, Ronald, Pascal K. Whelpton, and Arthur A. Campbell. 1959. *Family Planning, Fertility and Population Growth.* New York: McGraw-Hill.

Fryer, Peter. 1965. *The Birth Controllers.* London: Seeker and Warburg.

Gettys, James O., E. H. Atkins, and Charles C. Mary, Jr. 1974. A review of Family Health's latest evaluation of the demographic impact of the Louisiana Family Planning Program. *Journal of the Louisiana State Medical Society* 126(3):81–88.

Gettys, James O., Ben Freedman, and Ramson Vidrine. 1973a. The Louisiana Family Planning Program: An analysis of a statistical analysis. *Journal of the Louisiana State Medical Society* 125(3):77–83.

————. 1973b. The Louisiana Health and Social and Rehabilitative Services Administration replies. *Journal of the Louisiana State Medical Society* 125(5):173.

Gordon, Arthur. 1970. Louisiana's quiet revolution in family planning. *Today's Health* 48:38–41. Excerpted in *Reader's Digest,* January 1970, pp. 2–6.

Gordon, Linda. 1976. *Women's Body, Women's Rights: A Social History of Birth Control in America.* New York: Viking Press.

Grayson, W. Paul. 1981. The folklore of a medical community. *Louisiana Folklore Miscellany* 5(1):48–52.

Gulf South Research Institute. 1968. *A Study of the Louisiana Charity Hospital System* (prepared for the State of Louisiana).

Hardin, Garrett. 1969. *Population, Evolution and Birth Control: A Collage of Controversial Ideas.* 2d ed. San Francisco: Freeman.

Harkavy, Oscar, Frederick Jaffe, and Samuel M. Wishik. 1969. Family planning and public policy: Who is misleading whom? *Science* 165:367–373.

Harter, Carl L. 1966. Rationality in procreation and differential fertility. Ph.D. dissertation: Tulane University, New Orleans.

———. 1968a. Male fertility in New Orleans. *Demography.* 5:61–78.

———. 1968b. Rationality types in procreating: A typology for examining differential fertility. *Bulletin of the Tulane University Medical Faculty* 27(1):69–75.

———. 1970. The fertility of sterile and subfecund women in New Orleans. *Social Biology* 17:195–206.

Harter, Carl L., and Joseph D. Beasley. 1967. A survey concerning induced abortions in New Orleans. *American Journal of Public Health* 57(11):1847–1848.

Harter, Carl L., Virginia Ktsanes, Ann Fischer, and Joseph D. Beasley. 1965. *Family Survey of Metropolitan New Orleans: Instructional Manual.* On file, Tulane University Medical School Library. Mimeo.

Harter, Carl L., and Vestal W. Parrish, Jr. 1968. Maternal preference of socialization agent for sex education. *Journal of Marriage and the Family* 30:418–426.

Harter, Carl L., and Janice R. Roussel. 1969. The fertility of white females in New Orleans: A comparison of Protestants and parochial and secular-educated Catholics. *Milbank Memorial Fund Quarterly* 47(1):39–53.

Hawkins, C. Morton. 1969. A stochastic description of oral contraceptive usage. D.Sc. dissertation: Tulane University, New Orleans.

Heartwell, Stephen. 1972. A computer simulation model of a multi-state, multi-channel family planning outpatient system. D.P.H. dissertation: Tulane University, New Orleans.

Hellman, Louis M. 1971. Family planning comes of age. *American Journal of Obstetrics and Gynecology* 109(2):214–224.

Hendricks, Charles H. 1967. Delivery patterns and reproductive efficiency among groups of differing socio-economic status and ethnic origins. *American Journal of Obstetrics and Gynecology* 95:608–694.

Himes, Norman E. 1970. *Medical History of Contraception.* New York: Schocken (first published by Williams and Wilkins, Baltimore, 1936).

Holmes, Helen, Betty Hoskins, and Michael Gross. 1980. *Birth Control and Controlling Birth: Women-Centered Perspectives.* Clifton, N.J.: Humana Press.

Hougen, Lee R. 1974. An analysis of the cost effectiveness of training family planning clinic staff with prepared instructional materials in sites with and without trainers. M.P.H. thesis: Tulane University, New Orleans.

Hyatt Medical Management Services. 1980. *Current and Future Roles of the Charity Hospital System of Louisiana.* On file, University of New Orleans, Louisiana Collection.

Jaffe, Frederick S. 1969. Family planning in public assistance: What the federal regulations say and how to use them. *Family Planning Perspectives* 1(1):25–28.

———. 1973. Public policy on fertility control. *Scientific American* 229(1):17–23.

Jaffe, Frederick, Joy G. Dryfoos, and Marsha Corey. 1973. Organized family planning programs in the United States, 1968–1972. *Family Planning Perspectives* 5(2):73–79.

Jaffe, Frederick, and Steven Polgar. 1968. Family planning and public policy: Is the "culture of poverty" the new cop-out? *Journal of Marriage and the Family* 30:228–235.

Kahn, Rose. 1967. City's first family planning center to open June 26, *States-Item*, June 6; Lincoln Parish leads way for New Orleans family planning center, *States-Item*, June 7; High-risk mothers factor in state's infant mortality, *States-Item*, June 8; Family planning center, *States-Item*, June 9.

Kelso, Louis O., Inc. 1974. *Response of the Family Health Foundation to the Department of Health, Education and Welfare Audit.* New Orleans: Family Health Foundation, March 13, 1974.

Kennedy, David. 1970. *Birth Control in America: The Career of Margaret Sanger.* New Haven: Yale University Press.

Krause, Eliot A. 1977. *Power and Illness: The Political Sociology of Health and Medical Care.* New York: Elsevier.

Ktsanes, Virginia K. 1977. Assessment of contraception by teenagers: Final report on contract no. 1-HO-52833, National Institute of Child Health and Human Development.

———. 1980. The teenager and the family planning experience. In *Adolescent Pregnancy and Childbearing: Findings from Research*, edited by Catherine S. Chilman. Department of Health and Human Services, NIH pub. no. 81-2077, pp. 83–100. Washington, D.C.: Government Printing Office.

Lackey, Carolyn. 1978. Pica: A nutritional anthropology concern. In *The Anthropology of Health*, edited by Eleonor E. Bauwens. St. Louis: Mosby.

Landman, Lynn. 1968. United States, underdeveloped land in family planning. *Journal of Marriage and the Family* 30(2):191–201.

Lantum, Daniel N. 1970. To plan and design a family health program that can be integrated into the existing health services of Cameroon in 1970. D.P.H. dissertation: Tulane University, New Orleans.

Lelyveld, Joseph. 1970. Will we say "it just happened," when the world overpopulates itself to extinction? *New York Times*, July 19, 1970. Reprinted by Planned Parenthood–World Population, New York, 1970.

Lennox, Robert H., Rodney C. Jung, Joseph D. Beasley, and Verda D. Gray. 1964. A study to describe the characteristics of deaths associated with childbirth in metropolitan New Orleans and subsequently in the state of Louisiana: Instruction manual, Part 1. New Orleans: Maternal and Child Health Section, Department of Tropical Medicine and Public Health, Tulane University.

Levitan, Sar A. 1969. *The Great Society's Poor Law.* Baltimore: Johns Hopkins University Press.

Lipscomb, Nell I. 1969. Casework and family planning. *Social Casework* 50:204–209.

Littlewood, Thomas B. 1977. *The Politics of Population Control.* Notre Dame, Ind.: Notre Dame University Press.

Louisiana, Department of Health and Human Resources. 1980. Options for the Future of New Orleans Charity Hospital. Baton Rouge: Department of Health and Human Resources. Mimeo.

Louisiana, Division of Policy Planning and Evaluation. 1981. *A Benefit-Cost Analysis of the Family Planning Program of the Office of Health Services and*

Environmental Control. Project no. DPPE 81-03-04, pp. 1–61. Baton Rouge: Department of Health and Human Resources.

Louisiana, Health and Social and Rehabilitation Services, Division of Tabulation and Analysis. 1973. Report to the Medical Advisory Committee for Family Planning Services in Louisiana, Part I: Some Observations and Questions. New Orleans: Medical Advisory Committee. Mimeo.

Louisiana, State Legislature. 1965. Baton Rouge: Public Affairs Research Council. Unpublished report.

Luber, Tyana P. 1974. Sexuality of nurses: Correlations of knowledge, attitudes and behavior. Dissertation: Tulane University, New Orleans.

Mackintosh, Douglas R. 1975. How Family Health Foundation was Mau-Maued. *New Orleans* 9(8):45ff.

————. 1978. *Systems of Health Care.* Westview Special Studies in Health Care. Boulder, Colo.: Westview.

Mather, Frances Jean. 1975. A macrosimulation model of human fertility in a population with three contraceptive levels. Ph.D. dissertation: Tulane University, New Orleans.

Maultsby, Don M. 1971. Conjugal role structure, joint action and contraceptive adoption. Ph.D. dissertation: Tulane University, New Orleans.

McCalister, Donald V., C. Morton Hawkins, and Joseph D. Beasley. 1970. Projected effects of family planning on the incidence of perinatal mortality in a lower class non-white population. *American Journal of Obstetrics and Gynecology* 106:573–580.

McCalister, Donald V., Charles T. McGee, Theresa Forti, and C. Morton Hawkins. 1969. Family planning and the reduction of pregnancy loss rates. *Journal of Marriage and the Family* 31:668–673.

McCalister, Donald V., and Victor Thiessen. 1970. Prediction of the adoption and continued use of contraception. *American Journal of Public Health* 60(8):1372–1381.

McCalister, Donald V., Victor Theissen, and Margaret McDermott. 1973. *Readings in Family Planning: A Challenge to the Health Professions.* St. Louis: Mosby.

McClain, Carol. 1981. Traditional midwives and family planning: An assessment of programs and suggestions for the future. *Medical Anthropology* 5(1):107–136.

McCoy, Kenneth D., Jr. 1963. Constitutionality of state statutes prohibiting the dissemination of birth control information. *Louisiana Law Review* 23:773–778.

Medical World News. 1975. How Dr. Beasley's success story soured: Scandals in birth control empire led to conviction. April 21, no. 16, pp. 26–28.

Model Cities Agency. 1970–1972. Comprehensive Demonstration Plan for New Orleans. 3 vols. Mimeo.

Moore, Frank I. 1968. A model for the selection of indigenous personnel for family planning clinics in low income neighborhoods. Ph.D. dissertation: University of Oklahoma, Norman.

Moore, Frank I., Penelope Ballinger, and Joseph D. Beasley. 1974. Influence of postpartum home visits on postpartum clinic attendance. *Public Health Reports* 89(4):360–364.

Moynihan, Daniel Patrick, Paul Barton, and Ellen Broderick. 1965. *The Negro Family: The Case for National Action*. Washington, D.C.: Department of Labor.

Murray, Robert F. 1977. The ethical and moral values of black Americans. In *Population Policy and Ethics: The American Experience*, edited by Robert M. Veatch. New York: Irvington.

New Orleans Area/Bayou-River Health Systems Agency. 1980. Health Systems Plan. Mimeo.

New Orleans Department of Health. 1968. Survey of the New Orleans Department of Health. Mimeo.

Noonan, John T. 1965. *Contraception: A History of Its Treatment by the Catholic Theologians and Canonists*. Cambridge, Mass.: Belknap Press of Harvard University Press.

O'Connor, Stella. 1948. The Charity Hospital of New Orleans: An administrative and financial history, 1789–1941. *Louisiana Historical Quarterly* 31(1):5–109.

Onel, Aydin. 1972. Family health delivery system: Model for Burdur, Turkey. D.P.H. dissertation: Tulane University, New Orleans.

Owens, Beth. 1985. Abortion clinics, patients attacked. *Planned Parenthood Review* 5, no. 2, pp. 16–17.

Parrish, Vestal W., Jr. 1969. Attitudes toward maternal employment: An influence on desired family size in a Southern semi-rural county. Ph.D. dissertation: Tulane University, New Orleans.

——. 1973. Development of a community-focused family planning program: Agency and interpersonal relations. In *Readings in Family Planning: A Challenge to the Health Professions*, edited by Donald V. McCalister et al., pp. 237–245. St. Louis: Mosby.

Parrish, Vestal W., Jr., Jill Kaplan, Carl L. Harter, and Joseph D. Beasley. 1965. Family survey of Lincoln Parish: Instruction manual. On file, Tulane University Medical School Library, New Orleans. Mimeo.

Petersen, William. 1981. American efforts to reduce the fertility of less developed countries. In *Fertility Decline in the Less Developed Countries*, edited by N. Eberstadt, pp. 337–347. New York: Praeger.

Platou, Ralph V., Robert H. Lennox, and Joseph D. Beasley. 1964. Battering. *Tulane Medical Bulletin* 23(3):157–165.

Polgar, Steven. 1966. U.S.: The PPFA Mobile Service Project in New York City. *Studies in Family Planning* 15:9–15.

——. 1972. Population history and population policies from an anthropological perspective. *Current Anthropology* 13(2):203–211.

——. 1975. Birth planning: between neglect and coercion. In *Topias and Utopias in Health: Policy Studies*, edited by Stanley R. Ingman and Anthony E. Thomas, pp. 21–46. The Hague: Mouton.

Rainwater, Lee. 1960. *And the Poor Get Children*. Chicago: Quadrangle Books.

Rainwater, Lee, and William Yancey. 1967. *The Moynihan Report and the Politics of Controversy*. Cambridge, Mass.: MIT Press.

Reed, James. 1978. *From Private Vice to Public Virtue: The Birth Control Movement and American Society since 1830*. New York: Basic Books.

Reynolds, Jack. 1972. Evaluation of family planning program performance: A critical review. *Demography* 9(1):69–86.

Rock, John. 1963. *The Time Has Come: A Catholic Doctor's Proposals to End the Battle over Birth Control.* New York: Knopf.

Rosoff, Jeannie. 1969. View from Washington: Reorganization, consolidation or both. *Family Planning Perspectives* 1(1):18–24.

Sanger, Margaret. 1928. *Motherhood in Bondage.* New York: Brentano.

————. 1931. *My Fight for Birth Control.* New York: Norton.

————. 1938. *Margaret Sanger: An Autobiography.* New York: Norton.

Scofield, Leslie C., Jr. 1970. A proposal for a rural health auxiliary training program applicable to rural Brazil. D.P.H. dissertation: Tulane University, New Orleans.

Sear, Alan M. 1973. Clinic discontinuation and contraceptive need. *Family Planning Perspectives* 5(2):80–88.

Serfling, R. E., and F. J. Mather. 1973. The Family Health Foundation replies. *Journal of the Louisiana State Medical Society* 125(5):171.

Shapiro, Sam, Edward R. Schlesinger, and Robert E. Nesbitt, Jr. 1968. *Infant, Perinatal, Maternal and Childhood Mortality in the United States.* Cambridge, Mass.: Harvard University Press.

Signs: Journal of Women in Culture and Society. 1984. "Special Issues: Women and Poverty." No. 10. Winter.

Sorensen, Robert C. 1973. *Adolescent Sexuality in Contemporary America.* New York: World Publishing Company.

Southern Exposure. 1978. Sick for justice: Health care and unhealthy conditions, vol. 6, no. 2.

Stack, Carol. 1974. *All Our Kin: Strategies for Survival in a Black Community.* New York: Harper and Row.

Stycos, J. Mayone. 1977. Some minority opinions on birth control. In *Population Policy and Ethics: The American Experience,* edited by Robert M. Veatch. New York: Irvington.

Trahant, Yvette. 1981. The oral tradition of the physician. *Louisiana Folklore Miscellany* 5(1):38–47.

U.S. Commission on Population Growth and the American Future. 1972. *Population and the American Future: The Report of the Commission.* Washington, D.C.: Government Printing Office.

U.S. Comptroller General. 1975. *Improving Federally Assisted Family Planning Programs—A Case Study Showing Need for Additional Improvements.* Report to the Congress, April 15, 1975. Washington, D.C.: Government Printing Office, pp. 1–62.

U.S. Congress, House, Committee on Appropriations. 1969. *Department of Labor and Health, Education and Welfare FY '70 Appropriations.* Hearings before Subcommittee of Committee on Appropriations, FY '70. HR 13111, 91st Cong., 1st Sess. Relevant testimony, pp. 462–470 and pp. 522–527.

————. 1970. *Department of Labor and Health, Education and Welfare, Appropriations Bill FY '71.* Hearings before the Committee on Appropriations. HR 18515, 91st Cong., 2d Sess. Relevant testimony, pp. 296–317.

————. 1972. *HEW Family Planning Services and Population Research Program.* Hearings before Committee on Appropriations for Department of Labor and

Department of Health, Education and Welfare and Related Agencies, FY '73. HR 15417, 92d Cong., 2d Sess. Relevant testimony, pp. 4951–4965.

———. 1973. *Population, Health and Nutrition Programs Report*. Hearings before Subcommittee of Committee on Appropriations, FY'74, 93d Cong., 1st Sess. Family Health Foundation Report, pp. 1636–1690.

U.S. Congress, House, Committee on Interstate and Foreign Commerce. 1970. *Family Planning Services*. Hearings before the Subcommittee on Public Health and Welfare of the Inter-State and Foreign Commerce Committee. 91st Cong., 2d Sess. Relevant testimony, pp. 329–344.

U.S. Congress, House, Committee on Ways and Means. 1967. *President's Proposals for Revision in the Social Security System*, Hearings for the Committee on Ways and Means. HR 5710, 90th Cong., 1st Sess., pp. 1508ff.

———. 1969. *Social Security and Welfare Proposals. Part 3*. Hearings before Committee on Ways and Means. 91st Cong., 1st Sess. Relevant testimony, pp. 921–944.

U.S. Congress, Senate, Committee on Appropriations. 1967. *Appropriations for the National Institute of Child Health and Human Development, National Institutes of Health*. Hearings before Committee on Appropriations. 90th Cong., 1st Sess.

———. 1969. *Department of Labor and Health, Education and Welfare*. Hearings before Subcommittee of Committee on Appropriations, FY '70. HR 13111, 91st Cong., 1st Sess. Relevant testimony, pp. 462–470.

U.S. Congress, Senate, Committee on Finance. 1973. *Social Service Regulations, Part II: Hearings* before the Committee on Finance. 93d Cong., 1st Sess. Relevant testimony, pp. 375–387.

U.S. Congress, Senate, Committee on Foreign Aid Expenditures. 1965. *Population Crisis*. Hearings on S. 1676 before the Committee on Foreign Aid Expenditures of the Committee on Government Operation. 89th Cong., 1st Sess.

———. 1966. *Population Crisis, Part II: Family Planning Information Dissemination and Foreign Assistance Programs Reorganization*. 89th Cong., 2d Sess., pp. 474–494.

———. 1967. *Population Crisis, Part III*. 90th Cong., 1st Sess.

U.S. Congress, Senate, Committee on Labor and Public Welfare. 1966. *The Growth of the U.S. Population*. Hearings on S. 2993 Family Planning Programs before the Subcommittee on Employment, Manpower and Poverty of the Committee on Labor and Public Welfare. 89th Cong., 2d Sess.

———. 1973. *Quality of Health Care—Human Experimentation*. Hearings before Subcommittee on Health of the Committee on Labor and Public Welfare. Part 4. 93d Cong., 1st Sess., April–July. Forced sterilization.

U.S. Department of Health, Education and Welfare (DHEW). 1966. *Report on Family Planning: Activities of DHEW in Family Planning, Fertility, Sterility and Population Dynamics*. Washington, D.C.: Government Printing Office, pp. 1–35.

———. 1968. *Family Planning: Nationwide Opportunities for Action*. Washington, D.C.: Government Printing Office, pp. 1–40.

———. 1973. Audit of the Family Health Foundation. Mimeo. pp. 1–115.

U.S. General Accounting Office (GAO). 1975. *Improving Federally Assisted Family Planning Programs, DHEW.* Washington, D.C.: Government Printing Office, April 15.

U.S. *News and World Report.* 1969. Family planning campaign: The Louisiana story. July 28, 1969, pp. 55–57.

————. 1973. Subsidized birth control: Controversial but spreading. September 10, 1973, pp. 33–35.

U.S. Office of Economic Opportunity. 1968. *Need for Subsidized Family Planning Services: United States, Each State and County.* Prepared by Planned Parenthood–World Population, Center for Family Planning Program Development.

Varky, G., Frederick Jaffe, Steven Polgar, and Richard Lincoln. 1967. *Five Million Women—Who's Who among Americans in Need of Subsidized Family Planning Services.* New York: Planned Parenthood–World Population.

Ward, Martha C. 1971. *Them Children: A Study in Language Learning.* New York: Holt, Rinehart and Winston.

Weinberger, Casper. 1974. Population and family planning. *Family Planning Perspectives* 6(3):170–172.

Weisbord, R. G. 1973. Birth control and the black American: A matter of genocide. *Demography* 10(4):571–590.

Wells, John P. 1972. *An analysis of the organization and management of a developing state-wide family planning program.* Unpublished D.P.H. dissertation: Tulane University, New Orleans.

Westoff, Charles F., and Norman B. Ryder. 1970. Contraceptive practices among urban blacks in the United States, 1965. *Milbank Memorial Fund Quarterly* 48(2):215–233.

Westoff, Leslie A., and Charles F. Westoff. 1971. *From Now to Zero: Fertility, Contraception and Abortion in America.* Boston: Little, Brown and Co.

Whelpton, P. K., A. A. Campbell, and J. E. Patterson. 1966. *Fertility and Family Planning in the United States.* Princeton, N.J.: Princeton University Press.

Willson, Peters D. 1985. International family planning controversy broadens. *Planned Parenthood Review* 5, no. 2:31–33.

Wilson, Kathy. 1985. Anti-abortion movement threatens liberty. *Planned Parenthood Review* 5, no. 2:4–6.

Wolfe, Tom. 1970. *Radical Chic and Mau-Mauing the Flak Catchers.* New York: Farrar, Strauss and Giroux.

Appendix A

Estimated Federal Funding to
Family Health Foundation, January 1967 Through April 1974

Programs and Legislative Authorizations	*Amounts*
Louisiana Family Planning Program	
Title II—Economic Opportunity Act	$7,496,515
Title IV-A—Social Security Act	14,464,465
Title V—Social Security Act	11,112,085
Title X—Public Health Service Act	7,389,374
Total	$40,462,439
Neighborhood Health Clinics Program	
Title I—Demonstration Clinics and Metropolitan	
Development Act	$6,585,173
Title XVIII—Social Security Act	4,171
Title XIX—Social Security Act	835,715
Total	$7,425,059
International Program	
Title X—Foreign Assistance Act	$1,543,091
Parent-Child Development Program	
Title II—Economic Opportunity Act	$1,772,347
Research, Development and Training Program	
Title II—Economic Opportunity Act	$604,585
Title V—Social Security Act	993,392
Title III—Public Health Service Act	6,783
Title X—Public Health Service Act	360,312
Other—Department of Labor (Legislative authorization	
cannot be determined)	415,140
Total	$2,380,212
Grand Total	$53,583,168

Federal Funding Agencies
Department of Housing and Urban Development (HUD)
Department of State—Agency for International Development (AID)
Department of Health, Education and Welfare (HEW)
    National Institutes of Health (NIH)
    Social and Rehabilitative Services (SRS)
    Social Security Administration (SSA)
    Health Services Administration (HSA)
    Office of Child Development (OCD)
    Office of Economic Opportunity (OEO)
Department of Labor

Intermediary Funding Agencies
 1. City of New Orleans
 2. A city health corporation
 3. State of Louisiana
 4. A commercial insurance company
 5. A private university
 6. Community Action Agency (CAA) for Bossier and Caddo Parishes (the Shreveport area)
 7. Community Action Agency (CAA) for East Baton Rouge Parish
 8. Community Action Agency (CAA) for central part of state
 9. Community Action Agency for Orleans Parish
10. Community Action Agency for Webster Parish
11. Community Action Agency for Tangipahoa and other parishes
12. A private foundation

Source: U.S. Comptroller General, *Improving Federally Assisted Family Planning Programs—A Case Study Showing Need for Additional Improvements,* report to the Congress, April 15, 1975. Washington, D.C.: Government Printing Office, pp. 2–5.

Appendix B

Medical Services Offered by
the Louisiana Family Planning Program

A. *Medical History.* A comprehensive health history will be obtained and recorded in the patient's record. The history will include, but not be limited to

1. Data required by the National Center for Health Statistics.
2. Data required by the Federal Program funding the project (National Center for Family Planning Services).
3. Complete obstetrical history including menarche, menstrual history, last menstrual period, gravity, parity, pregnancy outcomes (number of abortions, premature and full-term births, stillbirths, neonatal deaths, and living children), and complications of any pregnancy and/or delivery.
4. Any significant illnesses, hospitalizations, and previous medical care and the indicated systems review, e.g., cardiovascular, renal, neurologic, hepatic, endocrine, hematologic, gynecologic (dysmenorrhea, metrorrhagia, menorrhagia, postcoital bleeding, vaginal discharge, dyspareunia), and venereal disease.
5. Problems relating to previous contraceptive use.
6. The following specific diseases:
   a. Thromboembolic diseases.
   b. Hepato-renal disease.
   c. Breast and genital neoplasm.
   d. Diabetic and prediabetic conditions.
   e. Cephalgia and migraine.
   f. Hematologic phenomena.
   g. Pelvic inflammatory disease.
7. Relevant family health history, e.g., significant recurrent chronic illnesses, genetic aberrations, and unusual health factors among family members.
8. Relevant psychiatric history, including previous history of mental depression.

B. *Contraceptive Information.* The patient will be given a review of contraceptive methods and their implications including

1. Instruction on basic reproductive anatomy and physiology.

175

2. Overview of methods of contraception available—including reversible (oral, IUD, diaphragm, foam, condom, and rhythm) and irreversible (tubal ligation, vasectomy) with regard to
   a. Relative effectiveness.
   b. Common side effects.
   c. Difficulty in usage.
3. Basic information concerning venereal disease.

C. *Physical Examination.* The patient will be given an initial physical examination including, but not limited to

1. Thyroid palpation.
2. Inspection and palpation of breast and axillary glands with instruction to the patient for self-examination.
3. Auscultation of heart.
4. Auscultation of lungs in any patient with respiratory symptoms.
5. Blood pressure.
6. Weight and height.
7. Abdominal examination.
8. Pelvic, including speculum, bimanual, and rectovaginal examinations.
9. Extremities.
10. Other, as indicated (based on history and previous medical record).

D. *Laboratory Services.* Initial laboratory services will be offered and provided as follows:

1. Mandatory services
   a. Hematocrit or hemoglobin.
   b. Urinalysis for sugar and protein.
   c. Papanicolaou smears.
   d. Culture for N. gonorrhea (patients with positive results should be recultured for test of cure in 7–14 days).
   e. Serology for syphilis.
   f. Pregnancy testing as indicated.
2. Optional laboratory and screening procedures
   a. Vaginal smears and wet mounts for diagnosis of vaginal infection.
   b. Microscopic analysis and culture of urine as indicated.
   c. Sickle cell screening as indicated. (The incidence of this disease is most significant among, but not limited to, blacks. Where sickle cell screening is carried out, provisions for hemoglobin electrophoresis and counseling for those with positive screening tests must be made available within the project or by referral.)
   d. Hemaglutination tests for rubella when indicated.
   e. Two-hour postprandial blood glucose for women receiving oral contraceptives who have a positive family history of diabetes mellitus or have had glycosuria in the third trimester of pregnancy.

E. *Prescription of Contraceptive Method.* The prescription of contraceptive method shall be according to the patient's choice, except where such choice is in conflict with sound medical practice. Factors to be considered in prescribing (by method):

1. Oral contraceptives to patients with no history of following:
   a. Physical or historical evidence of thrombophlebitis or pulmonary embolism.
   b. Liver dysfunction or disease (hepatitis or mononucleosis).
   c. Known or suspected carcinoma of the breast or reproductive tract.
   d. Undiagnosed abnormal vaginal or uterine bleeding.
   e. Hypertension.
   f. Convulsive disorders.
   g. Migraine.
   h. Visual problems or neuro-ocular disease.
   i. Diagnosed diabetes mellitus or prediabetes.
   j. Psychiatric depression.
   k. Class 3, 4, or 5 Papanicolaou smears.
2. IUD, except in case of contraindications such as:
   a. Known or suspected uterine pregnancy.
   b. Acute or subacute pelvic inflammatory disease.
   c. History of incapacitating dysmenorrhea or menorrhagia.
   d. Known or suspected cervical or uterine malignancy.
   e. Hypoplasis, stenosis, or distortion of the uterine cavity.
   f. Class 3, 4, or 5 Papanicolaou smears.

F. *Postexamination Interview.* The postexamination interview will include

1. Interpretation of clinical findings to the patient.
2. Instruction in the use of chosen and prescribed method of contraception (preferably both oral and written instructions).
3. Information concerning availability of emergency services.

G. *Contraceptive Follow-up.* Visits and services will be scheduled as follows, according to the method chosen.

1. Oral contraceptive patients will
   a. Return not later than three months after initial prescription and not less frequently than every six months thereafter, at which times the following services should be provided:
      (1) An interim history, including, but not limited to
         (a) Arm or chest pain and shortness of breath.
         (b) Headaches and visual problems.
         (c) Mood changes.
         (d) Leg pain or tenderness.
         (e) Vaginal bleeding and/or discharge.
         (f) VD history.
      (2) An examination of blood pressure and weight.
      (3) Laboratory examination as indicated.

     b. Receive follow-up contact by project personnel if they fail to appear for services as described above.

2. IUD patients will
    a. Return not later than three months following insertion, at which time the following services should be provided:
       (1) An interim history including but not limited to
          (a) Review of abdominal symptoms, vaginal bleeding and/or discharge and fever.
          (b) Other complaints of the patient related to the device.
       (2) An examination including visualization of the cervix.
       (3) Laboratory examinations as indicated.

3. Diaphragm patients will be seen within two to four weeks of initial fitting to confirm that the patient knows how to position the diaphragm correctly, followed by at least annual visits thereafter.

4. Other methods do not require a follow-up visit for medical review or examination prior to the required annual visit.

H. *Annual Visits.* All patients, regardless of contraceptive method chosen, will receive the services described below no less frequently than annually. (Patients failing to return for annual examinations will receive follow-up contact by project personnel and supportive services to facilitate their attendance.)

1. The patient's medical record will be available to the clinician, and an interim health history will be obtained which includes, but is not necessarily limited to
    a. Data required by the National Center for Health Statistics.
    b. Data required by the Federal Program funding the project (National Center for Family Planning Services).
    c. Any significant illnesses, hospitalizations, and medical care incurred since the most recent visit at which a medical history was obtained.
    d. Any indicated systems review, e.g., cardiovascular, renal, neurologic, hepatic, endocrine, hematologic, gynecologic (dysmenorrhea, metrorrhagia, menorrhagia, postcoital bleeding, vaginal discharge, dyspareunia), and venereal disease.

2. The annual physical will include all examinations required for the initial physical.

3. The annual laboratory services provided will include all mandatory initial laboratory services.

4. A postexamination interview should include
    a. Interpretation of the clinical findings to the patient.
    b. Additional instruction as required in the use of the chosen and prescribed method of contraception.
    c. Information concerning availability of emergency services.

I. *Problem Visits.* Patients will be encouraged to return whenever they have specific problems related to the contraceptive method or wish additional guidance or service, including additional supplies.

J. *Treatment of Vaginal Infections.* Vaginal infections will be treated through outpatient therapy.

K. *Treatment of GC.* GC will be treated where supplies for such treatment are not a cost to the project.

L. *Referrals.* Each project will be responsible for referrals (including the patient's acceptance by the service to which they are referred) in the following circumstances even though these services cannot be supported with project funds.

1. Medical problems indicated by history or physical examination.
2. All positive GC cultures and/or serology if not treated within the family planning clinic.
3. Vaginal infections which do not respond to usual outpatient therapy.
4. Patients with abnormal cervical cytology.
5. Patients with positive urine cultures.
6. Patients requiring social casework not appropriately handled by the project personnel.
7. For pregnancy related services when appropriate.
8. Patients suffering from anemia.
9. All infertility cases requiring more extensive workup for diagnosis and/or treatment.

M. *Emergency Services.* LFPP will make provision for handling such emergencies related to contraceptive services when the clinic is not in session. Such provision will include direct payment of the cost of such emergency care in these cases in which no third party is responsible.

N. *Inpatient Services.* LFPP will make provision for inpatient care of patients requiring such care as a result of complications arising from contraceptive services provided by the project. Such provision will include direct payment of the cost of such care in those cases in which no third party is responsible.

O. *Infertility Services.* LFPP will make provision for infertility screening and diagnosis. If these services are provided through referral, the project will make provision for payment. Infertility services will include

1. Complete history and appropriate physical examinations of both partners.
2. GC and serologic testing of both partners.
3. Basal body temperature monitoring.
4. Semen analysis.
5. Cervical mucus examination.
6. Vaginal smear for assessment of estrogen production.
7. Endometrial biopsy.
8. Hysterosal pingogram.

9. Referral for more extensive workup when indicated for diagnosis or treatment without reimbursement by project.

P. *Sterilization Services.* LFPP will provide either directly or by referral voluntary male and female sterilization procedures and counseling for those patients requesting such in accord with the following conditions:

1. The decision for performing sterilization as a family planning procedure is a matter between the patient and physician and must be the voluntary decision of the patient.
2. LFPP will ensure that the patient is provided the necessary information to arrive at an informed decision. Such information should include, but not be limited to
   a. Information concerning the irreversibility of the procedure.
   b. Review of temporary contraceptive methods available.
   c. Information concerning risks involved (complications and failures).
   d. Information and instructions concerning need for follow-up, particularly for males.
   e. Information concerning relative merits of male versus female sterilization in any specific situation.
   f. Information relating to the fact that sterilization does not interfere with sexual function or pleasure.
3. Consideration will be given to the following as contraindications for voluntary sterilization:
   a. The patient has physical, mental, or emotional conditions which could be improved by other treatment.
   b. The patient is suffering from temporary economic difficulties which may improve.
   c. The patient or couple feel that they are not yet ready to assume responsibilities of parenthood.
   d. The patient counts on reversing the operation in the case of change of circumstances such as remarriage or death of children.
4. Written *informed* consent will be obtained from the patient (or in some cases in which the patient is not competent to sign, such consent may be obtained from the appropriate legal guardian or authority) and placed in the patient's record.
5. If the patient is married, written consent of the spouse is desirable. However, there is no legal basis in most states for requiring the consent of a spouse, although many physicians and hospitals request joint consent in the case of married couples. Whenever there is doubt, legal counsel will be obtained for local guidance.
6. All males undergoing vasectomy will be provided appropriate postoperative semen analyses to confirm the absence of sperm. It is suggested that a semen sample be collected at four, six, and twelve weeks for analysis to confirm the absence of sperm.

7. If the provision of sterilization services is accomplished by referral, such provision will include direct payment of the cost of such care in those cases in which no third party is responsible.

Source: Family Health Foundation, *A Funding Request submitted to the Department of Health, Education and Welfare, The Louisiana Family Planning Program,* New Orleans, Louisiana, September 10, 1973.

Index

Abortion, 5, 17–18, 24, 67, 71
  and black militants, 91–93
  Catholic opposition, 29
  clinic referrals for, 29, 58
  contemporary controversies (1980s), 7, 144–145
  federal guidelines, 39
  folk methods, 13–14
  illegal, 5–7, 14–15, 22–23, 53, 58
  legalization, 27, 38, 142
Abused children. *See* Child abuse
Academy of Pediatrics, 45
ADC. *See* Aid to Families with Dependent Children
Adolescent pregnancies, 44, 57, 120
  contemporary controversies (1980s), 140, 142, 145–148
  and family planning objectives, 23, 83–85, 145–148
AFDC. *See* Aid to Families with Dependent Children
Africa, 21, 50
Agency for International Development. *See* U.S. Agency for International Development
AID. *See* U.S. Agency for International Development
Aid to Families with Dependent Children (ADC or AFDC), 39–40, 75
Airplanes for clinic use, 65
  alleged violations, 105–106, 108, 117
Alabama, 2
Alcoholism, 149
Alexandria, Louisiana, 63
Algiers-Fischer project (New Orleans), 55
AMA. *See* American Medical Association
Ambulances, 90, 112
American Medical Association (AMA), 8, 38
American Nurses Association, 38
American Public Health Association, 38, 102
Anthropologists and anthropology, 13, 17, 24, 47, 51
Antiabortion forces. *See* Pro-life forces
Asia, 21
Atlanta, Georgia, 42, 82
Auxiliary home visitor. *See* Outreach workers

Baldwin, James, 122
Baptist Church, 28, 52, 62–63
Bard (College) Center Fellow in Health and Nutrition, 140
Battered children. *See* Child abuse
Beasley, Joseph Diehl, 29–30, 44, 71, 75, 117
  on abortion, 58

appointments, awards and honors, 21, 72–73, 106–107, 112–113, 156(n7)
  and black militants, 95
  charismatic personality, 21, 25, 80, 125, 135–136
  fundraising skills, 25
  philosophy and objectives, 21–23, 36, 69–70, 91, 129
  schooling and early career, 19–20, 24–26
  trials and aftermath, 100–101, 105, 110, 112, 114–116, 123–130, 135, 140–141
Berrigan brothers, 125
Big C. *See* Charity hospitals
Bill of Rights Foundation, 125–126
Biostatistics, 24
Birth control, 78, 99, 126, 143, 150
  and abortion, 57–58, 144–145
  on demand vs. therapeutic, 7
  democratizing, 3, 5, 51
  folklore and myth, 13–18
  funding, 39–40, 109
  in Louisiana (1960s), 3–5, 9
  and racism, 30–31, 91. *See also* Genocide controversy
  Sanger coins term, 6
  See also Contraception and contraceptives; Family planning
Birth control movement, 5, 7–9, 69
Birth rates, 26, 50, 101–103, 137
Black community, 2, 27, 42–44, 58–60
  families, 47–50, 92
  men, 92–93, 95, 133
  women, 17, 43, 50–51, 55, 92–95
  See also Black militancy; Poor women; Racism
Black magic, 13
Black militancy, 59, 91–97, 133. *See also* Genocide controversy
Black Muslims, 59, 92–93
Black Panthers, 92
Blake, Davis, 69
Blake, Judith, 69
Bobo, James R., 42
Bond, Julian, 122
Brazil, 70
Brunswick Hospital Center, Department of Metabolic Medicine and Nutrition, 140

Cairo, Egypt, 70
Calcasieu Parish, 63
Cali, Colombia, 71
Cancer, 16, 56, 79, 83
CAP. *See* Community Action Programs
Cardiovascular disease, 57
Catholic Church, 5, 49, 99